Arden Blackburn's Mail Route
The Early Days at Christie Lake

Arden Blackburn's
MAIL ROUTE
The Early Days at Christie Lake

JOHN A. MCKENTY

ARDEN BLACKBURN'S MAIL ROUTE
Copyright © 2012, John A. McKenty

All Rights Reserved. No part of this publication may be reproduced, stored in a retrieval system or transmitted in any form or by any means—electronic, mechanical, photocopy, recording or any other—except for brief quotations in printed reviews, without the prior permission of the author.

The sketches of the Mud Lake bridge, the view from the rail line and Jordan's bridge used at the beginning of each chapter are done so with the kind permission of their creator Franc van Oort (www.francvanoort.com).

The photos for the front cover were prepared by
Mindy Brown of Images Inter Alia in Perth, ON.

Model names and designations mentioned herein are the property of the trademark holder and are used for identification purposes only.

ISBN: 978-1-55452-979-7
LSI Edition: 978-1-55452-980-3
E-book ISBN: 978-1-55452-981-0
(E-book available on the Kindle Store, KOBO & the iBookstore)

Cataloguing data available from Library and Archives Canada

To order additional copies, visit:
www.essencebookstore.com

For more information, please contact:
John McKenty
RR. 5 Stn. Main
Perth, ON K7H 3C7

Published by

This work is dedicated to Donna Walsh and George James, whose patience and perseverance kept it alive.

Neither snow nor rain nor heat nor gloom of night stays these couriers from the swift completion of their appointed rounds.
Herodotus 450 B.C.

Contents

Acknowledgements 9
Introduction 13
Chapter One — Christie's Lake House 19
Chapter Two — Comedy Kings of Christie Lake 43
Chapter Three — Christie Lake Flyer 67
Chapter Four — Christie Lake Bark Factory 89
Chapter Five — Hard Times Hit Christie Lake 109
Chapter Six — Christie Lake Camp 131
Chapter Seven — Christie Lake Bearcats 149
Chapter Eight — Christie Lake Community Club 167
Chapter Nine — Noonans' General Store 187
Chapter Ten — Jordan's Bridge 213
Chapter Eleven — Christie Lake School 235
Chapter Twelve — Christie Lake After the War 259
Epilogue 291
About the Author 293
Endnotes 295
Bibliography 299

Acknowledgements

Over time casual talk at Christie Lake had taken more and more of a historical turn. Less concerned with who was catching what or who was building where, long-time residents had turned their attention to days gone by and the people and stories that had shaped their community. As the "elder citizens" of the lake approached a considerable age, the need to provide a permanent record of what had gone before was becoming more and more apparent.

Stan Seymour started the ball rolling by interviewing folks such as Barbara Hutton, Elton Crandall Jr. and Jim Rogers. The quotes included in this book by these individuals are taken from Stan's audio tapes. Then George James and Donna Walsh picked up the ball from Stan convinced that the effort involved in preserving the story of the lake was worth the work.

Upon completion of my book *Follow the Crowd*, George James commented that he felt there was a story to be told about the community at Christie Lake. I must admit I was at first dubious, for although every community has its share of interesting historical vignettes, involving people connected by their very proximity, there isn't always a story.

George suggested I come out and talk to a few people to see if indeed there was something there. So it was that Donna Walsh, George James and I began a journey that turned us into friends and took us to the homes of some of Christie Lake's best-known inhabitants.

By the time we had spoken to Irene Kirkham, Gray Palmer and Terry Brooks, I knew that Donna and George were right. There was a story here. It was clearly evident that the link that had held the residents of the area together personally over the years was every bit as strong as the lake that had held them together physically.

This fact was reinforced as we spoke to Joe Noonan, Joanne Stiles, Ralph and Wendy Fish, Dave and Jim Rogers, Alan Jordan, Penny Nault, Rebecca Smith, Dave Hill, Ruth Brown, Les Peters, Peter Higgins, Bill Sproule, Jeff Nault, Judy Buehler (Lemieux), Penny Donaldson (Romeiser), Barbara Jordan, John and Hilary Fowler, Fran Laidlaw, Kay Pogue, Doris Kirkham and Gordon Hill. Some had lived at the lake their entire lives; some hadn't been back since their childhood, but all harboured fond memories of Christie Lake.

I value deeply the time we spent with these individuals and treasure the memories they shared of their families and friends. They took as much pride in regaling us with the antics of Dickie Patterson, as they did the accomplishments of the Marks family. While they spoke warmly of local icons such as Wib Noonan and Reg Sproule, they often reserved their warmest tone for their mailman, Arden Blackburn, whose route for over forty years connected the dots along the north shore of the lake. Half-a-century later I was privileged to travel the same route with Arden's son, Ken, who had often accompanied his dad in years gone by.

Although the Christie Lake Camp and the Boy Scout camp were not technically on the mail route of Arden Blackburn, I have included them because of the many connections they had with those who were.

In the beginning the name of the lake underwent numerous variations, including Myer's Lake and Christy's Lake. Much to the chagrin of George James, I have chosen to employ the most commonly used name and spelling—Christie Lake. When quoting a particular source, however, I have kept the spelling as in the original. Much more to George's liking is the fact I have maintained the spelling of Gravelly Bay with two l's.

In telling the story of the early days at Christie Lake I was greatly aided by the *Perth Courier*, where for many years the coming and goings at the lake were dutifully recorded by an observant writer using the pen name Rusticus, a Latin adjective meaning "rural, simple, rough or clownish." It is my belief the first person to fulfill the role of Rusticus was Joe or Gracie Marks and that when they passed on the role was picked up by Bob Marks' wife, Dot. That is, as I say,

Acknowledgements

just a conjecture on my part. Because the *Perth Courier* references are numerous, I have left them in the body of the narrative. All others have been footnoted.

In terms of family names, I have used the name by which the person would have been best known at the lake at that time. In the case where names have changed through marriage, I have included the individual's married name in brackets the first time their name appears in the text.

I thank everyone who took the time to speak to us. I hope that they consider this work a worthy reflection of the time we spent together. I thank especially Penny Nault, who has done a wonderful job of collecting information about the lake and was kind enough to share her files with us. As well, I am most grateful to Peter Higgins, who has done a masterful job of tracing the history of the McKinnon, Shepherd and Hill families, and to Gray Palmer, whose memories of the lake are both entertaining and informative.

Thanks to Debbie Sproule and Karen Rennie at the Perth Museum for their help in tracking down photos of the Marks family. I also thank Ralph Willsey for permission to quote from his newspaper interview with Bob Marks. And Franc VanOort for permission to use his prints.

No reference to Christie Lake would be complete without giving credit to two excellent books on the topic—Michael Taylor's *The Canadian Kings of Repertoire: The Story of the Marks Brothers* and Beverly Ensom's *Christie Lake Camp: The History*. Although not readily available, both are well worth tracking down.

I thank Beverly Ensom for permission to quote from her book and to Carole Gagne Ince, executive director of Christie Lake Kids, for her help in finding early photos of the camp. Thank you to Dr. Bob Chaplin and everyone who shared their photos with us. I tried wherever possible to note the source of each. Where there is no notation, the photo was either my own or from a box that over time the Christie Lake Association had collected.

Thanks to Franc Van Oort for allowing us to use his prints at the beginning of each chapter. Franc has done a masterful job of capturing some of the key elements in the surroundings at Christie Lake and I encourage everyone to seek out the full-sized prints at www.francvanoort.com or at the Riverguild Fine Crafts in downtown Perth, ON.

I'd also like to express my sincere gratitude to Timothy Fransky, Sherrill Brunton and all the wonderful folks at Essence Publishing. Bringing together a work with this many photographs, insertions etc. is no mean feat. Once again they proved themselves to be up to the task and then some.

Lastly, a tip of the hat to Donna and George, both of whom live at the lake. On far too many occasions I allowed myself to get sidetracked, only to have them gently bring me back on course. Others would have given up. Donna and George thought too much of the Christie Lake community to let that happen, and for that reason this work is dedicated to them.

John McKenty
Perth, Ontario

Introduction

Theirs was a bond born in nature. United by water, those who settled on the north shore of Christie Lake were eventually drawn into a relationship that transcended politics, religion and sometimes even family. For some the water was their livelihood; for others their playground. An unlikely mix of local characters, stage stars, railway executives and government officials, the community came together to work, to sing, to dance and, in the end, to celebrate the beauty that surrounded them.

Located approximately 15 kilometers southwest of Perth, Ontario and measuring 6.2 kilometres in length and 1.1 kilometres in width, Christie Lake is the third largest lake in what is known as the Tay Watershed. Connected as it is by the Tay River to Bob's Lake in the west and the town of Perth in the east, Christie Lake was part of a well-travelled route by the area's earliest inhabitants. While its twenty-eight islands provided the Algonquin and others with a welcome respite from a long journey, its fish, game and wild rice afforded them the sustenance they needed to carry on. Spread across 675 hectares, at its maximum Christie Lake reaches a depth of 18.3 metres.

Framed by steep slopes and broken cliffs, the rugged charm and unique character of the lake was a natural draw for those who arrived from Europe in the early nineteenth century looking to leave behind the overcrowded conditions of their homeland and to seek a fresh start in a new world.

While the Treaty of Ghent, signed on December 24, 1814, had brought an end to England's war with the American states, it had left the British Empire with the pressing question of what to do with thousands of now unemployed troops. Wary of disbanding its many soldiers and have them return home where post-war overcrowding and unemployment was already wrecking havoc, the British government decided to offer them grants of land in Upper Canada. Such a move was seen as not only helping to alleviate the labour and social unrest at home, but of forming a nucleus of loyal ex-soldiers who could quickly form militia units should the British colonies again find themselves under siege from their neighbours to the south.

To safeguard against just such an invasion, the British government decided to develop an inland waterway between Kingston and Ottawa which would be protected by the newly discharged soldiers. To provide assistance for the soldiers, the government, under the direction of Lord Bathurst, secretary of state for the colonies, also looked to populate the area with loyal British immigrants.

When Bathurst's plan received the enthusiastic endorsement of Lieut.-Gen. Sir Gordon Drummond, British administrator of Upper Canada, the colonial office in England announced a plan of assisted emigration designed to encourage those in Scotland and Ireland wishing to leave their present surroundings to do so. When announced in February 1815 the plan stated that persons desiring to go to the British colonies in Upper Canada would be conveyed there free of charge.

Furthermore the British government would supply the emigrants with provisions for the voyage and upon their arrival allocate each family a grant of a hundred acres. For the first six to eight months the settlers were to be allowed rations from the government stores while axes and other implements as needed would be provided at half price. Public support of a school teacher and minister was also to be included with the expectation that the travellers were to settle as a community.

When John Campbell, the Scottish agent in charge of the plan, officially posted the Proclamation in Edinburgh on February 22, 1815, it was an offer that caught the eye of twenty-four-year-old John Christy. Although the fee for going was steep (a deposit of 16£ for each male over seventeen years of age and 2£ for each married woman), Christy knew that after two years of settlement he'd receive his money back. It was an offer he couldn't resist.

Introduction

So it was that one month later, with his deposit fully paid, John Christy, along with his wife and daughter, joined over five hundred other Scots in Glasgow ready to embark on the adventure of their life. Their excitement, however, turned to frustration when the ships intended to take them to the new world failed to arrive. As time dragged on, the Christys and their fellow travellers found their scanty store of money and supplies fast disappearing. Disappointed with the ongoing delay, the group expressed their anger and dissatisfaction through their spokesmen Alexander McNab who demanded that additional living expenses be forwarded by the government to those who had been left stranded.

As it turned out, it wasn't until mid-June that the vessels destined to carry them on their journey began to arrive at Greenock the farthest inland point that could be navigated by an ocean-going vessel. When word came that the ships had finally reached Greenock, the Christys and their companions readied themselves to board the schooner that would take them from Glasgow to the waiting ships at Greenock.

The departure of the first contingent from Glasgow on June 24, 1815, was a bittersweet moment. The emigrants and their families had been met with much kindness from the Glasgow inhabitants. Hundreds of the town's citizens accompanied the travellers to the river to see them safely off. Set to leave Glasgow at three o'clock in the morning, many of the travellers had come down to the Broomielaw the evening before and remained on the wharf all night.

> *The air was calm and serene, but few were disposed to sleep. Interesting conversation filled up the passing hours, and the social glass went around oftener than once, for the "tee-total" scheme had not then been thought of. At two in the morning the embarkation commenced amidst hurry, noise and confusion. Soon after three, the steamboat taking the schooner in tow passed down the river amidst the shouts of thousands who lined the shore bidding Adieu to their departing friends. The scene to many of the emigrants was the most affecting they had ever witnessed. They were bidding a final farewell to their native land.*[1]

On August 3, 1815, John Christy and his family were among the one hundred and twenty-three settlers who set sail on the ship *Eliza* bound for Upper Canada. The voyage proved to be a difficult one. The conditions created by seasick passengers on a ship with limited sanitary conveniences made life unbearable for some, especially the children, many of whom contracted whooping cough and died before the ship finally arrived in Quebec City that September.

George Gray was just eleven years old when he made the voyage on the *Eliza* with his family. His father was older than many of the other travellers having turned sixty just before the family left Banff Shire, Scotland, and so much of the care of the Gray family fell to George's mother, who had her hands full with George and his four sisters and three brothers, including the youngest, eighteen-month-old Robert.

From Quebec City the Christys and the Grays were taken by steamboat to Montreal before making their way with sixty other families up the eighty-four miles to Cornwall. As though the delays and frustrations of the voyage were not enough, the travellers now faced the prospect of spending a long winter with nothing to do but ponder the uncertainty of where they'd be come spring. To add to their discontent, the winter quarters assigned them were far from adequate. As a result, about thirty families, including the Grays and the Christys, continued to make their way from Cornwall to the military settlement at Brockville.

Once in Brockville, according to Sir Sidney Beckwith, a quarter master general of the British forces in Canada during the 1812 war, the families were "accommodated in the barracks, in some adjoining huts hired by themselves, and in the neighbouring farm houses, where most of them procured employment."[2]

Come spring the settlers began the difficult trek northward to the settlement at Perth. On March 25, 1816, it was reported by Reuben Sherwood, chief surveyor of the new settlement, that the "the settlers have this moment arrived with their knapsacks and axes."[3]

With most of the commissioned and non-commissioned officers taking up residence in the military settlement at Perth, many of the Scottish civilians found themselves assigned to the outlying areas often connected to the town by way of water. Such was the case with the Grays and the Christys who, in June 1816, arrived at their allotted hundred acres located on Concession 2, Lot 2 and Concession 3, Lot 3,

Introduction

respectively, in Bathurst District at the foot of what was then known as Myers Lake.

The story goes that when an argument arose between the Christys and another prominent family as to whose name should adorn the lake, the two families decided to draw straws to settle the issue. When the Christys proved victorious, their name was given to the lake, although its spelling would be changed in 1908 by the Geographic Board of Canada.

> The Geographic Board of Canada has issued another report fixing the proper names of many places in the Dominion. The report just issued is of exceptional interest as a decision is given regarding the names of about fifty places in the Ottawa valley. Some of the board's decisions as affecting this district are:
> Christie Lake post office. Not Christy's Lake
> Fergusons Falls post village. Not Ferguson's Falls
> Smiths Falls railway junction and town. Not Smith's Falls
> (*Perth Courier* 04/10/1908).

Unlike the Gray family, the Christys did not remain at the lake. After meeting the residency requirements, John Christy was granted his deed from the crown on May 28, 1824, but eventually sold his property to James Doyle on July 1st, 1852, after which time he moved his family to Gloucester Township on the east bank of the Rideau River. The Christys were among a number of Scottish families to make the move. At the time it was reported: "To the east bank of the Rideau came a splendid migration in the 1840s of Scots who were disenchanted with the 'Scottish settlement' near Perth."[4]

Although the Christys left the lake that bore their name, other settlers quickly took their place, locating, for the most part, on the north shore where the gentler topography and fertile agricultural land proved to be enticing. Although few in number, this unlikely blend of Scottish and Irish emigrants survived, in large part, due to their ability to work together. Isolated as they were from the town, they became doctor and nurse, carpenter and counsellor for each other. They helped each another fix things, build things, plant the crops and bring in the hay. And when the work was done, they gathered to celebrate at picnics and dances often hosted by the Marks family at the head of the lake or the Noonan family at the foot of the lake.

Before long, word of Christie Lake and its beauty, not to mention its bounteous supply of fish, began to spread. As it did, the handful of residents who had settled there were joined by a large influx of summer visitors, many of whom were members of Perth's business and professional elite who came to the lake in their horse and buggies seeking a diversion from their life in town.

So it was that come the holiday weekend in May, the population around the lake literally exploded as those looking for a respite from the hustle and bustle of town joined those who lived at the lake. Mingling as they did at the Christie Lake station, Arliedale Inn or Noonans' store, this colourful mix of local residents and well-to-do vacationers developed a union that left an indelible mark on their community.

Nowhere was this relationship more apparent than in the person of their mailman. Six days a week Arden Blackburn's appearance at the lake signaled the arrival of everything from welcome news from a distant family member to medicine for Grandma's aching arthritis. Over time Arden would become much more than just the community's mailman.

◆ Chapter One ◆

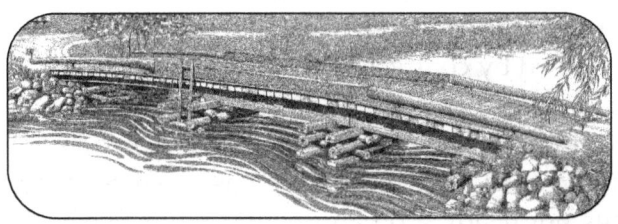

CHRISTIE'S LAKE HOUSE

In a country as vast as Canada delivery of the mail has always been a vital means of communication. It was for this reason that shortly after Confederation in 1867 the post office departments in New Brunswick and Nova Scotia were amalgamated with those in Ontario and Quebec, and *An Act for the Regulation of the Postal Service* was passed. At the time, the act created a federal government department headed by a cabinet minister to be known as the Postmaster General of Canada.

When the new legislation came into effect on April 1, 1868, it provided the newly-formed Dominion of Canada with a uniform postal service based on the British model created by Sir Rowland Hill, who had introduced the concept of charging for the delivery of mail by weight rather than destination. Originally set up as a centralized system, mail was delivered to a town's designated post office where the inhabitants from the surrounding area came to pick up their letters and parcels.

The first post office in Perth, Ontario, was located at the town hall and included a section of postal boxes for patrons, as well as a counter with wickets for picking up parcels, registering mail and conducting general business. Those living in the outlying areas, such as Christie Lake, were alerted by the local newspaper to the fact that they had mail awaiting them in town.

This system continued in Canada until October 10, 1908, when the country's first rural mail route was established between Ancaster and

Arden Blackburn's Mail Route

Hamilton, Ontario. Four years later, in 1912, the Government of Canada announced that all persons residing along well-defined roads over a mile in length were to be eligible for mail delivery. So it was that on May 13 of that year when the first such route was established in the Perth area. It was designated Rural Route No. 1 and its mail delivery assigned by contract to W. Cullen.

As rural mail delivery spread across Canada, it brought with it the need for additional post offices. The outlets located in outlying areas, often housed in general stores, served as a central drop-off location for residents not residing on an existing route. When Perth's fourth rural route, Rural Route No. 4, was laid out for the Christie Lake area, the post office was established at the farmhouse of George and Sarah Noonan. It was here that, for many years, a large crowd gathered each day to await the arrival of Arden and the mail.

A young and dapper Arden Blackburn in 1929 the year he began to deliver the mail on Rural Route No. 4. (Courtesy: Ken Blackburn)

Chapter 1 ◆ Christie's Lake House

No one had to explain to Arden Blackburn what the appearance of the mail meant to those living in the country. Born on May 23, 1911, Arden had grown up in the small hamlet of Prestonvale, northwest of Perth. As a youngster he witnessed firsthand the anticipation with which those around him waited for word from the outside world. It was an impression that stayed with Arden even after he left school to work at the local cheese factory. It was a job that would be short-lived, but, according to Arden, would leave a lasting effect (later in life Arden jokingly blamed the fact he was going bald on the salt from the cheese, saying it had been on his hands when he rubbed his head).

While turning eighteen meant many things to a young lad in those days, to Arden Blackburn it meant only one. He was now old enough to "draw" His Royal Majesty's mail. So it was that in 1929, shortly after his eighteenth birthday, Arden went to work for John Thomas, who held the contract for mail delivery on Perth's Rural Route No. 4. Thus began a tradition that lasted close to fifty years.

From the outset Arden went through his morning routine with military precision, picking up the mail each day in Perth and at exactly ten o'clock heading out the Glen Tay Side Road. Along the way he'd take a short left at Glen Tay, before turning around at the Miller farm and making his way to the foot of Christie Lake. From here he turned onto the North Shore Road, a road that, according to lake resident Gray Palmer, should never have existed.

Palmer maintained the intent had always been for the second, third and fourth lines in Bathurst Township to run parallel at about a mile apart, but because the engineer marking out the third line took a longer step with his right foot than his left, he ended up veering to the right, an action that resulted in the creation of what was known as a "forced road," one that ran across private property and along the shore of the lake.

Planned or unplanned, the North Shore Road was the thread that over the years Arden would use to weave together the lives of those who lived along its path. In total the route covered twenty-eight miles and included one hundred and forty stops and was, according to Arden's wife Sophia, "the heaviest route out of Perth." So punctual was Arden that residents at the lake told the time of day by the clip-clop of his horse's hooves.

Arden Blackburn's Mail Route

Nowhere along the route was Arden's appearance more anticipated than at the Christie Lake post office located in the kitchen of the Noonan farmhouse. From Monday to Saturday those who gathered there to await Arden's arrival filled their time exchanging tidbits of information and rumours regarding the latest comings and goings from around the lake and beyond. Often overseen by Amelia Rancier, who lived at the Noonans', the conversation continued unabated until Arden arrived and Sarah Noonan began to sort the mail into the wooden slots that lined the wall of her kitchen.

While Sarah ran the post office, her husband George did his part by serving as the township's pathmaster and ensuring that the North Shore Road was kept open. In the winter George Noonan often paid the local school lads to help clear the road of snow. Despite their best efforts, it was often said that come the next day the runners of Arden's cutter were the first marks on the freshly fallen snow.

"I don't recall any winter storm ever stopping Arden—it maybe slowed him down a little, but 'the mail did go through!'" mused long-time lake resident Bill Sproule.

Arden Blackburn with his horse and buggy in 1933 at the foot of Christie Lake. (Courtesy: Ken Blackburn)

Chapter 1 ◆ Christie's Lake House

From the Noonans' farm house Arden made his way to the post office at Brooke, located in the general store of Annie Perkins whose unmistakable walk was the result of having one leg shorter than the other. From here he headed eastward along the Sixth Line to the Wemyss post office, run by Reg Duffy and later the Camerons. The last leg of the journey saw him travel along the Fourth and Fifth Lines to the Lanark Road before finishing the route by travelling the final two and a half miles back to the post office in Perth.

As time went by, Arden came to know the lay of the land around Christie Lake better than most. Each year he watched as the warm spring weather brought the lake back to life. The annual return of the tourists and summer residents was a ritual that had been occurring at the lake since the turn of the century when the well-to-do citizens of Perth first discovered Christie Lake as a desirable holiday destination.

Drawn by the beauty of the lake and its plentiful fishing, as early as the 1880s Perth's professional and business elite had begun to arrive at the lake in their horse and buggies. While some chose to set up camp in makeshift tents on the shore of Gravelly Bay, others chose to stay at the boarding house of Alexander and Isabella Palmer.

CHRISTIE'S LAKE HOUSE

The subscriber wishes to inform the public that he will be ready to supply boats on hire as usual this season, Sundays excepted, but cannot furnish meals to guests. Parties visiting the lake must bring their own lunch.

Alex Palmer
Bathurst, May 22, 1894

Isabella Palmer had spent her entire life at the lake. It was Isabella's father George who, as an eleven-year-old boy, had arrived there with his family from Banff, Scotland, back in 1816. George had grown up at the foot of the lake and in 1845 married a young lady from the area by the name of Janet Kirkman. In the early 1850s George and Janet built a substantial stone home which they called Glen Lyon Cottage, which stands to this day at the entrance to Christie Lake.

Born in 1847 Isabella was the second of the six children born to George and Janet Gray. She grew up on the family farm at the foot of the lake and in 1870 married twenty-five-year-old Alexander Reid Palmer,

The stone house built by George and Janet Gray in the early 1850s that stands at the foot of Christie Lake to the present day. (Courtesy: Gray Palmer)

The view from Gravelly Bay in the early 1920s. (Courtesy: George James)

Chapter 1 ♦ Christie's Lake House

whose family had arrived from England in 1837. In 1876 the Palmers acquired the property east of the Gray's farmhouse where the abandoned Christie Lake bark factory had once stood. Alexander Palmer used the wood from the derelict structure to construct what he and Isabella called the Christie's Lake House, the area's first tourist home.

It wasn't long before word of Alexander and Isabella Palmer's rooming establishment began to spread.

> *Ho! For Christie's Lake on the 24th of May. One hundred and fifty people are expected at the Christie's Lake summer resort on above date to participate in yachting boating, angling, or a swing in a hammock in the cool shade, or perhaps better still a ramble over the verdant hills to the "cold spring" where Romeo and his Juliet, after refreshing themselves with the cooling waters, may inscribe their cognomens on nature's register, the silver birch, which overshadows the spring. Mr. Palmer has his beautiful resort in apple pie order, having had his boats thoroughly overhauled and repainted. A first class dance hall is convenient for those who may wish to indulge in a "tip of the light fantastic" (Perth Courier 05/17/1895).*

In August 1888 it was reported that the boarding house of the Palmers was "full to overflowing, and has been most of the season" (*Perth Courier* 08/24/1888). Among the crowd who gathered at the Christie's Lake House were the young men and women of the day who came to meet and teach the beginners "the intricacies and dizzy mazes of the square dance or the giddy whirl of the waltz."

Located adjacent to what was known as Gravelly Bay, the popularity of the Palmer establishment grew at a rapid rate. During the twenty years that Alexander and Isabella Palmer ran their summer hotel, their list of visitors read like a veritable who's who of Perth's most prominent citizens—Meighen, Stewart, Mendels, Hart, etc. While it was the natural draw of the lake that brought them there, it was the hospitality and warmth of the Palmers that brought them back.

The son of William Palmer and Mary Wilson, Alexander Palmer was said to be "a substantial citizen of Bathurst," whose "genial nature and likeable disposition" ensured that the Christie's Lake House remained a popular summer resort. For her part it was noted that Isabella Palmer "exercised an influence that was always for good.

She was always youthful in spirit. As a hostess, she was unique, for the whole neighbourhood felt that her name radiated a rare spirit of sociability, and at all times she took infinite pains to make everyone happy while visiting her home" (*Perth Courier* 02/06/1931).

Alexander and Isabella Palmer, early proprietors of the Christie's Lake House, standing at with a string of walleye pickerel. (Courtesy: Gray Palmer)

RUSTICUS—THE CHRISTIE LAKE REPORTER

My Dear Mr. Editor,
I once more enter my sanctum and take up my pen, which like the henchman's sword in time of peace, has grown rusty from disuse. However, I shall endeavour to scratch off a few items for your valuable paper, if you will allow me space (*Perth Courier* 08/12/1898).

Word of the lake and the Christie's Lake House was aided immensely by a scribe who went by the pen name Rusticus and whose weekly column in the *Perth Courier* detailed the various comings and goings from around the lake, as well as at the Palmer establishment. In May 24, 1892, the intrepid reporter noted that fishing at the lake was extremely good with some lads catching ten fish apiece,

Chapter 1 ♦ Christie's Lake House

including Perth's Tom Lee, who was said to have caught an eel that weighed fourteen pounds and was five feet long.

A Sunday afternoon swim in Gravelly Bay in 1928 with George Walker's cottage and boathouse in the background. (Courtesy: George James)

A Day at the Lake

I might venture to say that Saturday (June 13, 1896) was the banner picnic day at the lake so far this season, as there were no less than four different picnic parties drove up to have a day's outing. The largest group were the Sons of Temperance from Perth, but they did not all consist of sons as we noticed not a few daughters among them. This party took possession of Gravely Bay or "Picnic Point" and judging from the way they entered into the sports, which consisted of boating, picking strawberries, wandering through the shady bower and kicking football, we knew they were out for a day's fun, and had forgotten the care and turmoil of the little world they had left behind (*Perth Courier* 06/19/1896).

Arden Blackburn's Mail Route

The year 1892 saw the beginning of what was to be a longstanding tradition at the lake when a group of young people gathered on the holiday weekend in May to celebrate the Queen's birthday. From that time on this particular weekend became known as the unofficial opening of a new season at the lake.

It was to be a day marked by unpacking and house cleaning as summer residents arrived to scare away the winter visitors that had nested in the confines of their cottages. Once the bedding had been "aired" and the chores had been done, it was time to renew old acquaintances and to climb atop "Maiden's Leap" to catch the annual fireworks set off across the way on Ottawa Point.

> *We had a large number of visitors at the Lake on Coronation Day. In the evening of this ever-to-be-remembered day a large box fire was lit at Ottawa Point which illuminated the entire lake and presented a grand sight. After the fire had been going in full blast for several hours, a number of fireworks were sent skyward and this was much enjoyed by all who witnessed it. After the fireworks the party at Ottawa Point heartily sang 'God Save the King,' which concluded an enjoyable and patriotically spent night (Perth Courier 08/15/1902).*

As time went on, the Victoria Day festivities at the lake came to include a full program of games and activities, which began and ended at the Christie's Lake House. Each year a large crowd, sometimes said to be numbering near a thousand, gathered in front of the tourist home as Commodore deHertel opened the proceedings at three o'clock sharp. Following that, a number of activities, including boat races, swimming contests, a tug-of-war and a shoulder stone throw, created a whirlwind of activity.

In the evening everyone gathered once again in front of the Christie's Lake House, and the winners of the day's activities were presented with their prizes after which a huge bonfire was lit and the usual display of fireworks illuminated the lake. Inevitably the day ended with a "social hop" that lasted until the wee hours of the morning. In 1904 it was decided that the "Christie Lake Regatta," as the day had become known, should be an annual event.

Throughout the years, the fireworks display on the holiday weekend remained an eagerly awaited event at the lake with the required

CHAPTER 1 ♦ CHRISTIE'S LAKE HOUSE

pyrotechnics often supplied by James Brothers Hardware in Perth. Each year, according to Bill Sproule, Alan James, the son of store owner George James, arrived at the lake with his two-door "Dustpan" coupe fully loaded with the "ammunition" needed for the evening's extravaganza. As a youngster Bill waited expectantly for the "Sky Rockets," which were often saved for last. Launched from V-shaped racks set at various trajectories, according to Bill, the rockets exploded all the way over to Snake Island, in a display that produced "a thousand stars and deafening reports."[5]

A view of Judge McNeeley's cottage on Gravelly Bay in the early 1920s. (Courtesy: George James)

As the 19th century came to a close, more and more of Perth's citizens sought the relaxed pace and natural surroundings of the lake. The advent of the Industrial Revolution had heralded a transformation in Canada's cities and towns. Perth was no exception. By the turn of the century the town was a thriving centre of tanneries, distilleries, wagon makers and machine shops. Before long it was to become home to a number of large factories, including the Henry K. Walmpole Pharmaceutical Co., the Jergen Soap Co. and the Perth Shoe Co. Not surprisingly the Danners, Stewarts and other successful owners of such enterprises were afforded a lifestyle that could include a summer at the lake.

ARDEN BLACKBURN'S MAIL ROUTE

The rustling of the leaves on many a rocky headland, the whispering of the lonely pines scattered here and there among the rocks, the strange clearness of the water flashing under the noonday sun, or heaving relentlessly in the starlight under the gathering dusk. These are sights and sounds to store up and remember long after the lake has become only a memory. He who carries back to the city's dust and din at the summer's end, a memory such as this takes with him a treasure which a Carnegie cannot buy (Perth Courier 06/20/1902).

Eventually those who came to the lake in the summer began to erect permanent structures there. The first was R.J. Drummond, manager of the Bank of Montreal in Perth, who, in 1892, built a cottage on what was then known as Beuly Island, but later known as Ruby Island.

An early view of Ruby Island where Perth bank manager R.J. Drummond built the first cottage at the lake. (Courtesy: George James)

The following year, 1893, James Doyle, who had bought the original Christy property, subdivided a waterfront point at the foot of the lake across from the Christie's Lake House. Eventually to be known as Danner's Point, the bottom portion of the property was initially sold to Peter Hope, a well known Perth hardware merchant

Chapter 1 ♦ Christie's Lake House

and tinsmith, who in 1895 erected a cottage called Fern Cliffe. The upper half of the point was sold to Nicholas Andison, a Perth shopkeeper, who built a cottage first called Poplar Grove, but more commonly known as Breezy Crest.[6]

Once their summer homes were complete, Hope and Andison rented them out to other Perth businessmen, including the town's jeweler Anslow Rudd and David Hogg Jr., the local undertaker. Both the Hoggs and the Rudds returned to Christie Lake on a regular basis. At one point, it was reported that the Rudds had "become very much fascinated with the lake and thoroughly appreciated the beautiful scenery and fishing and boating privileges of old Christie's" (*Perth Courier* 08/03/1900). Given such a sentiment, the eventual news that the Hoggs and Rudds had purchased Fern Cliffe and Breezy Crest was not surprising.

In 1897 ownership of the Christie's Lake House also changed hands when Alexander and Isabella Palmer sold their home to the Anderson family. Shortly thereafter, it was noted that the weekly dinners and teas were still full to overflowing and that Mr. Anderson had installed "an up-to-date bath house in which he offers free baths to Perthites" (*Perth Courier* 06/22/1900).

That same year the Palmers subdivided three lots on Gravelly Bay and sold them to William Allan, William B. Hart and Benjamin Warren. While Allan erected a summer residence, known as Rockcliffe, the eventual summer cottage of the Truman and Chaplin families, Benjamin Warren sold his lot to the Findlay family, who built a cottage known as Bayview, later to become the Cuthbertson cottage. The third lot, that of William B. Hart, was sold to Col. A. F. Matheson in 1909 and then to William E. Danner of the Walmpole Pharmaceutical Co. in 1920, before it became the summer residence of George L. Walker in 1923.

By the turn of the century Christie Lake had also become a preferred destination for many church groups from Perth and area, including that of the Rev. Father O'Brien, whose picnic on June 16, 1899, was said to have been well attended. According to Rusticus, his reverence must have put in a special request for the day as it turned out to be a nice one.

As the reputation and popularity of Christie Lake spread, music and dancing remained an integral part of the festivities there. In 1895 when a group of young ladies drove out from Perth for an evening social, it was said as they made their way through the intricate passages of the Old Sixth, "their melodious voices resounded in the calm night air as they vibrated to the sweet strains of Tommy Atkins and Roll the Old Chariot Along" (*Perth Courier* 08/16/1895).

When it came to striking up a tune the men at the lake were not to be outdone and were often led by the unmistakable voice of Daley Reid. A mainstay of the Anglican Church choir in Perth, Reid's rich baritone could often be heard at the lake.

> *Strange fragments of melody floating across the lake at an early hour on Sunday morning gave one the impression that something new and terrible had struck the neighbourhood. Later, however, it steadied down into the stately cadence of "Nearer My God to Thee," and a "Night in Hades" (Perth Courier 06/20/1902).*

In 1899 the young men at the camp known as "Annie Lagu" on Hicks Island introduced those around the lake to a whole new form of musical entertainment when they brought to the lake a gramophone with over forty discs of the latest popular songs to the lake. "Sweet are the strains of music that are wafted to our ears over the water. The boys are good entertainers and can put up a capital fish story," it was reported at the time (*Perth Courier* 08/11/1899).

In June 1900 Perth's Col. James M. Balderson marched the 42nd Battalion Band and Boys' Brigade to Christie Lake in a spectacle long remembered by visitors and residents alike.

> *It was indeed a novel sight to see the scarlet tunics and accoutrements flashing in the sunlight as they rounded Noonan's curve, headed by the 42nd Battalion Band. On arriving at the Christie's Lake House they found that their captain had not forgotten one of the most important and most sought for conditions of a recruit's ambition after a fatigue march, the refreshing of the inner man. Captain Balderson, at his own expense, had arranged with host Anderson to have tables spread in the spacious dance hall for the accommodation of Company Three Boys' brigade and the 42nd Battalion Band, to which they did ample justice. After dinner a splendid program of*

Chapter 1 ♦ Christie's Lake House

field sports was dispensed with under the very efficient supervision of Mr. Thomas Barry, the 42nd discoursing the familiar strains of "long Live Our Gracious Queen," Tommy Atkins," "The Maple Leaf Forever," and "Soldiers of Our Queen," etc. to the great enjoyment of the resorters. Later in the day a skirmishing party was organized, the red coats scouring the woods for Boers, and as we have not seen Johnny Burns since we do not know what the result has been. After the sports of the day were ended Captain Balderson again refreshed his men by another square meal before returning to town. It was a banner day at the lake, to which great thanks is due Captain Balderson, and we tender him our thanks for the patronage he gave our lake on this the 81st birthday of our most gracious Majesty, our beloved Queen (Perth Courier 06/01/1900).

Over the years the 42nd Regiment Band and Cadets continued to hold their annual outing at Christie Lake in a day filled with what were said to be "sham battles, field manoeuvres and target practice." The return of the band to the lake each year drew a large number of town residents out to listen as bandmaster Jacobs ran them through a program of musical favourites, before setting up in the hall at the Christie's Lake House, where dancing was enjoyed by all until the wee hours of the morning.

Whether inspired by the musketry skills of the regiment or not, there were those at the lake who fancied themselves to be sharpshooters, a sentiment questioned by those who knew better. While it was said that Daly Reid could put "a hole through a five-cent piece at fifty yards while standing on his head," it was also noted that when Frank Hicks raised his rifle, most scurried for cover as he was "the only known man who could shoot in a circle" (*Perth Courier* 08/07/1903).

At the time a safer and more fashionable amusement at the lake was the progressive euchre parties hosted by the young ladies. Held at the Christie's Lake House, each table featured a vase filled with fresh flowers and some exquisite artwork courtesy of Jessie Hart daughter of Perth's pre-eminent bookseller John S. Hart.

The duplicates were very appropriate being made of the bark of our beautiful silver birches which abound on the shore of our lake. The gentlemen's duplicate was a diamond shape while the ladies wore a heart of course. On each duplicate was a sketch in watercolour of some pretty scene of the lake or adjoining country. The beautiful and artistic handiwork was the work of Miss Jessie Hart of "Sunbonnet Alley" (Perth Courier, 08/04/1899).

At the end of twelve games the hostess rang a bell and refreshments were served, following which the winners were announced and received napkin rings made by the young ladies that also displayed sketches of the lake fashioned by Miss Hart. The winner of the "booby" prize was decided by the drawing of a card, after which the tables were cleared and the dance lovers kicked up their heels to their hearts' content.

Once again the men were not to be outdone, and when George Stanley of Perth held a get-together for his friends in August 1900, a British flag was said to fly from every branch on Cook's Island. At the same time illuminated Chinese lanterns of all colours and shapes "lent their dazzling halo to one of the most bewildering and enchanting views we ever beheld on old Christie's" (*Perth Courier* 08/06/1900).

Not all the revellers who came to the lake were adept at navigating it, a fact borne out by a group from the Scotch Line who had some difficulty in determining which way was which.

Boatloads of merrymakers could be seen at all hours heading in all directions, and apparently going everywhere. One boat arrived on shore during the afternoon stern first, the occupant being happily ignorant that that was not the natural and accepted way for a boat to go. He was at once shown his mistake (Perth Courier 06/20/1902).

The popularity of Christie Lake as a destination for an enjoyable outing was given a substantial boost with the arrival on the scene of the bicycle. By the time George James and his friend Daley Reid opened their hardware store in Perth in 1893, "wheels" were all the rage. The modern bicycle, with its improved safety, greater comfort and reasonable price tag, meant more and more folks were leaving town for a day at the lake.

Ho, for a bicycle! What can compare to a bicycle run from Perth to Christie's Lake on a fine day and then cool off with a stroll over the

Chapter 1 ◆ Christie's Lake House

green hills or a stretch under a nice, shady tree; or better still, a pull on the lake. But oh! What an appetite! Won't you relish one of Mrs. Anderson's wholesome dinners. Many of Perth's best-known families, including the Hart's, the Mendel's and the Shaw's were said to have booked space. Mr. Anderson, owing to an increase in patronage, is obliged to erect another building with six spacious sleeping apartments. On the top of this building there will be deck or look out with a rail on which hammocks will be swung and easy chairs for the comfort of the guests (Perth Courier 06/23/1899).

With the increased number of young men and women seeking the seclusion of the lake, rumours abounded that many a proposal between an amorous young man and a fair maiden was tendered amidst the beauty of Gravelly Bay, a favoured location for smitten lovers.

Mervyn Hicks on Hicks Island with a nice catch of pickerel.
(Courtesy: Fran Laidlaw)

Arden Blackburn's Mail Route

It was here many moon's ago fair 'Wanetta' vowed to her brave that she would ever be true, and kindle his camp fire and broil his venison steak, etc., and I am quite certain Mr. Editor, that many fair promises are made at the present day in the shady precincts of this same old spring (Perth Courier 07/20/1900).

Before long Ruby Island wasn't the only island at the lake to be inhabited. In 1901, four lads from Perth—Mervyn Hicks, Art Johnston, Matt Donaghue and Will Noonan—built a clubhouse at the foot of the lake on what was to become known as Hicks Island. The structure, which included a combined living and dining room, as well as a couple of bedrooms, also sported a large double door at the front through which a boat could be pushed and then stored for the winter. The "Breezy Time" cottage or camp, as it was called, was to serve as a summer residence for the Hicks family for many years.

When the Breezy Time Camp was officially opened on August 5, 1901, there were a number of invited guests in attendance, including Alex and Joe Marks from Lake View Farm at the head of the lake.

The four Breezy Time boys placed before their guests such a spread as would tempt the appetite of the most fastidious epicure. After merry songs, sparkling speeches and thrilling stories, a vote of thanks was tendered to the Breezy Time boys whom we have to congratulate on their comfortable club house which they have so beautifully decorated (Perth Courier 08/09/1901).

At the opening Joe Marks sported a badge presented to him by the Breezy Time boys making him an honorary member of the camp. The badge contained the boys' motto: "Nequam Somnambulum," which they said meant "We never sleep."

When Mervyn Hicks, a manager at the Wampole Pharmaceutical Co., married Matilda Forgie, the couple lived in the first of the Wampole homes to be built on Burchell Avenue in Perth, but spent their summers on Hicks Island with their three daughters, Dorothy (McLaren), Mary (Kerr) and Kathleen (Pogue).

"It was a wonderful way to grow up," mused Kathleen Hicks.

Kathleen's father was a man of many talents. For over forty years Mervyn Hicks served as timekeeper at the old Perth Arena; he sang at the annual hockey banquets and he acted in plays at the Balderson

Chapter 1 ♦ Christie's Lake House

Dorothy Hicks (McLaren) paddling with Maltilda Hicks, fashionably dressed as always, sitting in the back of the canoe. (Courtesy: Fran Laidlaw)

Theatre. When he found a free moment, he loved to hunt and fish. His wife Matilda, on the other hand, was less taken with the outdoor life and maintained a fashionably-dressed appearance, even at the cottage where she was often seen wearing a hat and carrying a parasol.

Shortly after the Breezy Time boys built their camp on Hicks Island, John and Martina Jordan, whose family had bought the original Christy farm from James Doyle, sold the property across from Hicks Island to two civil servants from Ottawa, R.R. Farrow (Customs Department) and F. H. Cunningham (Fisheries Department).

In 1902 Cunningham and Farrow put up a double cottage known as Olford Lodge and Waveney Cottage. Located on what was to be known as Ottawa Point and built by Wesley James of Perth, the cottage was said to be "one of the finest on the lake." Shortly after their arrival, the Cunninghams and Farrows wasted no time in reinforcing the lake's propensity for music. That summer when a severe storm struck, it was noted that "between the peals of thunder, the strains of sacred songs could be distinctly heard from Ottawa Point" (*Perth Courier* 08/08/1902).

In April 1902 the Christie's Lake House was sold again, this time to Gerald Mullen, a businessman from Brantford, and Karl Bayard

Steers, a stage director for one of the theatre troupes of the Marks brothers. Although Mullen and Steers announced they intended to paint, decorate and refurnish the premises from cellar to roof and to have it lighted by electricity, by the end of the summer their partnership had fallen apart and it was announced that Steers was returning to the theatrical profession and had left for Perth where he was to rejoin the R. W. Marks Dramatic Co.

That December auctioneer John T. Devlin held an "Insolvent Sale" to liquidate the contents of the summer hotel which was then sold to the Norris brothers, who redid the interior of the house and built a new verandah around the dance hall which had been made much larger by the elimination of several adjacent rooms.

The year 1903 saw a flurry of building activity at the lake. It was that year that George Findlay and William Allan both built their cottages near Maiden's Leap. Findlay was a popular Perth butcher and it was noted that his arrival at the lake was going to be "a great convenience for the Christie's Lake House and cottagers to have a dispenser of fresh meat in our midst" (*Perth Courier* 06/26/1903).

A view from Gravelly Bay showing the original Rockcliffe cottage of William Allan with Maiden's Leap to its left. (Courtesy: Bob Chaplin)

Chapter 1 ♦ Christie's Lake House

Front and back view of Rockcliffe Cottage which became the Truman/Chaplin cottage. Top L. – R. Robert Cameron Chaplin, Edward Thomas Truman, Grace Brodieure, Betty Chaplin, Mayselle Truman, unidentified man, Sheila Chaplin. Bottom: Mayselle Truman with her grandson, Bob, the son of Cameron and Betty Chaplin. (Courtesy: Bob Chaplin)

Shortly thereafter Perth sash manufacturer Alexander Kippen built a summer dwelling in the same bay near what was known as Sandy Beach. Kippen, a well-known Perth carpenter, supplied most of the material from his planing mill in Perth. Next to him was to be the cottage of George Walker, who operated a drug store adjacent to the Balderson Theatre in Perth. In those days when someone in Perth said "meet me at the fountain," everyone knew they meant the soda fountain in Walker's store.

It was in 1903 that a couple of local lads with extensive military backgrounds also put up a combined boathouse and cottage at the foot of the lake next to the Christie's Lake House. The long narrow building, erected for Lt. Col. Edward deHertel and Col. James Balderson, eventually served as a retail outlet for Lloyd Jackson before becoming the site of a girls' camp.

> We are pleased to note the completion of Messrs. deHertel and Balderson's new boathouse and cottage which is a decided adornment to the lake. As your correspondent has not made the acquaintance of the architect it would be unwise to attempt to describe the new structure, suffice it to say that it is a dandy and is built in the most convenient spot in the lake (Perth Courier 05/15/1903).

When Balderson, deHertel, and a number of the boys gathered in the newly built cottage one Saturday evening, a dispute arose as to what to name it. While "Bachelor's Rest" and other names were suggested, it was finally and unanimously decided to call it "The Barracks." Having tapped their military leanings to christen their cottage, the lads combined their first names to do the same with their boat, declaring it to be the "Jim Edward." They also announced that they intended to set up a wireless telegraphy between the Breezy Time Camp on Hicks Island and their newly-constructed Barracks.

Both deHertel and Balderson were well known in the area and both would serve a term as mayor of the town of Perth. Born there in 1861 Edward deHertel had left Perth to join the staff of Lord Strathcona in the Hudson's Bay Company. Following the Northwest Rebellion of 1885, however, he returned to Montreal before making his way back to Perth in 1900 where he became the commanding officer of the 130th Lanark and Renfrew Battalion.

Chapter 1 ♦ Christie's Lake House

James Morris Balderson, b. August 5, 1862, opened a law office in Perth in 1894 and was elected town councilor in 1899 and mayor in 1902.

Born in Perth in 1863, James Morris Balderson, commanding officer of the 42nd Lanark and Renfrew Regiment, came by his military leanings naturally enough, for his grandfather had fought in the Battle of Waterloo. In 1894 the younger Balderson opened a law firm in Perth in partnership with Arthur Meighen and in 1902 was elected the town's mayor.

Shortly after he arrived at the lake, Balderson was asked to put his political skills to use by umpiring a baseball game between a team from Christie Lake, which included three Marks brothers, Ernie, Tom and Alex, and a team from Perth.

The most important event which occurred at the lake since the last Courier issue was the baseball game on Tuesday between "our baseball pets" and our friends from Perth town. Great interest had been shown previous to the game and it was no wonder that such a large crowd of spectators flocked into the baseball grounds. The game was certainly enjoyed by everyone—or rather everyone but the pets—because it was interesting all the way through. The town opponents proved far too many for those from around these shores, and as a result the score was in the majority for the visitors, and a large majority at that (Perth Courier 08/01/1902).

Despite the lopsided score in favour of the Perth team, it was said that, as an umpire, the mayor "gave general satisfaction," which was a good thing, for the Marks boys, who held considerable sway around the lake, took their baseball very seriously. In fact, the only thing the Marks boys liked better than being on a baseball field was being on a theatre stage.

♦ Chapter Two ♦

COMEDY KINGS OF CHRISTIE LAKE

The Marks boys were not only familiar figures around Christie Lake; they were, in fact, well-known right across the country. Six of them had ended up in the world of show business, a feat that led *Maclean's* magazine to hail them as "the most remarkable theatrical family in Canadian history." According to the magazine, "The dazzling Marks brothers were the greatest impresario performers of our small town stage in the era before the nickelodeon."[7]

By the time Arden Blackburn began to deliver the mail to Christie Lake most of the brothers had retired from the stage, but that didn't mean Arden wasn't well aware of who they were. His wife, Sophia, often told the story of how Gracie Marks, the wife of one of the brothers, waited in the big trunk near the mailboxes at the Marks' homestead at the head of the lake.

"'She would get in the trunk and when Arden came along she would pop up and have a hot cup of coffee for him,' Sophie recounted."[8]

It was a gesture typical of the dramatic flair for which the Marks family was well known. Billed as the "Canadian Kings of Repertoire," the brothers spent forty weeks of the year on the road playing the small town show circuit throughout Canada and the northern United States, before returning to Christie Lake each summer to relax, to recharge and to rehearse the shows they'd run the following season. With their high top hats, Prince Albert coats, patent leather shoes, over-sized diamonds and handle-bar moustaches, the brothers were an unmistakable sight at the lake.

As surely as the family of John Christy had given the lake its name, the family of the Marks brothers gave it its character. Growing up at Christie the brothers loved nothing better than to entertain, to play ball and to be at the lake. Often accompanied by an entourage of artists, agents and other show business personnel, or what folks at the lake called "the actor people," over the years the brothers left an indelible mark on the place they called home.

The affinity of the Marks boys for the things they held dear was deeply rooted in their formative years at the lake. Although neither of their parents, Thomas nor Margaret, ever stepped on a stage, the Marks home at Christie Lake was often filled with laughter and song as members of the community gathered to hear Margaret Marks sing an Irish lullaby or Thomas Marks recite the latest happenings from the local newspaper.

Thomas Marks and Margaret Farrell, parents of the famous Marks brothers, owned a farm on the north shore of Christie Lake.

Chapter 2 ♦ Comedy Kings of Christie Lake

Thomas Marks had been one of ten children raised at the lake by Robert and Sarah Marks who arrived there in the late 1820s from County Mayo in Ireland. Settling on Concession 5 Lot 2 in Bathurst Township, Robert Marks had christened the area the "Killarney of Canada," a description that stayed with the lake down through the years. It was Robert and Sarah's second son, Thomas, born on the Bathurst Township homestead in 1833, who was to be the father of the celebrated brothers.

From an early age Thomas Marks worked on the family farm and before long grew to be an imposing figure standing over six feet tall. His strength earned him the reputation of being the strongest man in Lanark County. On November 19, 1853, Thomas married Margaret Farrell, the daughter of Thomas and Eleanor Farrell, and the couple purchased a farm on the 3rd concession of South Sherbrooke Township, a property that came with nearly two miles of prime Christie Lake waterfront.

In addition Thomas and Margaret also purchased a tract of land some three miles away on which they cleared one hundred acres and built what was, for the time, a rather substantial log cabin to serve as their residence. Within a few years, however, the couple fell victim to the ravages of a fire that originated in a nearby tannery and completely destroyed their home and outbuildings.

Following the fire, those who lost their homes were summoned to Perth to receive sufficient funds to help them start over. When Thomas Marks was called forward, he drew his large frame to its full measure and refused the money, declaring all he needed to carry on was his strength. No one was more surprised at such an assertion than the government official who claimed Thomas' name would be recorded in Ottawa "as the most honest man in Lanark County."[9]

When Thomas and Margaret Marks built their next home they located it on the north shore of the lake above a bay that would henceforth be known as Marks Bay (and later as Station Bay). It was here at Lakeview Farm that Thomas and Margaret Marks raised their family of seven boys—Robert William (R.W.), Tom Jr., John, Joseph, Alex, McIntyre (Mack), Ernie—and two girls—Ellen Jane (Nellie) and Olivia Mariah (Libby).

Arden Blackburn's Mail Route

Lakeview Farm the original home of the Marks brothers and the eventual site of Arliedale Inn. (Courtesy: Penny Nault)

In their early years on the farm the Marks children watched as their mother often used her considerable talent to entertain a community gathering. A naturally gifted singer with an inherent flair for fun, it was said that Margaret Marks brought the soul of Ireland—its music and its laughter, its tenderness and its dreams—to Christie Lake. It wasn't long before the hospitality of the home of Thomas and Margaret Marks was a recognized fact around the lake.

"Those who were guests left with memories of songs and family affection which linked all to one another by bonds of close kinship blessed with comradeship and understanding," it was said (*Perth Courier*, 08/02/1951).

Although the boys' father had no formal education, over the years Thomas Marks taught himself to read.

"'My father couldn't write and mother had to teach him to sign his name,'" recalled his son Tom Jr., "'but he was a splendid reader and he read the paper to us without mistake.'"[10]

Before long, the senior Thomas Marks' reputation as a reader and a story-teller had spread around the lake, and on any given Sunday morning at least a dozen neighbours would appear on the Marks'

Chapter 2 ♦ Comedy Kings of Christie Lake

doorstep waiting to hear him read aloud from the latest edition of the newspaper. In the warmer months, the group gathered on the verandah while Thomas, nestled in a rocking chair, recounted the latest news or regaled them with the latest fiction. In the winter, the proceedings moved indoors where folks sat at the kitchen table or clustered around the wood stove waiting anxiously to hear the next sentence.

"'I remember when I was a youngster,'" recalled Tom Marks Jr., "'seeing as many as thirty horses tied in front of the house on a Sunday. People would come from far and near to listen to my father. Most of them stayed all day and, though it never entered my head at the time, I've often wondered since, how we managed to feed them all.'"[11]

In time the senior Thomas Marks came to be held in such high regard by residents around the lake that when he ran for councillor in the late 1860s, he polled the largest number of votes ever recorded in the municipality. It was a position he would hold for nearly twenty years.

The impact of Thomas and Margaret Marks upon the character of Christie Lake was immeasurable. Over the years their dramatic and musical acumen brought to the lake a spirit of camaraderie and celebration that permeated the fabric of the community and laid the groundwork for the careers of their sons.

The first of the Marks boys to catch the show business bug was the couple's eldest son, Robert William, better known as R.W. Born in 1855, by the time he was nineteen R.W. had grown restless on the farm and was using his father's horse and buggy to tour the district selling sewing machines and five octave harmonicas.

One evening in 1876, R.W. and several other young men from the area went to the village of Maberly to catch a show being put on by a travelling magician known as King Kennedy. As R.W. recalled it:

> "The show was all right but the men were evidently travelling in hard luck. After the show I asked them what they would ask for a week's engagement. They would not sell it out for a week, but offered me half interest in the show at a low price and I took them up. I knew a number of good villages in the locality, and with my father's democrat and horses I started on the road with the company. I made money right from the start, and the next season had control of the company myself."[12]

Thus began a chapter in Canada's theatrical history the likes of which would never be seen again. Despite his lack of formal show business experience, R.W. had kept a watchful eye as folks gathered at his family's homestead on Christie Lake; he saw what they wanted. They wanted to be entertained; they wanted to be transported from the reality of their day-to-day lives; they wanted to laugh.

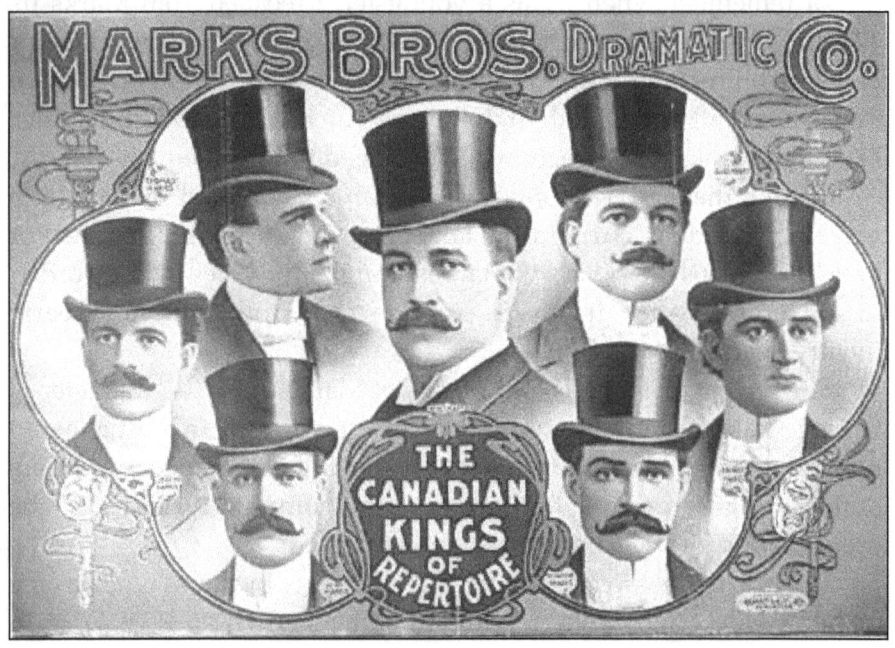

L. – R. Joe Marks, Tom Marks (top), John Marks (bottom), R.W. Marks, Alex Marks (top), McIntyre Marks (bottom), Ernie Marks. (Courtesy: Perth Museum)

"'The comedian's jest is the great universal tonic,'" maintained R.W. "'Above everything else the world wants to laugh and the man who can sell tickets to a real side-shaking giggle is a benefactor on his way to a fortune.'"[13]

Truer words were never spoken and R. W. Marks had the smarts and physical presence to back them up. Like his father, the six foot two, broad-shouldered R.W. cut an imposing figure. It was one that served him well in days ahead when he was called upon to be both promoter and bouncer.

Before long R.W.'s brother Tom joined him on the road and in 1882 the two Christie Lake boys recruited a pair of Kansas ladies, Emma

Chapter 2 ◆ Comedy Kings of Christie Lake

Wells and her sister Jennie (Ray), to accompany them. The foursome, linked on both a personal and professional level, led a troupe that combined dancers, musicians, comedians, acrobats and melodrama. With R.W.'s shrewd business sense and intuitive feel for what the audience was looking for, the troupe's family-oriented performances proved to be a successful recipe for fame and fortune. Widely-hailed in towns such as Pembroke, Arnprior, Almonte, Carleton Place, Smiths Falls and Perth, by 1885 the Emma Wells Concert Company, as they were known, was deeply entrenched in the entertainment psyche of rural Eastern Ontario.

In 1886 R.W. and Tom returned to Christie Lake for what was to be an annual ritual of work and play. While they spent the early part of the summer relaxing and renewing old acquaintances, by late summer they began to gather the members of their troupe together at the lake for what was to be a mix of work and play; it was a time to rehearse new plays, to work out musical routines and to construct the scenery and props needed for the upcoming shows.

That summer when Emma Wells came to the lake she bought a waterfront property from R.W.'s father, Thomas, for a hundred dollars. Naming it "Red Cedar Wild," Emma immediately commissioned the building of a summer residence.

In the meantime to accommodate the activities of his company R.W. had a rehearsal hall built on the crest of a hill with an unsurpassed view of the lake. Here R.W. and Tom mapped out routes and selected plays for the fall tour. Here the actors, musicians, dancers and comedians perfected their parts, while other company members, assisted by residents from around the lake, created and painted the scenery. Despite the challenges in transporting such equipment across the country, the Marks brothers continued to feature elaborate stage settings and costumes in their shows, much of it designed and produced at Christie Lake.

It wasn't all work, however, and while at the lake R.W. and his brothers enjoyed a well-earned respite from the rigours of the road. Here they reveled in the company of family and friends, often taking them about the lake in their latest boats. R.W., who was known to enjoy the odd nip of whiskey, was said to have kept a bottle in his boat should just such an occasion arise.

"My father always had two or three bottles in his sailboat," recalled R.W.'s son Bob.

"He took out the minister one time, and he says, 'Have a little drink, it won't hurt you.' Well he (the minister) almost got fired. This was the English Church minister," mused Bob who chuckled about the incident years later.[14]

Come the end of summer it was time for the company to head out and so R.W. gathered family and friends for a farewell picnic that served both as a thank-you to the folks around the lake, as well as a final rehearsal before hitting the road. Before long, the picnics and rehearsals hosted by the Marks brothers became among the most highly-anticipated events of the year by the residents from around the lake and beyond.

While R.W. had inherited the physical stature of his father, his brother Tom had inherited the Irish wit of their mother. On stage Tom Marks brought to life a host of comedic characters, his favourite being

L. – R. Ella and Tom Marks with their daughter Arlie and dog Buster. (Courtesy: Perth Museum)

Chapter 2 ♦ Comedy Kings of Christie Lake

Jiggs from the well-known comic strip "Bringing up Father." On the road Tom was often accompanied by his pet bulldog Buster. It was said that "Buster provided the sort of entertainment that kept spectators coming back for more and gave Tom the kind of publicity which eventually turned fanfare into dollars."[15]

Life on the road wasn't all fun, however, and there were times that a young Tom Marks longed to be back at the lake.

"Never in all my life," he declared, "have I been as ill as I was one night with one of the worst diseases in the world, barring love. I was suffering from homesickness. I could smell the wind off the lake and see the lights shining on the water in front of the farm house. I was tempted. I wanted to…buy a one-way ticket home. I'll never know why I didn't."[16]

In 1886 Tom married Ella Maude Brokenshire of Wingham, Ontario, an accomplished pianist with a gift for scoring musical adaptations of plays and illustrated songs. In 1895 the couple welcomed the birth of their daughter Arlie. With Tom now heading up

May A. Bell Marks who in 1898 married R.W. Marks and took up residence at Christie Lake. (Courtesy: Perth Museum)

his own troupe, Arlie usually toured with her parents often joining them on stage.

Following the birth of Arlie, Tom's parents hosted a family reunion at R.W.'s rehearsal hall. All of the Marks children were there along with eighty families from around the lake. The dancing lasted until 4:30 a.m.

> *Chinese lanterns glimmered and flags of all nations, with scenery from the various Marks shows, decorated the spacious hall built for rehearsals. Tom Marks, 'Canada's Own Comedian,' entertained with mirth-provoking songs (Perth Courier 06/05/1895).*

By the mid-1890s the relationship of R.W. and Emma Wells was coming to an end. Following the death of her sister Jennie Ray in 1896, Emma Wells severed all ties with R.W. Although the death of her sister no doubt weighed heavy on her and played a role in the rupture of her relationship with R.W., it was obvious that the attention being paid by R.W. to his new leading lady, May Adelaide Bell, who had joined the troupe in 1894, also added to Emma's resolution to declare a parting of the ways.

Following Emma's departure, R.W. married May A. Bell at a ceremony in Kingston, Ontario, in December 1898. At the time May A. Bell was twenty-seven, while R.W. was forty-five. An established stage beauty in her native New York City, where she performed with the likes of well-known Canadian comedienne Marie Dressler, May A. Bell was a versatile performer, equally adept as a vocalist, pianist and dancer.

While she had grown up in Brooklyn as part of a strict religious family, by 1890 May A. Bell was nineteen, married and pregnant. On December 13 of that year she gave birth to a son, George Whitman, who, along with his wife, "Tiny," were frequent visitors at Christie Lake where it was said May A. Bell was the originator of many happy events and was held in "popular esteem" by her neighbours and summer residents alike.

The departure of Emma Wells from Christie Lake was not to be a quiet one. While she begrudgingly sold her share of the property, now known as "Red Cedar Villa," to R.W. for six hundred dollars, family records indicate that in a fit of rage she threatened to haunt the shores of Christie Lake and in particular "Red Cedar" for as long

Chapter 2 ◆ Comedy Kings of Christie Lake

Two different views of R.W. and May A. Bell Marks' Red Cedar Villa.

as R.W. remained there. It was a threat folks seldom took seriously, but few ignored.

It was R.W.'s niece Bettie, daughter of his brother Ernie and his wife Kitty, who was the first to claim a strange encounter at Red Cedar. As a youngster Bettie often went there to visit her aunt and uncle. While there she partook of the opportunity to play in the "green room" where the costumes, wigs, jewellery and other assorted theatrical equipment was stored.

"That room was like Aladdin's Cave to a five-year-old," recalled Bettie.

On one such visit Bettie complained to her aunt May A. Bell: "It's no fun today; there's no little girl to play with me."

"Where's that little girl I heard you talking to the last time you were here?" asked her aunt, assuming the voice on that previous occasion had been a friend that Bettie had brought along.

When Betty explained that the young girl had already been in the room when she got there, the implication of such a statement left her poor aunt so shaken that her face turned completely pale.

"As I remember, the little girl was attired in an old-fashioned dress, and we laughed and played all afternoon—yet I never saw her again," recalled Bettie Marks.[17]

On yet another occasion, Bettie recalled how she and her brother, Ted, along with some of their teenage friends, were seated around a table at Red Cedar using a Ouija board. As the evening wore on, the board had begun to lose its appeal.

It was then that Ted asked, "Is there anybody here that shouldn't be?" and got a strange response from the kerosene lamp mounted on the ceiling above their heads.

"All of a sudden, and for no explicable reason that I can think of, a flame shot from the lamp right up to the ceiling. The flame was so intense that we ran screaming from the room fearful of the consequences should we remain, that is, all but Ted, who was knocked out of his chair. He was just as upset as the rest of us, so there is no doubt in my mind that any of this was his doing," recalled Bettie.[18]

As such incidents found a lasting place in the folklore of Christie Lake, residents wondered if the spirit of Emma Wells had indeed returned to haunt R.W. and the lake.

Chapter 2 ◆ Comedy Kings of Christie Lake

Taken from the dock at Red Cedar Villa ca. 1900 - R.W Marks, Ernie Marks, Tom Marks, Jack Marks, Joe Marks and two of the Matheson girls who were their cousins. (Courtesy: Penny Nault)

May A. Bell Marks with son, Robert Jr., sitting in front of Red Cedar Villa ca. 1911.

> **"Ten, Twenty, Thirty" by Robson Black**
>
> Down on the shores of Christie Lake, eleven miles from Perth, Ontario, lives Robert ("R.W.") Marks, a six foot showman. Before his doorstep spreads one of the rarest estates in all Ontario, an estate of flowing waters, of scattered islands and granite headlands, of long ghost walks of silver birch where the rabbit plays "his comedy lead" and the hawk signs up for forty weeks of "heavies." This is the place—this Christie Lake—where the Marks family of players and managers has grown from childhood, where their dramatic companies are assembled at midsummer, where the second edition of the Marks name, adding new patterns to the family heirloom, will probably pass along the enterprise to indeterminable generations. Around the lake shores the actors have their cottages, their motor boats race the waters in the early morning and the pitch of night. They fish together, work together,—as pleasant a family as ever tanned and fattened under the summer sky. And now since the railway came within catapult throw of the big Marks' home, they are building a rehearsal hall, warehouse, and painting studio where the entire Marks enterprise will be housed when the forty weeks of road tour are ended and another forty in process of planning (*Canada Monthly,* May/October 1915).

Despite the occasional preternatural disturbance, life was good on Christie Lake for R.W. and May A. Bell Marks. Here the couple's two children Mary Marguerite ("Maizie" b.1901) and Robert ("Bob" b.1910) were born and grew up. When a photograph of a young Bob Marks was chosen as the "Most Beautiful Child" in the *Toronto Sunday World* photo contest in 1914, it seemed he was well on his way to following his parent's footsteps.

Bob's big stage moment came at the age of twelve when he was to play opposite his mother at Montreal's York Theatre. Just before the performance, however, young Bob was hit by a car with enough force to knock him out. Being the trooper he was, Bob got himself up and in costume in time for his curtain call as Little Willie. He managed to play his part without incident through to the heart-wrenching final act in which Little Willie leaves this world.

Chapter 2 ♦ Comedy Kings of Christie Lake

At this point Willie's mother played by May A. Bell cried, "He's dead! He's dead!" and fell upon him. Unfortunately she landed right where the car had hit him, causing young Bob to yell out in pain.

"You're dead!' exclaimed May A. Bell.

"I know, but I got hit by a car and I'm sore," retorted Bob, who then followed the script and appeared to have passed away.[19]

Despite Bob Marks' early success as a comedian, his aspirations for a life on the stage were not to be. His sister, Maizie, who also appeared on stage at an early age, fared somewhat better eventually running a successful dance school in Auburn, New York, where she moved following her marriage to Elton Crandall. Elton and Maizie had met there in 1918 when she had was performing at the town's Jefferson Theatre. At the time Elton had been playing sax and clarinet in the orchestra, and when the time came for the orchestra to meet the actors and actresses, Maizie and Elton struck up an immediate and lasting relationship.

The marriage of Maizie Marks and Elton Crandall at Christie Lake, as later described by their son Elton Jr., was a typical Marks affair.

R. W. Marks on the beach at Red Cedar with daughter Maizie ca. 1904.

Arden Blackburn's Mail Route

In 1920 my father came by train from Auburn N.Y. to Christie Lake and arrived at the station and there was quite a crowd gathered because everyone heard that the Marks girl was going to be married and they all came to see who this foreigner was coming to marry a Marks and dad alighted, of course all dressed-up when all the people there didn't wear shoes. They were all shoeless because it was getting to be summertime. It was in May and there was a horse and wagon that took my dad over to Red Cedar Inn past Arliedale and at that time at the top of the hill from the station there was a bridge over the railway tracks and they went right past Arliedale Inn and then across the land over to Red Cedar Inn. Dad and mother were married in Red Cedar Inn in May 1920 and spent their honeymoon there. And, as the story goes...in the morning my grandmother (May A. Bell) came in and my mother

A young Elton Crandall Jr., son of Elton Crandall and Maizie Marks, holding his prize catch of a Northern Pike. (Courtesy: Elton Crandall Jr.)

Chapter 2 ◆ Comedy Kings of Christie Lake

was crying in tears and my grandma said, "Did he touch you?" And my mother said, "Why no, and he got up this morning and went fishing with my brother."[20]

Maizie became an American citizen by virtue of her marriage and, following the ceremony, she and Elton returned to the States to live. For the next twelve years Maizie operated a studio in Auburn and taught ballroom dancing. Each summer, the couple returned to Christie Lake and the cottage they had been given as a wedding present. Known as Restmore, it became the eventual summer home of the Orser family. It was here that the Crandall's son Elton Jr. and his wife Betty, along with their three daughters, also spent their summers.

On October 16, 1904, the community around Christie Lake was shocked and saddened to learn of the death of Thomas Marks Sr., the patriarch of the Marks family. His passing, it was announced, was the result of an apoplectic stroke. The news came as quite a surprise to both family and friends as the elderly Thomas had worked right up until the day of his death.

Devastated by the loss of their father, the Marks brothers continued to build homes and cottages on land that had been part of the original family farm. The one exception was Joe Marks, the head of the third Marks Dramatic Co. to be on the road. Unlike his brothers, when Joe Marks decided to establish a summer residence at the lake, he selected a lot, not on the farm, but on a small island opposite Red Cedar Villa. Known as Ruby Island, the property was purchased by Joe from R. J. Drummond in 1902. Joe immediately christened it the "Bachelor's Retreat."

While Joe Marks had studied to be an Anglican minister, he had left six months prior to ordination to return to Christie Lake and his favourite pastimes of fishing, hunting and sailing. Folks around the lake loved to tell the story of how Joe once caught a nineteen inch fish with a garden rake on the south shore of his island.

When Joe officially opened his island retreat, George Griffin manned the barbecue, while Billy Patterson was the master of ceremonies and Thomas Newell dished out the ginger ale. Joe, who liked nothing better than to visit his island, was often seen on the lake in "Marvel," the canoe he had purchased in Peterborough.

Joe Marks in his canoe just to the left of his cottage on Ruby Island.

One day, Joe Marks, who had a penchant for recalling stories of days gone by at the lake, was burning leaves on the island when he uncovered an old fireplace used by native people in times past. Joe told how the island had been the camping ground of an Indian named Stevens, who had come to the area to hunt usually accompanied by his wife. John Newell, an old friend of Joe's, was said to have remembered when Chief Peter Stevens occupied the island and his braves with their women camped on the adjacent shore.

In 1905 the Bachelor's Retreat was forced to revert to the name of Ruby Island when Joe Marks did follow a familiar Marks pattern and married his leading lady, Mabel Grace Marintha Andrews. Because R.W.'s wife May A. Bell would brook no confusion in their names, Joe's wife became known as Gracie. A theatrical star of considerable stature, Gracie Marks was a skilled comedienne and an especially talented child impersonator. Following their marriage Joe's canoe and Gracie's rowing skiff were often seen in close proximity to each other and to their island.

Ernie Marks, the fourth of the brothers to lead his own troupe, also married his leading lady, Katherine ("Kitty") Reynolds of Brockville, Ontario. A versatile singer and comedienne, Kitty Marks

CHAPTER 2 ♦ COMEDY KINGS OF CHRISTIE LAKE

was just sixteen at the time and recalled her engagement to the twenty-three-year-old Ernie.

> *When Ernie and I became engaged in 1900 his parents gave a reception for us at the farm. They had a huge table in the dining room. About twenty people could sit at it. I can still see the family as I looked down the table that night, and remember being just a little breathless at the glitter of diamonds and other jewelry. It was like a picture you see of an ambassadorial reception or something. But this was deep in the Ontario bush.*[21]

While most gatherings at the lake may have lacked the opulence of the scene at the Marks household, they did, however, carry their own sense of gaiety and excitement. When Peter Hope sold his Fern Cliffe cottage to Perth jeweler Anslow Rudd in 1907 and Nicholas Andison sold the adjacent Breezy Crest cottage to David and Mary Louise Hogg in 1908, both the Rudds and the Hoggs often hosted "at homes" at the lake for their friends from town, including the Perth Women's Institute.

A rare view of the parlour in R.W. and May A. Bell Marks' Red Cedar Villa taken in 1899. (Courtesy: Elton Crandall Jr.)

Tables had been erected on the lawn and everything that could add to the enjoyment of the day was done. Mr. Rudd, with his fine motor boat and trailer, spared no trouble to give everyone a sail on the beautiful lake. Mr. Hicks also did the grand with the services of his fine row boat. Tea was followed by hearty votes of thanks from various members of the society to Mr. and Mrs. Hogg and to all who had in any way aided them in their untiring efforts to give pleasure to their guests. Witty and complimentary speeches were made by Colonel Balderson, Captain Matheson, Dr. Wilson and Mr. Leaver and a Scottish song from Mr. Wilson closed the formal proceedings of this delightful day (Perth Courier 07/15/1910).

CHRISTY'S HAUNTS—1909

Many surprises were in store for your humble scribe. We saw improvements on all sides: at George Noonan's, our genial postmaster, we saw that a new telephone system had been installed and following the line we reach the "Barracks" which was once the bachelor quarters of two leading patrons of our lake. It is now comfortably converted into a store and grocery and refreshment quarters operated by Mr. Lloyd Jackson, who runs a daily stage to and from Perth. Here also a telephone station has been installed with long distance connections to any part of Ontario. Looking to the right where we expected to behold the old Christy Lake House, the greatest surprise of all meets our gaze. The Dance Hall and "Sun Bonnet Alley" have been removed and where the hotel stood, a new dwelling to all appearances has been erected, painted and decorated in first class style. A new windmill has been set in motion, supplying water for sanitary and other purposes. Passing on around the shore another surprise awaited me. I beheld three trim new cottages almost on the waterfront, erected and equipped for Col. Jas. Balderson, whom we learn is sole owner and proprietor. Rounding Picnic Point and the "Fairy Tree" where the Sun Bonnet girls used to bathe and bask in the sun, we see three stately cottages owned and occupied by Messrs. Kippen, Findlay and Allan and their respective families (*Perth Courier* 07/09/1909).

Chapter 2 ♦ Comedy Kings of Christie Lake

A family gathering on the verandah at Red Cedar Villa in 1923 with a young Elton Crandall Jr. on the lap of May A. Bell Marks while his mother Maizie sits across from them.

In 1909 Col. Balderson bought the Christie's Lake House from the Norris brothers and renamed it Hillcrest. Among the many renovations he undertook were the repair and repainting of the ground's familiar windmill. Inside a large tank was installed to supply water to the residents and a bathroom added for convenience. A new boat house and three additional cottages facing the lake were also built. At the time it was noted that one of the guests with a "splendid Kodak," had taken several photos of the lake and cottages which he then displayed at Lloyd Jackson's store in the Barracks.

That same year, Col. Balderson also helped establish the Perth and Christie Lake Telephone Association. At a meeting held at Dewitt's store in Elliott Dennis Noonan was named chairman and Balderson appointed secretary of a committee formed to solicit subscriptions for the new endeavour. Shortly after the drive for the telephone company was launched, it was announced there had been a generous subscription from Tom Marks towards the building of the line. "Tom is always to the front," hailed the local newspaper.

Arden Blackburn's Mail Route

> **The Christy Lake Telephone Company**
>
> The Christy Lake and Perth telephone will be in shape to do business in a few days. The wires are all strung and new long distance telephones of the latest type are being installed. There will be six phones at present: at Geo. Noonan's and Jackson's store at Christy Lake, and on the third line at William Stiller's, Thos. DeWitt's, Geo. Korry's or Dennis Noonan's, Alf. Chaplin, Manion, and in the Bell central office, Perth. The lake people and farmers will be greatly convenienced by this new departure and it ought to be a paying investment (*Perth Courier* 06/11/1909).

At a fundraising picnic staged that summer on behalf of the Christie Lake Telephone Company, over four hundred were in attendance, which proved to be a huge financial success. While Tom Marks and members of his troupe provided the musical numbers, the day also involved another favourite Marks' activity in the form of a baseball game, this one between a team from Christie Lake and one from Harper. The game came close to being called when the ball landed in the large pile of wood and brush that had been collected for the evening bonfire. The proceedings had to be halted until the debris was removed and the ball was recovered.

> **Announcement**
>
> Tom Marks and his company will present the great comedy "Bringing Up Father" at his summer cottage, Arliedale, on August 15th. The grounds will be decorated and a stage erected for the occasion. Proceeds will be devoted entirely to charitable purposes (*Perth Courier* 07/20/1917).

Tom Marks could afford to be generous towards the community where he had grown up. Besides the money earned from his dramatic endeavours, Tom had also made some wise investments. When western Canada came into its own and real estate and oil were prime commodities, Tom had been there—holding both land deeds and oil stock. He also acquired extensive mining interests in British Columbia, thanks, no doubt, in part to the advice of his brother John who had left

Chapter 2 ♦ Comedy Kings of Christie Lake

Christie Lake to find his fortune in the gold fields of the Klondike. The only brother to never enter show business, John Marks returned only occasionally to the lake, choosing instead to reside in British Columbia where he owned mines in the area surrounding Hedley.

When all was said and done, Tom Marks probably owed his investment success more to good luck than good advice. In 1911 when an acquaintance offered to sell him five hundred shares of stock in the "Dingman Well" for a dollar a share, Tom had no notion of what would happen next. When "all hell broke loose," as Tom put it, and the well began to spew forth its liquid gold with increasing regularity, Tom immediately assigned another member of his troupe to take charge of the upcoming engagements, while he himself headed to Calgary.

"I sold my stock as soon as I got in," he recounted. "I rated myself as a smart financier since I got twenty-nine dollars a share for it."[22]

In the end, Tom Marks' generosity towards the telephone company and other local endeavours was but one more example of the impact he and his brothers had on the community at Christie Lake. Aware of the widespread influence the boys had, few were surprised that when the train came to Christie Lake it stopped at the doorstep of the Marks family.

◆ Chapter Three ◆

CHRISTIE LAKE FLYER

Arden Blackburn knew only too well what the sound of a train could do to a horse. Whenever he got to the railway tracks, Arden checked his watch, and if his sons were with him he had them get out of the buggy and walk. He didn't want them along for the ride should the horses get spooked.

It was shortly before Arden began to deliver the mail in 1929 that he heard about John Patterson, a well-known Christie Lake farmer killed at the train crossing on the edge of Perth. Patterson had gone to town in his horse and buggy. Later that night when he headed for home, it started to rain. Many surmised that Patterson, who was hard of hearing, might have had his vision blocked by his umbrella making it difficult, if not impossible, to detect the approach of the oncoming train. Others wondered if his horse had bolted leaving Patterson stranded on the track. His horse would later be found in a farm yard on the 3rd Line of Bathurst, uninjured and still wearing its harness.

It wasn't long after he began his route that Arden received yet another chilling reminder of the train's power. Living as he did in Perth, Arden pastured his horses at Clifford Munro's farm at Dewitt's Corners. One morning Arden arrived at the farm to discover that three of his team had broken free sometime in the night. Much to his dismay, the lifeless bodies of the horses were found lying beside the

Arden Blackburn with his horse Queen and brother-in-law Ernie McPhee. (Courtesy: Ken Blackburn)

tracks. They had been killed sometime in the early morning, two and a half miles west of Glen Tay, by what was known as the "Merchandise Freight," a fast-moving train that passed through Glen Tay shortly after midnight. The train crew reported the accident at their next stop in Smiths Falls. Once alerted, the section foreman at Glen Tay had found the horses shortly thereafter.

Despite its inherent dangers, the train was a much anticipated addition at Christie Lake. While surveying for a rail line to run along the north shore of the lake had begun as early as 1905, it wasn't until May 1912 that the CPR actually commenced grading work. Once started the most difficult part of the construction proved to be the section from Christie Lake to Crow Lake, where the presence of the Canadian Shield meant extensive blasting was required in order to cut a path through the rock.

As the work got underway, residents in the area watched various blasting crews set up camp on the shore of the lake. The largest was

Chapter 3 ◆ Christie Lake Flyer

that of the Huff and Shea company, located at what was then known as Smith's Creek and overseen by Mike Sullivan, a veteran railroader and miner, who had engineered some of the most difficult track through the mountains of British Columbia.

Arden's wife Sophia on the road to Christie Lake in her husband's horse and buggy. (Courtesy: Ken Blackburn)

Construction on the new CPR line is progressing steadily. Shea and Huff are preparing for another big blow out. Mike says that there will be very little of the mountain left when he next touches off the battery which will let off the big blast. A steam shovel is on the way to scrape up the debris.
Murdock Bros. have completed their No. 2 camp on Mack Marks' place and operations are brisk at this end. Mr. Hansen is doing some heavy work at the head of the lake (Perth Courier 09/13/1912).

Other camps at the lake included one on the Stiller property run by the Murdock brothers and one on "Sunny Ridge" under the direction of an English engineer by the name of Boston.

Arden Blackburn's Mail Route

We had the pleasure of visiting Mr. Boston's camp on "Sunny Ridge," a very pleasant location near the mouth of the upper Tay. We were met by Mr. Boston's lieutenant, Mr. Harry Vincent Doherty, and loyally entertained. This camp boasts one of the choicest chefs along the line being imported from China. We also had a run to "Mud Lake," where Mr. Hamilton has charge of the pile driving party, which is a CPR outfit. In one place, Mr. Hamilton informs us he touched bottom at seventy-four feet. Mr. Huff, of Huff & Shea, has perhaps one of the best located and most comfortable camps along the line. We also visited there last week and were met by Mr. Huff and his right hand bower, Mike Sullivan, who took pleasure in showing us around and made us partake of a sumptuous repast. We are invited with a number of the cottagers this week end, to a novel feast at which a whole roasted pig will be served (Perth Courier 07/26/1912).

The blasting created such a stir among residents around the lake that George Noonan began to arrange sightseeing tours. George would load up his boat with curiosity seekers at the foot of the lake and then take them to Marks Bay so they could catch the explosions first hand.

A distant view of the completed CPR rail line that runs along the north shore of Christie Lake. (Courtesy: George James)

Chapter 3 ◆ Christie Lake Flyer

One group to avail themselves of this service was the Lanark County Council, who did so June 20, 1913. Accompanying them were several prominent Perth citizens who were only too happy to view the work and to show off their recently acquired automobiles. Among the motoring entourage at the lake that day was John A. Stewart, mayor of Perth, who provided two of his automobiles for the excursion, one of which was being driven by Lawrence James of the James and Reid Hardware. Also with the group was County Coroner Dr. Dwyre in his Studebaker, Senator Peter McLaren in a Russell and mill owner T. A. Code, who was there in his new Hupp.

When they arrived at the lake, the gentlemen gathered at the Noonan farmhouse, where some were helped onto a supply boat being towed by Alex Marks, while others followed in George Noonan's motorboat. At the time it was noted that County Reeve Tom Greer, feeling a particular pride in what he considered to be the finest lake in his township, naturally fell into the steering job at the stern of the boat.

"Tom instantly threw off forty years, and in fancy memory carried him back to the days when he used to run logs on lake and stream" (*Perth Courier* 06/27/1913).

The first stop of day for the councilors was the Shea and Huff camp. While the CPR had first feared it would have to dig a tunnel through the mountain, it was later decided to cut the line around the slope instead. At the time of the group's visit, a steam shovel was busy digging its steel jaws into the cracked debris of the mountainside. The endeavour was fraught with danger, a fact reinforced while the dignitaries were present by a couple of workers who were having wounds dressed, including an unfortunate Swede who had had his shoulder bruised by a stone hurled in a blast.

It was well known around the lake that, just a few months previously, three of the men had lost their lives in a premature explosion at the Murdock camp.

> *The tragedy was one of those unfortunate affairs that are present in all railway construction camps whose men are concerned with blasting. All were experienced with dynamite. An inquest was held at the home of Geo. Noonan, Christie Lake, the jury returning a verdict of death by accidental discharge of a charge of dynamite* (*Perth Courier* 01/07/1913).

The battle between man and nature was a daunting one and, while the rugged slope of the lake proved to be a formidable challenge, the muck at the bottom of Mud Lake proved to be an even greater one.

"Engineering science will conquer Mud Lake at a heavy cost, for the most advisable right of way to a railroad has to be secured at almost any cost," noted the local newspaper (*Perth Courier* 06/27/1913).

Although it was only two or three feet in depth, Mud Lake sat on a bed of semi-liquid muck estimated to be twenty feet deep. Under that was a thick stratum of soft blue clay sitting on various layers of sand and gravel. All of which made it almost impossible to find solid footing for the piers needed for the construction of the bridge. In order

A crew at work on the Mud Lake bridge in 1914.

Chapter 3 ◆ Christie Lake Flyer

to reach bedrock the centre pier had to be set at a depth of one hundred and three feet below the water level, while the pier on the west shore had to be down fifty-six feet and the east side thirty feet.

The footings for the Mud Lake trestle were erected within reinforced concrete caissons (shafts) built during the winter months when the ice could be used to carry the construction cranes and other heavy equipment out to where the work was being done. Immense boilers were operated on the west shore to run the cement mixers and air pumps needed for the construction of the caissons.

Once complete the concrete shafts were used to house the men from the Foundation Co. of New York who had the arduous and dangerous task of putting up the piers. When completed the Mud Lake trestle had two large trusses spanning the lake supported by three piers. When the work was complete, an inspection was conducted and the new line officially opened on June 29, 1914.

From then on two passenger trains arrived at the lake daily— 12:33 p.m. from the east and 3:05 p.m. from the west. To ensure the safety of its passengers and crew, the CPR hired lads from around the lake, including Morley White, to walk the track and inform them of any rocks that had been shaken loose by the rumbling of the trains.

Once in operation, the stretch of rail line along Christie Lake afforded the train's passengers a compelling vista of sparkling water and beautiful pine trees. According to well-known Ottawa journalist Austin Cross, it was "a stretch of sand beach and a rolling panorama of outdoors that filled the eye and satisfied the soul."[23]

The excitement of the arrival of the train to Christie Lake was sadly tempered for the Marks family by the loss of Alex Marks, whose lifeless body had been found adrift in his boat just weeks prior the rail line being opened. Despite his dashing good looks, Alex had never been comfortable in the spotlight, choosing instead to fill the less demanding role of advance agent. Over the years, he had travelled ahead of R.W.'s troupe securing concert halls and accommodations, providing newspaper editors with recent reviews and making sure a couple of young lads went about the town plastering it with handbills.

On the day of his death Alex had been making the trip from Lakeview Farm to the foot of the lake to meet W. J. Rabb, who was to

Two views of a train at Christie Lake. Above: CPR publicity photo showing a train crossing Mud Lake. Below: a Howard Fogg print depicting a train rounding Christie Lake.

Chapter 3 ◆ Christie Lake Flyer

build some cottages for the Marks family. When he passed his brother-in-law Morley White (married to Nellie Marks, one of the two Marks sisters) on the way down the lake everything seemed to be fine, but when the noon hour came and Alex had not returned, his sister became anxious. When inquiries determined that Alex had not turned up at his intended destination, Morley White started out in a rowboat to look for him. He eventually found him in what was then known as George Farrell's bay.

The cause of death was given by the coroner, Dr. Dwyre, as a cerebral hemorrhage. It was assumed that his engine had stopped somewhere out on the lake (a detail borne out by the fact that when found the gas and electrical start were still turned on). It appeared that when Alex attempted to restart the engine, he was felled by a heart attack. When found his body was lying over the side of the boat with his arms in the water. Unable to lift the body back into the boat Morley White was forced to row back for help. Alex Marks, although married for a brief period, had remained a bachelor for most of his life and had been a familiar figure that would be missed around the lake.

> **Freight Trains Collide at Christy Lake**
>
> The first accident which has occurred on the new C.P.R. lakeshore line between Glen Tay and Trenton happened at Christy Lake shortly before eight o'clock last Monday morning. Luckily no one was killed or injured although considerable damage was done to the rolling stock and tracks. A west bound freight was taking the siding a few hundred yards west of the depot and before it had completely cleared the main line, a freight train bound east crashed into the former. Neither of the trains was proceeding at any speed, which luckily prevented a more serious accident. Immediately after the accident happened a telephone message was forwarded to the C.P.R. auxiliary crew at Smiths Falls, as well as to the work train crew (numbering about fifty) at Mud Lake bridge. Both of these trains hurried to the scene and the crews were soon at work clearing the main line. This was accomplished shortly

> before the time due for the arrival of the noon express. The cars struck by the freight engine were loaded with flout and it was strewn from fence to fence. The cylinder of the engine and other forward parts were badly damaged while the ties at the switch were torn to splinters. Road Master Miram Long was early on the scene of the wreck and superintended the work. Several freight trains in transit were delayed all along the line. The accident attracted a large number of summer visitors at the lake as well as many of the farmers from the surrounding country (*Perth Courier*, 08/27/1915).

When the Christie Lake train station was erected in 1915, it was but a stone's throw from the home of R. W. Marks, whom many credited with having used his influence to bring the train to the lake in the first place. Adjacent to the station was a steep set of stairs and a wooden slide that connected the station's platform to the water's edge. While the slide was intended to provide visitors with a means of getting their trunks and luggage down to the water, over the years it became a source of great fun for the local youngsters, including the Greer children whose father Gilbert would become the station foreman. While living in the station house, the younger Greers often played at the bottom of the slide learning to swim at an early age, a fact that continually confounded the American tourists who thought they were too young to be in the water and were continually hauling them up the hill to their mother.

That year when the end of season dance was held at the Noonan's, many residents commented favourably on the station and noted that it was well-equipped on the inside and the view from it to the lake was said to be a "feast for the eyes." It was also noted that John Mitchell, a well-known Perth carpenter, had already removed the buildings that once occupied by the construction crew at Mud Lake.

"John says there is enough good lumber in the buildings to build four fine houses in Perth," it was reported at the time (*Perth Courier*, 08/27/1915).

The arrival of the train brought a steady stream of visitors to the lake, including a number of CPR executives, who initially came in private rail cars, but some of whom eventually built summer homes

Chapter 3 ◆ Christie Lake Flyer

A crowd gathers on the platform at the Christie Lake station.

A young Harold Peters, who would eventually work for the CPR, resting on the station stairs that went down to the water. (Courtesy: Les Peters)

Arden Blackburn's Mail Route

A couple has their picture taken at the Christie Lake station.

on the lake. Notable among them was William Neal, the sixth president of the CPR, who first spent his time at the lake in a well-appointed rail car, flying to Toronto or Montreal as need be, but eventually built a cottage on land purchased from R. W. Marks and later to be the residence of Gord Hill. Over the years, the lake was to become Bill Neal's refuge from the boardroom of the CPR. He liked nothing better than to relax and spend his time reeling in a good-sized bass or pickerel.

Chapter 3 ◆ Christie Lake Flyer

> **The President of the CPR**
> **As remembered by Jessie McKinnon (Hill)**
>
> We had a very aristocratic lady at the lake, she thought she was very aristocratic anyway. She lived in the cottage across the bay from us, Mrs. Danner, whose husband was president of the company that made medicines. It was a big company and danged important, I guess, in the town...one day Mrs. Danner was crossing the bridge at Jordan's and Mr. Neal was one of the fishermen and he had his rod across the bridge so that she couldn't quite get past it, and she honked her horn imperiously, and he took his time to move, and move his fishing rod and she turned to him and said, "Do you know who I am?"
> And he said, "I can't say lady, but where I come from I am some pumpkins myself."
> And he was too; he was president of the CPR of Canada, Mr. Neal.[24]

Other CPR officials to build summer homes at the lake were Henry Suckling, the company's treasurer, and Web Krauser, a purchasing agent with the company's supply operation in Montreal. While the rail line was being built, many of the executives had been entertained by R. W. Marks who began to operate a summer hotel as well as a boat livery at Red Cedar Villa.

The increase in population brought on by the railway precipitated a flurry of building activity at the lake. Down the hill from the train station, Mack Marks, who was living at Lakeview Farm with his wife, Laura, and two daughters at the time, built two cottages. Not far away Morley White built a couple of cottages, including one for himself, which would become the cottage of Judge Blair, and one for Ernie Marks, known as Fair Haven, which would later become the Briggs residence and then that of Joe Noonan. Acknowledged to be a great carpenter "with a good eye for the ladies," Morley White was affectionately known as the "mayor" of Christie Lake.

While there is nothing to indicate that R. W. Marks or any of his brothers held any strong religious convictions or were regular churchgoers, they did realize that those who did constituted the lion's share of the audience for their family-oriented entertainment. As a result each

A young Bill Sproule leaning against the sign for the Christie Lake station along with Alan James. (Courtesy: George James)

Sunday while on the road R.W. had his troupe dress in its finery and parade through whatever town they were in before making its way to the church. It was a blatant attempt to convince the members of the congregation that "the players were also god-fearing individuals who embodied the very essence of their wholesome productions."[25]

When at the lake the Marks boys made a conspicuous attempt to take part in the various church picnics and services held there. Shortly after the train station was built, Rev. Coles from St. Stephen's Anglican Church in Maberly began to hold services there on Sunday evenings. On one such occasion, he remarked that he would be "pleased to see more worshippers in attendance from the lower end of the lake." It was then that R.W. invited the Rev. Coles to move the service to the verandah at Red Cedar Villa where a weekly collection was then taken up for Canadian prisoners of war in Germany.

Chapter 3 ◆ Christie Lake Flyer

Another church group to enjoy the lake was the choir of St. James Anglican Church in Perth, who came out for their annual picnic. On such occasions, R.W. often gave the members of the group a trip around the lake in his gasoline launch, a beautiful inboard mahogany, appropriately named the Maizie after his daughter.

The young men's class from St. Paul's United Church in Perth also came to the lake for a fireside evening. Accompanied by Bryant Robinson on piano and Will Erwin on fiddle, these young men raised their voices in the singing of old-time hymns following which they usually listened to a guest speaker.

At one particular gathering, their guest was former Perth resident Col. J. W. Spalding, deputy commissioner of the R.C.M.P. Throughout his talk that evening Col. Spalding held the rapt attention of the young men as he described the efforts of the famous police force to establish law and order in the tumultuous Canadian west. What he didn't mention was the time he shot lake resident Tom Marks in the foot.

According to Tom the incident occurred when he and his troupe were working their way through the towns and villages of the Northwest Territories. When the two lads from Lanark County crossed paths, Tom and the colonel decided to hook up at the Prince

An unidentified young lad standing in front of what was to be the residence of Joe Noonan. (Courtesy: George James)

Albert Hotel for a drink or two. While sitting at a table in the hotel Tom was accidently shot in the foot by a .22 calibre revolver that Spalding had taken from a drunken reveler earlier in the day. Carefully tucked away in the Colonel's pocket, the weapon had somehow been discharged. Fortunately, according to Tom, the bullet glanced off an eyelet on his shoe and penetrated only a few inches into his foot.[26]

It was just such adventures and misadventures that made the relative peace and quiet of Christie Lake a welcome respite for the Marks brothers and their various associates. While some of their many guests rented a cottage from R.W., others, such as George Carruth and Webb Chamberlain, eventually established permanent summer homes at the lake.

George Carruth whose "Kilties" played for the theatre troupe of Tom Marks and who for many years coached the Christie lake ball team. (Courtesy: George James)

Chapter 3 ♦ Christie Lake Flyer

At the time, Chamberlain, who was the leading man in the troupe of Joe Marks, had met and married Louise McCormick, the organist at the Ashbury Methodist Church in Perth. The couple subsequently built a cottage called Rustic Point, just west of Portage Bay, on land owned by the Marks family. Not long after his arrival at the lake, Chamberlain, who would go on to find fame as a playright, was engaged at the Royal Alexander Theatre in Toronto when he discovered that someone had tried to steal the engine from the boat.

At the time, the boat had been raised out of the water and hoisted close to the boathouse roof. When the thief or thieves attempted to pry the engine loose, one of the pulleys gave way, causing the boat to come crashing down and sending the would-be perpetrators on their way. The boat then say in the lake until Chamberlain arrived to rescue it.

Another of the Marks entourage to put down roots at the lake was George Carruth. In 1915 when Tom Marks needed a band to travel with his troupe, he hired Renfrew's Pipe Major George Carruth and four of his kilted lads to furnish some good ole "Scotch music." On the day of a show, the "Kilties," as they were known, paraded in front of the theatre while playing a few numbers and did the same that evening just prior to the performance inside.

When Tom invited the "Kilties" to come the lake, Carruth fell in love with the area, eventually building a cottage called "Vimy Ridge," later to become the Romeiser cottage. Well-known for his role as a Scottish comedian, Carruth entertained his Christie Lake neighbours by playing the bagpipes each night from his front steps, a gesture that may or may not have been well received.

In the summer of 1917, Carruth and his wife enjoyed a pleasant surprise when the private rail car of General Manager Price of the CPR pulled into the Christie Lake station. Inside was Price, his wife, his two daughters and his private secretary. Price, who was there to visit Henry Suckling on the occasion of the opening of Suckling's new summer home, was quite surprised when he accidently met his cousin, Mrs. Carruth, whom he had not seen for twenty years.

While the picnics and fun days hosted by the Marks family continued over the years, the organization of such events eventually fell to Tom and Ella's daughter Arlie and her husband, Jim Perrin.

Arden Blackburn's Mail Route

Arlie Marks, daughter of Tom and Ella Marks and her husband Jim Perrin who in the later years often hosted the Marks family picnics. (Courtesy: Perth Museum)

> *On Thursday of this week at 2 p.m. sharp, the clarion call of a bugle might be heard for the gathering of the clans to "Arliedale" the starting point for Jim Perrin's picnic. About 3 p.m. Jim's launch swung out from the dock with eight boats in tow, heavily laden with jolly picnickers and select viands...We headed to the upper Tay, landing at Hanna's Acre," where others joined us. A ball game by the "Petticoat club" was pulled off, with a corn roast and dancing on the green, after which a plenteous spread that would whet the appetite of an epicure was placed before us. Well did we eat! I would say yes, after which the camp fire was danced and preparations were made for the return trip. R. W. Marks and Morley White assisting with their launches to tow the party back. We are safe in saying that every member of the large party thoroughly enjoyed themselves (Perth Courier 08/24/1917).*

On another occasion, Perrin and Henry Suckling's son, Guy, entertained the cottagers to a rare treat by way of a floating bonfire.

Chapter 3 ♦ Christie Lake Flyer

Heaps of brush and other debris being piled on a floating raft in "Marks Bay" and as soon as the crowd had assembled a torch was applied and the forked tongues of flame flew heavenward while the sparks shot in different directions. The children gamboled on the sandy beach while the youths and fair maidens tipped the light fantastic to the strains of the gramophone. Presently a large campfire was lighted and corn was roasted and passed around. Baked beans and roasted potatoes were also dished up and all washed don by a mug of Mrs. Ballantyne's fragrant coffee (Perth Courier 09/07/1917).

Such events set the tone for life around the lake, particularly for the summer residents whose limited stay at the lake was a much anticipated time of relaxation and socialization. Get-togethers were frequent and often involved food and dancing. Typical were those that took place at Silver Oaks, the summer home of the Listers, where the genial Dick Lister could always be counted on for a hearty welcome. Often the Lister's spacious verandah served as a dance floor after which the guests were treated to cake and sandwiches. On one such occasion, the guests were pleasantly surprised.

Of course, we looked for cake; when to our surprise, choice pickerel and bass, secured by Dick's drag net and spuds, from we don't know where, were passed around. Did they taste good? Well, just ask Morley White. After that cake, sandwiches and a bowl of choice coffee was the top notch of an elegant repast. A wigwam erected the day previous by the ladies, added to the scene when Dick applied the torch. We all voted it the best yet (Perth Courier 09/07/1917).

Even the popular outdoor magazine *Rod and Gun* arrived at the lake in the person of Mr. H. G. Taylor, who, in 1919, spent three weeks at Christie Lake with a party of fourteen made up primarily of family and fellow fishermen. In the January 1920 issue of the magazine Taylor proclaimed his time at the lake to be "a real trip, with real fishing. Just what you look forward to and hope to get, but very seldom find" (*Perth Courier* 01/16/1920).

A fishing party from Rochester N.Y. staying at Red Cedar Inn display the results of their efforts in July 1927.

To prove his point, Taylor went to great lengths to describe the wonderful bass of Christie Lake.

> *They are valiant fighters every single last one of them and just when you think you have them tired out and you are trying to bring them around to the net they will bore to the bottom and sulk, followed by another deep plunge. They all break water and jump into the air four or five times before they are landed* (Perth Courier 01/16/1920).

By the time the roaring twenties arrived, the lake's most prominent citizens were ready to retire from the road and to pursue a less hectic life on its shores. As the decade progressed, one by one the Marks brothers returned to their roots at Christie Lake, there to take up residence alongside the neighbours they had entertained for so many years.

The exceptions were John Marks, who remained in the west, and Ernie Marks, who in 1921 closed his touring company and moved to Oshawa, where he bought the old movie house, to be known as the Marks Theatre, and became the town's highly popular mayor. With

Chapter 3 ◆ Christie Lake Flyer

the return of the Marks brothers to Christie Lake, a remarkable chapter in Canada's entertainment history came to an end.

> **THE SUMMER OF '22**
>
> Well sir, I wish to inform you a real boom has struck this end of the lake and the sound of the hammer and saw is heard in the land and many changes have been made since I last wrote. On looking across the bay from Ruby Island I note that Chris Allen has erected a kitchen to is bungalow and adjoining him George Marks has built a comfortable home for summer or winter and it shall be known as "Tiny Cottage." Next to him Mr. Solokoff has in completion a splendid summer home and next is the summer cottage of Rev. Mr. Clayton who is now busy building a boathouse. Across the bay Joe Marks is building a summer and winter home on "Portage Point," the most attractive point of land on old Christy's. Then we come to "The Pines" the palatial home of Mr. and Mrs. Morley White while next is Fairview the summer home of Mr. and Mrs. Ernie Marks. Ernie is with us at present enjoying the breezes while he has a manager looking after his theatre in Oshawa. We then come to Arliedale Cottage on the point which will be occupied by Jim and Arlie Perrin this summer. On rounding the point into Marks' Bay we behold Bell View Cottage, the beautiful home of Mr. And Mrs. Behan erected by Morley White last winter. Then appears "Vimy Cottage," the home of Mr. and Mrs. Carruth and then we touch the "Club House" and at the top of the hill "Red Cedar Villa" and down the hill "Sunset" and "Sunrise" cottages all the property of R. W. Marks. Several other cottages appear until we come to the birthplace of the Marks family now the property of Tom Marks and many are the changes which have been made. He has put in waterworks having running water in every room, bath etc. and also installed an electrical plant and renovated the house generally from top to bottom and is now ready to entertain and accommodate visitors and tourists who may come his way. A rural mail route is being arranged and also a telephone system is being rushed to completion...Mr. Allan

> our new CPR agent is on duty daily at the station ....and Mrs. Noonan has opened her store at the lower end of the lake for the summer and is always ready and willing to wait on customers (*Perth Courier* 06/16, 1922).

◆ Chapter Four ◆

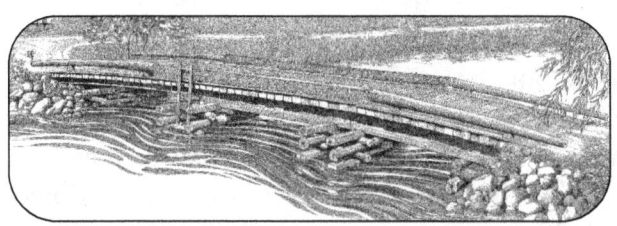

CHRISTIE LAKE BARK FACTORY

When R. W. Marks retired to Christie Lake, he used his time to oversee his various rental properties, including Sunrise and Sunset, the double cottage he built for his children, Maizie and Bob, as well as the Annex or Club House which he operated as Red Cedar Inn. Among R.W.'s many show business guests at the time was noted Canadian author Wilson Pugsley MacDonald. MacDonald was Canada's first pop poet, a slim, dapper man who barnstormed from town to town reading his poetry and singing his songs. With his well tailored suits, walking stick, grey Homburg and monocle, MacDonald, much like his host, cut a striking presence at the lake.

> **FROM THE *TORONTO STAR*, APRIL 2, 1927**
>
> Christie Lake has made a bid for the George Young marathon swim. *The Star* has received from the proprietor of the Red Cedar Inn, Mr. R. W. Marks, manager of the May Bell Marks and Marks Brothers Theatrical Companies, a letter which reads as follows: "We have decided to $25,000 to have the George Young swimming contest take place at Christie Lake. The temperature of our water is better than that of the large lakes. A date in July or August will be agreeable."

> Where is Christie Lake? Everyone who has gone from Toronto to Montreal in the daytime on the C.P.R. has seen it. This 25 miles of water and wooded islands is 11 miles from Perth, 149 from Montreal, 186 from Toronto.
>
> Who is Robert Marks? A generation ago in Ontario that question would have been as unnecessary as the query today "Who is Henry Ford?" He is the eldest of the famous theatrical family of the seven Marks brothers who came from a farm back of Perth to the top rung of travelling showdom...
>
> It is half a century since this veteran actor left Perth for the tallow candles, kerosene lamps and calcium lights of many stages in all parts of North America...
>
> If the George Young swim takes place under such auspices there should be no doubt of its publicity success.
>
> The veteran Thespian who has lured them into the big tent or the opera house has proved his ability to put on a show that will attract the thousands.

In 1927 when R.W. attempted to lure Toronto swimmer George Young to race at Christie Lake, the seventeen-year-old Young had just created an international sensation by becoming the first person to swim the twenty-two mile channel from Catalina Island to the California mainland. His feat had been part of a marathon sponsored by chewing gum mogul and sports magnate William Wrigley Jr.

When he dove off the banks of Catalina Island, Young did so alongside others who were Olympic champions and world record holders. Yet, in the end, only Young went the distance. When the triumphant Canadian stepped onto the shore, after an incredible and grueling fifteen hours and forty-five minutes, his fame was instantaneous. "The "Catalina Kid" made headlines across Canada and the United States. Offers poured in for publicity appearances, product endorsements, and even a motion picture contract.

When Young returned to Toronto following the marathon, 150,000 people gathered to greet their hero. With many in Canada eager to see him in action, the *Toronto Star* confirmed it had received a letter from R. W. Marks offering $25,000 to have the George Young swimming contest take place at Christie Lake. Despite the support of the newspaper, R.W.

Chapter 4 ♦ Christie Lake Bark Factory

Two different views of the clubhouse, also known as the Annex, and the boat house at Red Cedar Inn. (Courtesy of Penny Nault & Les Peters)

lost out on his bid to have Young come to Christie, when the Canadian National Exhibition in Toronto announced a twenty-one mile Marathon Swim, to be billed as the first "Professional Swim Championship of the World" and to be held as part of the CNE. Sporting a cash prize of $30,000, the Toronto offer was too good for Young to turn down.

GRAND OPENING
Arliedale Inn

The most modern summer hotel in Lanark County situated at Christie Lake—"The Killarney of Canada. Main line C.P.R. 100 yards from door.

The Arliedale Inn will open for business on

Wednesday, June 14th

Reservations given prompt attention.

The Hotel is newly furnished throughout—electric lights, hot and cold running water in every room.

REASONABLE RATES

Per Week—$15.00.   Per Day—$3.00

SPECIAL SUNDAY DINNER

Will be served from 4.30 p.m. to 7 p.m. Flavelles Premier Milk Fed Chickens prepared by a competent chef.

BIG DANCE ON WEDNESDAY JUNE 14TH

Hotel will open with a grand Jitney Dance with music provided by Halcyon Orchestra. Admission Free.

DANCING—10c.   LUNCH—25c.

Taxis will run from Perth to and return—$1.50 round trip. Train connections—C.P.R. night train will stop and take passengers for Perth and Smiths Falls.

Dancing every Wednesday and Friday during June, July and August with a different orchestra at each dance specially engaged from far and near.

HELEN MARKS,   LINDSAY E. PERRIN,
   Hostess.   Manager.

Chapter 4 ♦ Christie Lake Bark Factory

The original Marks homestead renovated and enlarged by Tom Marks in 1923 with a store on the right.

While R.W. may have longed for the kind of recognition that such a race would have brought to the lake, his brother Tom sought a quieter retirement. In 1921 Tom returned to Lakeview Farm, the original Marks homestead, on Christie Lake. By then folks around the lake had begun to refer to the bay as Station Bay because of its proximity to the train station.

Once back at the lake, Tom Marks made substantial changes to the old farmhouse, equipping it with electricity and running water and renaming it Arliedale Inn after his daughter Arlie. Here he ran a store and tourist home said to be an enterprise more for his amusement than for any real business purpose. "It was a subdued existence for one with the turbulent and exciting past of the old trouper. There amid that pleasant sort of placid scenery that mooing cows must love and lady nature poets simply dote upon, sits the hard-boiled veteran showman."[27]

When Tom Marks opened Arliedale Inn to the public in 1922, he announced that any Perthites wishing to avail themselves of the "drowsy days and glorious nights" at Christie Lake could now utilize a taxi service to do so. The Christie Lake Taxi would pick up them up at the Hicks House in Perth, said Tom, and bring them back at any hour for a reasonable rate. Reservations for the taxi were to be made by card at Arliedale Inn.

R.W. Marks' Cole automobile parked outside Red Cedar Villa in the early 1920s. *(Courtesy: Elton Crandall Jr.)*

Chapter 4 ♦ Christie Lake Bark Factory

With revelers now arriving by horse and buggy, as well as bicycle, train and motor car, the dances at Red Cedar Inn and Arliedale Inn remained highly popular events. Each Wednesday evening a gold piece was given to the best step dancer at Red Cedar Villa, while at Arliedale the dancers strutted their stuff on a platform set up just beyond the front porch. The platform was covered in a wax said to glisten in the bright glow of the Delco lamps connected to the lighting system of the inn. Here the crowd danced to the latest hits played by the Burns Orchestra until Tom Marks let the wooden-hinged curtain drop on the inn's refreshment booth, signifying the evening was over.

Tom Marks Birthday Party—Jan. 11 1926

Tom Marks, who on January the eleventh was not quite "old as the hills" around Christy's Lake (this date being his birthday), got the surprise of his young life when a party of between fifty and sixty of his neighbours, drove to his place, and all piled out with violin, saxophones, coronets and banjos. Tom was right on the job, and dug up one of his old drums and joined the band. The fun then began, and until the wee small hours, "swing your own," and "balance to your partner" were the watch words. After wishing Tom he would have as many more birthdays when they could all meet again and spend a pleasant evening, all returned to their various homes, unanimous that they had enjoyed the time of their lives (*Perth Courier* Jan. 22, 1926).

Following his retirement, Tom Marks spent many pleasant moments in his easy chair on the verandah at Arliedale Inn. Puffing on his 'Havana' he kept a watchful eye on all passersby and gave a hearty welcome to his numerous callers.

R.W.'s son, Bob Marks, recalled how his Uncle Tom would saw the back off the rockers on one of the chairs on his verandah.

"He'd get a nice looking girl and say, 'Won't you sit down?' She'd sit down and rock and whoop! She'd go head over heels," chuckled Bob.

"I said, 'You're going to be sued for that, boy.'"

Two different views of Restmore the cottage of Elton Crandall and his wife Maizie (Marks) ca. 1928.

Chapter 4 ♦ Christie Lake Bark Factory

Well about two years later, according to Bob, Tom got on one himself by mistake and went head over heels.

"Break that god damn rocker up!" Tom snarled.

"Aw, we had a lot of fun there at Christie Lake. I'm not kidding ya," recalled Bob Marks years later.

The serenity of Tom Marks' pastoral existence at the lake was severally tested one October evening in 1923 when a young lady rushed to his door with news that there was a body lying at his front gate. Enlisting the aid of brother-in-law Morley White, Tom hurried to the gate to discover the lifeless body of John Behan. The sixty-three-year-old Behan, a supply man for the CPR, was a summer resident who often came to the Arliedale store in the evening for milk.

This particular evening, for whatever reason, Behan had brought his shotgun along and while he was going through the gate, it was reported that the gun "was, in some manner discharged, the contents lodging in the unfortunate man's body."[28] A few years later, life at the lake took one of its more interesting turns when Morley White, who had built the Behan cottage, married John Behan's widow.

With the coming of the 1930s, life around the lake had settled into a familiar pattern. Across from R.W.'s Red Cedar Inn stood Lake View Cottage the home of Mack Marks. Down the hill from him was the summer residence of the Sucklings. Next was Tweedledum occupied by Mrs. Felix Shaw and her daughter and Tweedledee owned by retired banker Mr. Eardley-Wilmot. Around the bay was Vimy Ridge, the summer home of Mr. and Mrs. George Carruth. Next was Fair Haven, the summer home of Ernie and Kitty Marks and their three sons. Next was "White Eagle," the home of Morley White, and then Peek-a-boo Camp, home of Chloe and Bill Phillips. Next to them was Restmore Cottage owned by R. W. Marks and next to Restmore was Rustic Cottage, the summer home of Webb Chamberlain and his wife. Then there was Ruby Island, home to Joe and Gracie Marks. On May Bell Point were the Reids of Ottawa.

A frequent visitor with the Marks family at the time was Chris Allen, who, in his trapper outfit, could often be seen in his boat fishing for bass. When he wasn't on the water, Allen was on the road. A talented singer, dancer, comedian and raconteur, Allen had been hired by R. W. Marks in 1898 and spent over twenty years with the Marks brothers before leaving in 1922 for a successful film career in Hollywood.

Folks in Perth eventually had the opportunity to see Allen on the silver screen at the Balderson Theatre when he appeared in the Gene Autry movie *The Old Barn Dance*. The problem was that many in the audience didn't know who Allan was. So following the first screening of the picture, Bill Hamilton, manager of the theatre at the time, made an announcement explaining to those in attendance that Mr. Allen had played leading roles for many years in the theatrical troupe of Tom Marks and made Perth and Christie Lake his home between engagements.

The 1930s saw the presence of the Marks family greatly reduced at the lake. Both Alex and McIntrye Marks had died in their forties, Alex in 1914 and McIntyre in 1920. While one of the Marks sisters, Libby, passed away in 1916, Nellie, wife of Morley White, passed away in 1934. Tom Marks died in 1935 at the age of eighty-one, his wife Ella having predeceased him in 1931. Their daughter Arlie, after whom Arliedale had been named, would die in Chicago in 1941.

Following the death of Tom Marks, Arliedale Inn was sold in 1938 to well known Drummond township auctioneer Clayton Hands and his business associate Jack Newson. At the time it was announced that the gentlemen were going to operate the inn under the same name and were to renovate the building. Thirty-three acres of land were included in the sale and it was noted that Mr. Hands intended to erect a number of cabins and a dining hall, as well as operate a store and rental boat outlet.

Jack Newson ran the lodge for the next nineteen years until it was sold to Neil Stewart in 1957. Eventually Arliedale Inn became the private residence of Bill and Anne Groome. They later sold it to a gentleman by the name of Schafer who in the seventies tried unsuccessfully to receive approval to build a thirty unit motel on the property. Not long after the request for a building permit was turned down in 1979 Arliedale Inn burned to the ground.

In March 1937 an era at the lake ended with the passing of R. W. Marks at the Great War Memorial Hospital in Perth. Although ill for over two years, the eighty-four-year-old R.W. had remained at his Christie Lake home until a week before his death. His wife, May A.

Chapter 4 ◆ Christie Lake Bark Factory

Bell, had died in Toronto General Hospital in 1932 at the age of sixty-one. Although R.W.'s son, Bob, continued to operate a tourist home at Red Cedar Inn for a few years after his father's death by November 1949 Bob Marks had torn down the inn and used the material to build additional cottages.

> MONTREAL 149 Miles   TORONTO 188 Miles   KINGSTON 55 Miles   OTTAWA 55 Miles   BROCKVILLE 47 Miles
>
> **RED CEDAR INN**
> R. J. MARKS, Manager
>
> Red Cedar Inn 500 yards from Christies Lake Station C. P. R. Beautiful view of the islands from rooms. White sand safe bathing beaches. Ideal for children.
>
> Three completely furnished cottages on the lake shore for rent by day, week, month or season, surrounded by an acre of land and shade trees. Running water in some of the kitchens. Good fishing in front of all cottages. 62 lots for sale, 3 beautiful islands, 3 camp sites, 3500 feet of shore line.
>
> For reservations, booklet and photos write R. W. Marks, Prop., Christies Lake, Lanark County, Ont.
>
> Standard Hotel, on main line of the Canadian Pacific railway and connecting with the new Madoc to Ottawa Highway. 12 passenger trains daily. Good connection from all above cities.
>
> SEASON OPENS MAY 15th
>
> CHRISTIES LAKE
> LANARK COUNTY, ONTARIO
>
> The best Fishing in Ontario—Small mouth black bass, pickerel, pike, sunfish, rainbow trout, perch, rock bass, whitefish, bullheads and chub.
>
> Reduced rates for fishing. Angling License, $1.00 (one dollar), for three (3) days for non-residents. R. W. Marks, Provincial Game and Fish Warden, No. 120.
>
> Boat livery, bait and licensed guides for hire. Free parking space for cars. Tent space for rent. Ice cold living spring water. Dancing pavilion.
>
> Excursions daily among the 27 islands. 50c fare.
>
> Daily mail, Bell telephone, C. P. R. Telegraph. Grocery store for supplies.
>
> Motor Routs:—Montreal to Perth, Kingston to Perth, Ottawa to Perth, Brockville to Perth, Toronto to Perth and 12 miles to Red Cedar Inn, 4 miles from No. 7 Highway.

An advertising flyer for the Red Cedar Inn, the home of R.W. and May A. Bell Marks. Their son, Robert J. Marks, managed the inn. *Perth Museum Collection.*

Married to Dorthea (Dot) Romeiser, a young lady who designed clothes for Eaton's, Bob Marks became increasingly eccentric over the years, often wearing a homemade hearing aid, which, with its combination of batteries and wires, made him look like a Martian. Having inherited his father's predilection for the odd drink, Bob often ended up losing some combination of money and property in his frequent poker games, before he eventually landed at Lanark Lodge outside Perth. Once there the sixty-eight-year-old told folks he looked older than he really was "because his nose had been broken…and he didn't like wearing his new teeth."[29]

By this time Joe Marks was also gone, having passed away in 1944 at the age of eighty-two, his final years spent quietly at his Christie Lake home with his wife, Gracie, who, following Joe's death moved into Perth. With the sudden loss of Ernie Marks on June 21, 1952, and his wife, Kitty, on January 1964, the curtain closed on the final run of Canada's best-known theatrical family.

The impact the brothers had on the Christie Lake community cannot be underestimated. From the people they brought to the lake, to the rehearsal picnics and farewell parties they hosted, to the baseball games they played, they left a legacy that lasted long after they were gone. It has been said that if there is a monument to the memory of Canada's most famous theatrical family, it is the lake that their Irish grandfather dubbed the "Killarney of Canada."

Joe and Gracie Marks who lived year round at Christie Lake.

Despite the loss of its best-known citizens, life at Christie Lake carried on even in the dead of winter.

> *Sleighing parties and dancing parties are all the go round here. The profession is giving a delightful informal dance Tuesday evening, but there is much dissatisfaction among the young people. The hesitation and cheek-to-cheek dances are banned (Perth Courier 02/24/1922).*

Chapter 4 ♦ Christie Lake Bark Factory

While ice races were held on a "kite track" in Station Bay, in 1926 the Perth Ski Club organized weekly Saturday afternoon outings to the lake.

"The wintertime was a very social thing," recalled lake resident Ernie Rogers. "We did nothing but go the neighbours and sat and played cards and played till two or three o'clock in the morning because all you had to do in the wintertime was cut wood or take care of your animals."[30]

A few of the boys enjoying a game of hockey in Gravelly Bay. L.-R. Mortimer Reid, F. Maher, Bob Code, Jim Prentice, Alan James. (Courtesy: George James)

Over the years many lake residents braved the winter cold to cut ice from the lake. Charlie Peters, who did so in Station Bay, became well-known in the area for his unique method of getting the ice into the boxcars that waited at the station before hauling the frozen cargo to Perth. Peters had his team of horses haul the ice up the slide at the station and once the ice was at the top, he'd untie the horses and walk them around to the other side of the boxcar. With the doors on both sides of the train open, Peters ran the rope through the boxcar and re-attached it to the horses that then pulled the ice up a ramp and onto the floor of the boxcar.

Still other area residents used the frozen surface of the lake to draw lumber from the nearby bush. For many years the area around Christie Lake had served as a rich source of timber, with the result that a number of sawmills had sprung up nearby, including Adam's Mill at Glen Tay and Allan's Mill at Grant's Creek.

Kenny Kirkham hauling a rather large tree with his team of horses. (Courtesy: Doris Kirkham)

One of the earliest industries at the lake was, in fact, a bark factory established under the direction of Thomas Aspden, an enterprising Englishman, described as being "four sheets square to the wind" due to his multiple endeavours. A chemist by trade, Aspden had immigrated to Canada from England in the 1850s. In 1858 he and fellow Englishman William Benson established Canada's first corn milling operation known as Canada Corn Starch Works (later to be Casco).

In 1861 Aspden quit the starch works and moved from Montreal to Perth where he applied for a patent for "a new and useful arm or method of obtaining by compression the liquor for making a concentrated extract of tanning liquor from the stems or branches of wood and leaves of hemlock, oak and other trees" (*Perth Courier* Mar. 26 1869).

Chapter 4 ♦ Christie Lake Bark Factory

In 1868 Aspden established the bark factory along with Captain John Manion and Perth businessmen William J. Morris, Alexander Morris and John S. Hart who served as the company's treasurer. George Templeton, whose son James established a tannery in Perth, was the first manager of the works and Robert Brown its engineer. The factory, itself, was housed in a long building located on a seventeen acre strip of land at the foot of the lake that the group purchased from Oliver Burns who had settled at the lake in 1828.

At the factory tannin (tannic acid) was extracted from the bark of the hemlock trees which grew in abundance around the lake. Hundreds of barrels of the extract were then sent annually to Boston, Montreal and other destinations, including the Templeton tannery in Perth where it was used in the tanning of hides for leather. During the winter twenty-five to thirty men were kept busy cutting, hauling and piling the large stock of peeled bark which was needed to keep the plant running during the open season. A welcome source of income for area farmers, the company paid from $3.00 to $4.00 per cord for bark, some of which came from as far away as Westport.

A sketch of the bark factory at the foot of Christie Lake. Opened in 1868 to extract tannin from the bark of the hemlock, it closed in 1874. (Courtesy: Gray Palmer)

Arden Blackburn's Mail Route

In January 1870 local resident Isaac Corry (Korry) wrote his brother in Utah:

> *There is quite a business up at Gravely Bay at the foot of Christie's Lake where they erected a large factory for extracting the juice from hemlock bark. They consume about ten thousand cords of bark in the year and about two thousand cords of firewood in the year. The juice of the bark is sent to England and other foreign markets for tanning purposes.*[31]

Once the factory was in operation, the company regularly hired about a dozen men, some of whom found the work there to be a bit on the dangerous side. Such was the case for George Graham who was injured and taken to the nearby home of the Gray family.

> *It appears that while engaged in starting some machinery, driven by a 50 horsepower engine, his right foot became entangled in one of the large pinion wheels and in an instant the greater portion of the member was destroyed rendering amputation necessary, which was performed by Dr. Howden, assisted by Dr. Kellock. The utmost promptitude on the part of Mr. Thomas Moffatt on cutting off the steam supply prevented a much more serious accident if not complete destruction of life. Mr. Graham, we are informed, although much depressed from the nature of his misfortune, is progressing fairly. He is at present lying at George Gray's, 3rd Line, where he is receiving much kindness and attention on the part of the family as well as from Mr. Aspden on the part of the company. He will remove to town as soon as possible* (Perth Courier, June 25, 1869).

Despite the occasional mishap, the factory operated until November 11, 1871, when a fire completely destroyed the building and its contents. It was an estimated loss of $25,000 of which only $6,000 was covered by insurance, thus leaving a considerable loss for the plant's owner at the time a Mr. J. Cook. Fortunately $20,000 worth of hemlock bark stored throughout the neighbourhood had not been lost.

Chapter 4 ♦ Christie Lake Bark Factory

> **HEMLOCK BARK**
>
> The Cook Extract Company will pay cash for any quantity of Good Sound Hemlock Bark delivered at their Works at Myer's Lake, Bathurst.
>
> Parties having contracts for bark delivery will be pleased to know that we are rebuilding our Bark Works, and will want all the bark they can bring, for which they will be paid in Cash on completion of their contracts.
>
> THE COOK EXTRACT CO.
>
> Perth, Dec. 13, 1871

While the Cook Extract Company rebuilt the factory at Christie Lake, within a few years it again closed down this time due to the diminishing supply of bark.

Despite the unfortunate loss of the bark works, the lumber trade around Christie Lake continued to flourish. At the turn of the century, as domestic and overseas demand for Canadian wood and wood products increased, cutting operations proliferated around the lake. With each passing winter more and more women and children were left alone as the men took their teams and worked the shanties. In 1891 it was reported that when John Ritchie was finished "shantying" for the winter, he had taken over three thousand logs.

Typical of the lumber camps in the area was that overseen by James Robinson who was engaged in bringing out logs for Ritchie. Located about a mile from Christie Lake, the shanty there was made of logs stuffed with moss to keep out the cold. Inside was a long table made of rough boards and two benches that ran the full length down both sides of the room. At the rear of the room were two beds each sufficient to hold a dozen men.

After a hard day in the bush, the men returned to the shanty for a well-deserved meal of pork, beans, potatoes, bread and tea. After supper, it was said, "the men dry themselves, smoke, play cards or pass the time away in good-natured raillery. Like most other camps, this one possesses some remarkable people and animals" (*Perth Courier*, January 24, 1902).

Old-timers in the area, such as Tom Scott, reminisced fondly about the camaraderie and fresh air of the spring drives. Despite the hard work and danger inherent in such ventures, shanty life spelled excitement and adventure to the young men of the area, many of whom were said to be "better fed in the shanty than they were at home, with pay to boot."[32]

Carl Adams and his men bringing a raft of logs across Christie Lake in 1928. (Courtesy: Penny Nault)

In 1894 when Thomas McMunn of Bolingbroke brought a raft of one hundred and forty cord of sawed wood to the foot of the lake, it was reported to be "a considerable job" to pile such a quantity on the beach. A few years later when a drive from Bob's Lake passed through Christie Lake, it was said that while the current drives are "but ghosts of the drives of years ago...an 8,000 log drive has about it, too, something of the breath of the big woods, and the freshness and earnestness and life of the lumber trade" (*Perth Courier* 05/30/1902).

Not all of the logs floated down the river and across the lake completed the journey and one family, the Jordans, redid the entire floor of one of their houses with the wood recovered from the bottom of the lake, most of it still bearing the marks from the spurs of the lumbermen's boots.

Chapter 4 ♦ Christie Lake Bark Factory

A load of logs being gathered at the old dam near Bolingbroke on August 17, 1928. (Courtesy: Penny Nault)

One of the busiest mills in the Christie Lake area was the mill of John Ritchie. Built in 1859 the Ritchie mill was located on the Tay River, a mile off the Scotch Line and seven miles from Perth. At the turn of the century, it employed upwards of twenty men who in the summer turned out oak and elm lumber and in the winter worked the Ritchie timber limits. Bob Scott had gone to work for John Ritchie in 1900.

"If there was a daytime head-wind on the lake, we worked nights when it was calm. If the wind was fair that was our good luck," recalled Scott (*Perth Courier* 10/21/1965).

Those, like Scott, who worked the lumber trade were a hearty lot who loved the outdoors and whose language was sometimes on the rough side, a fact of some concern to John Ritchie, a devout Baptist, who worried about what his children might hear. It was for this very reason that the Ritchie children began to spend their summers at Christie Lake.

◆ Chapter Five ◆

HARD TIMES HIT CHRISTIE LAKE

During the summer, when his four children were not in school, John Ritchie didn't much like the thought of them hanging around his mill. As a result, in 1897, he purchased land from James Doyle for $35 and constructed a one-room cottage at the foot of the lake. Since it was also used by Ritchie's sister and her husband when they came home from doing missionary work in India, the cottage became known as India Villa.

It was here that the Ritchie children began to spend their summers surrounded by fresh air and clean water and well away from the men at the mill. John Ritchie was so convinced the lake was an ideal spot for youngsters that when he met Jessie McKinnon, another ardent Baptist, whose lovely voice filled the church each Sunday, he invited her to send her children to the cottage as well. The invitation was a welcome one for Jessie McKinnon, who at the time was a widower with four young children.

So began a summer tradition whereby the four McKinnon children joined the four Ritchie children to spend their summers at Christie Lake under the watchful eye of the oldest Ritchie daughter. Once or twice a week a wagon load of food was sent to the lake to feed the lot and together the eight children shared summers full of discoveries and adventures, including the time Ernie Ritchie shoved his hand into the hole of a hollow tree only to find it inhabited by a family of skunks, all of whom made poor Ernie pay dearly for his curiosity.

The fact that her children were able to enjoy their summers at the lake was no doubt a relief for Jessie McKinnon, who had been left a widow in 1888 when her husband Donald was struck down by yellow fever while on a business trip to Louisville, Kentucky. His sudden death had left Jessie alone with the couple's four children—Donald who was thirteen at the time, Grace who was nine, Walter who was six and Jean who was four.

Jessie McLean had been a teacher at the Perth Public School when she first met the irrepressible Donald Sylvester McKinnon, a travelling salesman who attended local fairs and demonstrated the Osborn sewing machine. When he met Jessie McLean, McKinnon wrote home to his family saying that he had met a young lady who sang like a "nighthawk," although he no doubt meant a nightingale.

Married in the Presbyterian Church in Lanark in December 1874, the couple moved to Ottawa where they opened a store on Sparks Street selling pianos. They then relocated to Toronto where Donald continued to sell pianos and sewing machines.

By the time John Ritchie announced in 1910 that he intended to sell his various properties and head out west, the McKinnon children were all fully grown. Despite the passage in time, the announcement struck a chord with Walter McKinnon, who was now a bond dealer in Toronto, but still harboured fond memories of his summers at India Villa. So it was that while Carl Adams bought the Ritchie sawmill, Walter McKinnon purchased the Ritchie cottage.

The third of Jessie and Donald McKinnon's children, Walter Laughlin McKinnon had been born in 1882 and began work in 1901 as a school teacher at the one-room school located on the 3rd line of Bathurst just north of where the Althorpe Road crosses the Tay River. He taught there until Easter of 1902 when it was announced that he resigned his position to pursue further education.

That fall Walter McKinnon entered McMaster University in Toronto, a Baptist institution, where his attendance was financially supported by another Baptist family from Perth, the Farmers, one of whose members served on the faculty at the university. It was while

CHAPTER 5 ◆ HARD TIMES HIT CHRISTIE LAKE

at McMaster that Walter McKinnon met Winifred Emily Phillips of Courtright and the two were married on February 2, 1905.

Following his graduation in 1906, McKinnon became the business manager and municipal bond editor of the *Financial Post of Canada* and later a salesman for stock brokers Brent, Noxon and Co. So successful was he in his financial dealings that not only did he accumulate enough capital to purchase India Villa, but in 1911 he opened his own company, known as W.L. McKinnon and Co., dealers in government and municipal bonds.

The original India Villa bought by Walter McKinnon from John Ritchie in 1911. (Courtesy: Peter Higgins)

No one was happier about Walter McKinnon's purchase of India Villa than his daughter Jessie (Hill) who was to inherit both her grandmother's name and her love of the lake. As soon as school was out that June, young Jessie enjoyed her first train ride to the lake, an adventure she never forgot.

At five o'clock in the morning we reached Perth and my father took us out of the train, and I suppose we walked from the station to the Hotel

Perth where we slept until the livery stable was open, which would be about 9 o'clock in the morning. Mr. Cameron's livery stable was where we picked up Mr. Cameron and a team of horses and a big wagon with a fringe around it, The wagon had to take all of our possessions and ourselves on the eleven mile trip to Christie Lake along the gravel road. This is the way we got to Christie Lake. There my father helped Mr. Cameron unload everything and tucked us all away.[33]

From that time on, as soon as the school year ended, Jessie and her mother, as well as her sister Jean (Higgins) and brother Jack, headed to Union Station hauling everything they needed to get them through the summer. As Jessie put it, they "couldn't afford to buy two sets of things" and so they were forced to drag along bedding, cooking utensils, dishes, nearly everything they owned. Once at the lake the McKinnon children literally exploded from the wagon.

Walter and Winifred's daughters, Jean and Jessie, enjoying some time at the cottage in 1912. (Courtesy: Peter Higgins)

Chapter 5 ♦ Hard Times Hit Christie Lake

"We were so excited to arrive at Christie Lake. We just took off from the wagon and did our exploring of all the changes from the year before, and what our treasures were and where they were," recalled Jessie.

While Walter McKinnon remained in Toronto during the week to tend to his business affairs, he'd arrive at the lake late Friday evening to spend the weekend with his family. Once there he spent his time fixing things around the cottage or cruising the lake in his new motor boat said to be equipped with the latest fittings and engine. When he ordered the boat he gave instructions that it be shipped to the Bathurst train station. No one was more surprised than Walter McKinnon when it ended up in Bathurst, New Brunswick. Come Sunday evening Walter left the lake by train, having booked a sleeping berth so as to arrive back in Toronto well-rested for work that Monday.

Walter and Winifred McKinnon take the children for a cruise in Walter's boat Old Put-Put in 1913 L.-R. Jack McKinnon, Don Shepherd, Walter & Winifred McKinnon, Jean McKinnon, Jessie McKinnon. (Courtesy: Peter Higgins)

Shortly after the McKinnon family started coming to the cottage young Jessie McKinnon was startled by the tremendous blasts caused by the construction of the railroad. Although the explosions were at the other end of the lake, Jessie recalled how they rattled the dishes in the McKinnon cottage two and a half miles away.

When the line was complete, Jessie and her family no longer arrived at the station in Perth, but rather the Christie Lake station where they descended the steep wooden steps to the water. Here they were met by George Noonan who transported them to the cottage in his motor boat, while George's son, Wilbur, took their luggage and other belongings in his horse and buggy.

> **BERRY PICKING IN 1915**
> **AS REMEMBERED BY JESSIE MCKINNON**
>
> We spent a good part of our summer months picking berries at the railway where the trains ran, near the train tracks, there were wonderful crops of raspberries. We would pick every container that we owned full before we would leave the berry patch. One day we were surprised to see a brown bear lumber up to the berry patch. We children were quite disturbed about it, but Mother just went on picking and the bear didn't pay any attention to us and went away when he had all that he wanted. This went on for many, many years until the railway people got an idea that they had to burn all of the brush that was surrounding the tracks and they burned all the berry bushes, so we were out of raspberries.

Shortly after Walter McKinnon bought the Ritchie cottage, his brother-in-law Harry Shepherd bought the adjacent property. An engineer from Brockville, Ontario, Shepherd had married Walter McKinnon's sister Grace. The couple had four children—Don, Lawrence (Law) and twins Bud and Marnie. With Walter's help the Shepherds built a ramshackle one room cottage that had only curtains for privacy and an attached kitchen. The area occupying the two cottages was designated as Oak View and it was here that the three McKinnon children and the four Shepherd children reunited each summer for a carefree time of swimming off the dock, playing

Chapter 5 ◆ Hard Times Hit Christie Lake

Two different views of the Shepherd cottage. An earlier photo on the top ca. 1912 and a later version ca. 1950s. (Courtesy: Peter Higgins)

on the swing, digging in the sand box and bouncing on the teeter-totter.

No one approached summer at the cottage with more anticipation than did Jessie's mother Winifred. According to young Jessie, her mother was an avid fisherwoman who sank bundles of brush along the shore of the lake in order to create a habitat for minnows which she would then use to catch bass.

The summer that Jessie was twelve years old, however, her mother was forced to leave the cottage and return to Toronto where her sister had suffered a stroke. The McKinnon children were left at the lake on their own with their aunt, Grace, nearby to look after them. As fate would have it, while her mother was away, Jessie took sick with an ear infection that caused her to suffer an extremely high temperature. It left her aunt Grace with her hands full looking after her own children, as well as tending to the McKinnon children, one of whom was very sick. To make life easier for Jessie's aunt, George Noonan's wife, Sarah, came over to help look after the children.

Walter McKinnon's wife, Winifred, the mother of Jack, Jean and Jessie Mackinnon. (Courtesy: Peter Higgins)

Chapter 5 ♦ Hard Times Hit Christie Lake

"Bless her heart. She was a wonderful friend; she would come over when I was sick and give me bed baths," recalled Jessie.

When Jessie was well enough to travel, her aunt Grace decided she should return to Toronto to be with her mother. The problem was that Grace couldn't leave the other children to take Jessie to the train station. Once again Sarah Noonan came to their aid.

She came at three o'clock and Mr. Noonan and she took me up to the head of the lake. I had no money. I had no train ticket. My father arranged from Toronto that I could be taken back to Toronto and he would look after the funding of it, so I went up there... That was a wonderful memory of mine. I never forgot to be grateful to Mrs. Noonan, and Mr. Noonan, too. He just drove the boat, but she was a real nurse, as well as a loving mother.

Eventually both Jessie and her mom returned to the lake where each weekend Walter McKinnon arrived in his big black Buick honking his horn as he came up the hill so that the children could be lined up to meet him starting from the youngest to the oldest. Once there, Walter, or "A" as he was known, would give them each a quarter. On several occasions when he arrived at the lake Walter McKinnon was accompanied by friends from Toronto, many from the YMCA where he was an active member. On one such occasion he brought the choir from the Bloor Street Baptist Church to perform a show in the band shell at Perth.

Although not a musician himself, Walter McKinnon shared the lake's affinity for music, turning his garage at the cottage into a recreation room where folks often gathered in the evening for entertainment and dances. Each year a grand party was held for the opening of the cottage and friends from around the lake were invited to attend. While the band played, refreshments were served including doughnuts which the musicians hung on their music stands according to Jessie's cousin Marnie Shepherd (Milne).

Young Jessie McKinnon couldn't recall a time when her father, a self-taught handyman, wasn't walking around the cottage with a hammer and a saw. Early on he put a verandah on the side of the cottage and one on the front which gave the family a little additional room. He also put up a "his and hers" outhouse fitted with ceramic toilets and sinks and connected to a septic tank. A night light was provided by means of dry cell batteries hooked to flashlight bulbs.

Oakview as it appeared in the 1940s.
(Courtesy: Peter Higgins)

Then there was the barn he built for the family horse, Minto, which Minto initially shared with a cow. Intended to provide the McKinnon family with milk, the cow was often the unwanted cause of Jessie's sister Jean having to stay at home while the other children went out to play. For when Jessie's mom milked the cow, her sister Jean had to hold the cow's tail so it didn't brush against her mother's face. On more than one occasion, recalled Jessie, Jean was invited to go somewhere with her friends, only to have to decline because she "had to stay home and hold the cow's tail."

To the delight of the girls, their mother eventually grew tired of milking the cow and the family started to walk with their quart pails over to the Jordan's, where Mrs. Jordan scooped their milk out of a vat that stood on a stoop by the farmhouse door. When their pails were full, the McKinnon children headed for home. One day as they were walking back from the Jordan's, Jessie's brother took a notion to swing his pail around. Afraid to stop swinging it for fear he would spill the milk, he kept it up all the way home where, it was said, his mother was surprised to find the pail full of buttermilk.

Chapter 5 ♦ Hard Times Hit Christie Lake

> **TORONTO AND DISTRICT AMATEUR BASKETBALL ASSOCIATION**
>
> Recognition of the valuable services he has rendered to basketball in Ontario was given W. L. McKinnon last evening, when he was elected Honourary President of the new Toronto and District Amateur Basketball Association. Mr. McKinnon is a former President of the old T. and D. Association, which loses its identity with the formation of the new organization. He has done much in the interests of the game, both as a player and as an executive. He still plays being captain of a team in the Central "Y" House League. Mr. McKinnon is a native of Perth and head of the firm of W.L. McKinnon and Co. bond dealers, Toronto (*The Globe* 11/19/1926).

Often the centre of attention Walter McKinnon liked nothing better than to have a crowd at the cottage. When it came time to round everyone up for a swim off the dock or a game of tennis, he'd use his

Walter McKinnon, known as "A," playing tennis on the court he had installed at Christie Lake. (Courtesy: Peter Higgins)

megaphone to summon them to the activity. An athlete of some note, McKinnon had a tennis court installed at the cottage with a back screen to keep the balls from getting lost in the junipers. At one point McKinnon even announced the formation of a summer camp to be run by his daughter Jessie.

> **CHRISTIE LAKE VACATION CLUB**
>
> A new development is taking place at Christie Lake this year beginning this week at "Oakview Cottage" owned by Mr. and Mrs. W.L. McKinnon of Toronto, which will be used as the headquarters of the Christie Lake Vacation Club. Miss Jessie McKinnon, daughter of Mr. and Mrs. McKinnon, will be in charge, and Mrs. Wm. DeWitt will cater to the membership of the Club. The idea is taking well for the entire accommodation is already booked for the summer by the members of the club, the majority of whom come from Toronto, Kitchener and Ottawa. Mr. Robert McNairn, son of Prof. McNairn of McMaster University, Toronto, will assist in the entertaining of the members. Mr. McNairn is a second year student at McMaster University (*Perth Courier* 06/28/1929).

In 1919 the original Shepherd cottage was shoved down the hill to the lake to be used as a boat house and Harry Shepherd hired a local carpenter, Bill Mitchell, to put up a new building up on the hill. The new cottage had a spacious living room with a large fireplace built with stones that the Shepherd boys, Don and Law, had helped their dad collect. There were three bedrooms off the living room with curtains on the doorways, as well as a small kitchen and back porch. Across the front was a veranda, the length of the cottage complete with wooden rocking chairs and a hanging swing. There was no hydro, only oil lamps and no indoor plumbing, just a two-seater at the back in the cedar trees. The outside of the cottage was shingles and the porcupines used to come up on the veranda to chew them. The Shepherds had been told by the Jordans that it was because of the salt in the wood.

Chapter 5 ◆ Hard Times Hit Christie Lake

A group enjoying themselves on the dock in front of the McKinnon boathouse in 1937. (Courtesy: David Hill)

With no running water in the cottages, the McKinnons and Shepherds brought water from the lake using a gas engine located in the pump house at the bottom of the hill. The water was pumped up the hill to a large elevated storage tank and when the tank needed to be refilled someone had to go down the hill and crank the engine to start it. Another person then stayed up top and watched the tank. When it was full, the person at the top of the hill shouted to the one at the bottom to shut off the engine.

The summer of 1923 was a difficult one for the Shepherd family. That May Harry Shepherd passed away, leaving his wife Grace a widow with four young children—Don (fourteen), Lawrence or Law (nine) and the twins Bud and Marnie (two). Finding herself in the same position her own mother had once been, Grace Shepherd looked forward to summers at the cottage and the supportive presence of family and friends.

According to Grace, there were only two seasons in the year—getting ready for school and getting ready for the lake.[34] When it came time to head to the lake, Grace gathered up her mother, the senior Jessie McKinnon, and her four children and boarded the train for Christie Lake. During one particular trip, Grace bemoaned the fact that she hadn't brought a washcloth to wipe the children's faces. Much to everyone's surprise their ever-resourceful grandmother lifted her long skirt to reveal a number of items pinned to her slip, including a washcloth.

The trip to the cottage was an event that always brought with it a great degree of excitement for the Shepherd youngsters, none more so than the time that Don and Law decided to bring their pet rats along for the ride. When the porter informed the boys they couldn't bring the cage containing the white rats into the parlour car, they had to put them on a shelf in the lady's washroom, a move that caused quite a commotion.

As fate would have it, during the trip a gravel train broke down on the track ahead and all passengers, including the Shepherds and Grandma McKinnon, had to be transferred from the train they were on to one up ahead. Grace and Law and the twins went first carrying their hand baggage, while Don went back to help his grandma. Much to everyone's surprise Don couldn't find her. As it turned out she had gotten off the wrong side of the train and was now trundling along in the ditch carrying the cage of white rats. It was a sight to behold and one that was still fresh in the minds of everyone even after they reached the lake and were safely ensconced in George Noonan's boat, baggage and all.

Summers were a time of much joy for the McKinnon and Shepherd children, a time of renewing old friendships and seeking new adventures. Each morning, the children walked or went by boat to Noonans' farm to await the arrival of Arden Blackburn and the daily mail. As they waited for Sarah Noonan to put the mail in the pigeon holes, they listened as the adults talked of various goings-on. In the early thirties when talked turned to the sad state of the world's financial affairs, it's doubtful the Shepherd or McKinnon children even took notice of the topic or realized the impact it would have on their lives.

Chapter 5 ♦ Hard Times Hit Christie Lake

Some folks watching the action on the tennis court at the McKinnon cottage in 1936. (Courtesy: Peter Higgins)

The years following Black Tuesday (October 29, 1929) were tough ones for financial investors such as Walter McKinnon. For many in Canada the twenties had indeed roared. During the decade a multitude of companies had started with investment money raised on the Toronto Stock Exchange. Between 1922 and 1926 Canadian companies had issued new shares to a value of over $700 million. It was a heady time for investors and financial managers. Profits and share values climbed. To take advantage of the boom, investors began to borrow in order to buy additional shares.

Eventually the bills came due. As cautious investors started to sell off stocks in order to cash in on their high values, others followed suit. By late October 1929 the number of stocks offered for sale outnumbered the demand for new shares. Suddenly, the value of stocks fell dramatically. The stock market crashed. Many Canadians lost all they had worked for during the past decade.

As the thirties progressed, times got tougher and tougher for those with little to no money to spend. As demand for Canadian

Above an early view of the wash house at the McKinnon's ca. 1915 and a view of dining room ca. 1944. (Courtesy: Peter Higgins)

Chapter 5 ◆ Hard Times Hit Christie Lake

products declined, warehouses filled with unsold goods. Factories closed down or cut back. Workers were laid off or forced to take pay cuts. Fewer could afford to take vacations. Fewer came to the lake.

CHRISTIES LAKE HOUSE FOR SALE

The above popular property is offered for sale very reasonable. Would make a splendid private summer home. There is another small cottage that goes with the property, also a large garage boathouse and ice house etc. This is one of the best properties on Christies Lake (*Perth Courier* 08/19/1932).

Investors such as Walter McKinnon were forced to issue difficult announcements to an already uneasy clientele. In many cases they tried to cushion the blow. In June 1933 when he announced his firm was taking over the bond business conducted in Perth by the late Tom Farmer, Walter McKinnon took the opportunity to remind folks of the current economic climate.

A FINANCIAL DEPRESSION

We are all in the midst of the world's worst financial depression. As a consequence many problems have arisen extremely difficult to solve. Even the safest and best of investments have problem features of one kind or another. W.L. McKinnon and Co. stands ready to assist the clients of the late Tom Farmer and of Tom Farmer Company in solving any of these problems. They also assure the clients of the same confidential treatment of their business as has always been accorded to them in the past...
The clients of the late Tom Farmer and of Tom Farmer Company are invited to bring their investment problems and their advice as to what funds they have available for investment to W.L. McKinnon and Co. whose offices will be across from the Town Hall Building in the same location as Tom Farmer Company now occupies.
Perth, Ontario, June 10th, 1933

Arden Blackburn's Mail Route

The Perth office of W.L. McKinnon and Co. was to be managed by McKinnon's son-in-law, Joe Higgins, who had married Walter and Winnifred's daughter Jean. Joe was an avid hockey fan and supporter of the Perth Blue Wings and in his official capacity as treasurer of the team's executive was said to have given "freely of his time and ability in financing matters in a way that won plaudits from those associated with him" (*Perth Courier* 04/19/1940).

In 1940 when Joe Higgins accepted a position with the Dominion Abrasive Wheel Co. Ltd. in Mimico, Ontario, he was replaced by Jim Wright as the new manager of the McKinnon office in Perth. Wright, who had worked in the Toronto office of W.L. McKinnon Co., had married Margaret McLean of Perth, who had also worked in the Toronto office as secretary to the company solicitor.

Following the sudden death of Winifred in 1942, Walter McKinnon married his long-time secretary Nettie Aldridge and continued his civic-minded activities, serving as one of the principal fund raisers for the move of McMaster University from Hamilton to Toronto and also for the building of Yorkminster Baptist Church in Toronto. He was also on the executive of the Victory bond effort in both wars and at one time was said to have been offered the position of Minister of Finance in the government of Mitch Hepburn, an offer he declined.

Despite a valiant attempt to appear otherwise, by the end of the forties, the seventy-two-year-old McKinnon was in financial difficulty, and on June 2, 1952, much to the shock and dismay of many was forced to declare bankruptcy. It was an announcement that left area residents, including those at the lake, feeling anxious about their financial investments. Particularly worried were those who had recently sold their bonds back to McKinnon on the understanding they'd be issued new ones.

Like many Norman Sargeant of McDonald's Corners maintained he had relied entirely on the goodwill of W.L. McKinnon and Co.

"I traded with James Wright, manager of McKinnon and Co.'s office here," said Sargeant. "I never paid too much attention to the course of the deal. I just assumed that the bonds I bought would be put into safekeeping. I thought they would go into the safe at some future date. I thought everything was purely routine" (*Courier* 11/24/1954).

Chapter 5 ◆ Hard Times Hit Christie Lake

Following an investigation by the Ontario Securities Commission in December 1953 McKinnon was charged with various counts of theft and fraud, including eleven transactions totaling $44,000 conducted with residents in the Perth area, many of whom claimed they had transferred their bonds to the McKinnon office in Toronto upon being warned of recent robberies in the area. Some said they had lost their life savings. All claimed they had not given the McKinnon firm permission at any time to sell or exchange their bonds.

McKinnon's court hearing was delayed by a serious automobile accident that left him hospitalized shortly before the announcement of his financial collapse. When the hearing finally commenced in Perth in December 1953, it was said McKinnon expressed his sorrow about the savings his investors, particularly those from the Perth area, had lost.

"I never had so much grief in my life as I have experienced in losing money for my clients. My savings for the past 40 years are gone. I am completely broke," stated McKinnon at the time (*Perth Courier* 12/17/1953).

Throughout the hearing McKinnon was represented by prominent Canadian lawyer J. J. Robinette, who had been the lead prosecutor in the trial of Igor Gouzenko and had represented Evelyn Dick in the famous overturning of her murder conviction in 1946. Robinette argued that the evidence submitted by the Crown could not be classed as theft or fraud since the bonds that were supposedly stolen by Walter McKinnon had actually been bought by him.

Robinette pointed out that the books at the McKinnon firm were "scrupulously honest, and that all bonds excepting those purchased by Mr. McKinnon were returned to the rightful owner." The essence of the situation, according to Robinette, was the promise people had received from McKinnon that they would at a later date receive new bonds for those that they had sold him.

"There is no law condemning a man who breaks promises," Robinette reminded the court (*Perth Courier* 12/17/1953).

When McKinnon came before Judge F. W. Wilson in the Judges Criminal Court of Lanark County, he pled not guilty. The trial was an emotional one that dragged on through much of 1954. Once again Robinette reminded those concerned that all books and records had been properly kept. There had been no attempt at concealment. There were no inaccurate entries. The "badges of fraud" usually looked for in such cases simply were not there, maintained Robinette.

"There is always a tendency to cry "Fraud' in a case of bankruptcy where promises are not kept...but it is not a crime to breach a contract," maintained Robinette who pointed out that the custom of "delayed delivery" where bonds are accepted for exchange before the replacements are turned over was, in fact, a common and acceptable practice in the bond business.

In rebuttal Crown Attorney J. A. Klein maintained McKinnon was well aware that he was "playing a game of musical chairs—and that at any given point the music might stop" (*Perth Courier* 12/02/1954).

According to Klein, what McKinnon had perpetrated was "a general scheme to swindle, as far as necessary to keep himself afloat, the people whose securities he was able to get into his hands—especially people who were at that station of life when they would repose complete trust in him, people who wouldn't know how this bond business was done, people who wouldn't ask questions."

Amid the high emotions and financial complexities of the trial, there was another issue that had captured the attention of folks at the lake. Many wondered how a bankrupt McKinnon could afford such high-priced legal help. Robinette publicly countered the rumours and finger-pointing by declaring there was absolutely no evidence that his client had "salted away" any money.

"As a matter of fact, my fees have been paid by Mr. McKinnon's son-in-law," pointed out Robinette, who said he simply wanted to set the record straight.

Despite the fact that those called as character references for McKinnon, including Christie Lake's John Jordan, extolled his character and accomplishments, the accused was sentenced to one year determinate and six months indeterminate in the Ontario Reformatory.

"You have been defended with great ability," Judge Wilson told the accused in passing sentence, "but I can't overlook the gravity of your offences. You have committed a grievous and protracted wrong, not just against stock speculators but against the aged, the blind and the crippled, with the result the life savings of many of these people were wiped out."

Chapter 5 ◆ Hard Times Hit Christie Lake

It was noted that McKinnon, who stood erect and composed during the judge's address, sat and wept when sentence was passed. In the days ahead, while there were those at the lake who claimed Walter McKinnon was away on business, there were those who knew better.

◆ Chapter Six ◆

CHRISTIE LAKE CAMP

The downfall of Walter McKinnon wasn't the first time the topic of crime and punishment had been the centre of conversation at Christie Lake. Back in 1899 when someone busted into the lake's first cottage, the culprits drew a rather public reprimand.

> *The parties who broke into Mrs. Drummond's cottage, Ruby Island, and helped themselves to working utensils etc. should have been thoughtful enough to return them to the cottage and not leave them lying around the island. Mrs. Drummond would be very much obliged if they would return the hatchet (Perth Courier 06/23/1899).*

In the world of justice the desire to make things right often comes with a desire to ensure they aren't repeated. The line between retribution and rehabilitation is always a fine one, a fact recognized by Ottawa's Jack McKinley who, when he became the judge for Ottawa's Juvenile Court in 1922, encountered many boys whom he felt needed "adjusting and reclaiming," rather than punishment.

In many cases what the boys required, according to Judge McKinley, was a change in environment, along with some appropriate adult direction. To accomplish this McKinley envisioned a summer retreat, away from the hot city streets, where the measure of success

Ottawa's Judge McKinley, the driving force behind the formation of the Christie Lake Camp for underprivileged children.
(Courtesy: Carole Gagne Ince and Christie Lake Kids)

would be in "giving the boy responsibility, handling him with friendship, teaching him the general principles of good citizenship and doing so with the help of the open air."[35]

To achieve what he had in mind, Judge McKinley approached the Ottawa Kiwanis Club for help. When the Club gave its enthusiastic support, McKinley's probation officers began to visit the homes of deserving boys and make the necessary arrangements for them to go to camp. The Ottawa YMCA agreed to let them use its facilities at Golden Lake after the regular Y program was over. So it was that on August 1, 1922, several boys boarded a Grand Trunk rail car bound for Golden Lake where camp director Ace Milks led them through three weeks of baseball, swimming and campfires.

The camp was such a success that the directors decided to look for a permanent home. It wasn't long before Milks announced that he had found the perfect spot, an eighty-eight acre site situated on Christie Lake. The property he said had everything: a good long

Chapter 6 ♦ Christie Lake Camp

shoreline with several places for swimming and boating, a spacious field for sports and a large elevated area for tents or cabins shaded from the sun by huge old oak trees.

On May 29, 1923, Judge McKinley and Ottawa businessmen Harold Fisher and E. R. Bremner purchased the Christie Lake property for $1,200. To be known initially as the Christie Lake Boys' Camp, and then simply as the Christie Lake Camp, over the years it proved to be a welcome refuge for many underprivileged youth seeking a reprieve from the temptations of the city and a clean start amid the refreshing water of the lake.

An early view of the camping huts at the Christie Lake Camp. (Courtesy: Carole Gagne Ince and Christie Lake Kids)

That July when the first campers arrived by bus, they were greeted by sleeping huts made with a wooden frame covered with canvas. There were eight bunks in each hut with a cot in the middle for a staff member. There was also a large dining hall, featuring a fireplace and a large verandah overlooking the lake, and a headquarters for the new Camp Director, John ("Jack") Carmichael. Known as "Chief," the twenty-two-year-old Carmichael was an employee of the boys' department of the Central YMCA in Toronto, but had moved to Ottawa to work as a probation officer and act as camp leader. Before long the camp was open to all under-privileged boys regardless of whether they had been in trouble with the law or not and they began to arrive at the lake by train rather than bus.

> *"I can still see the mobs at the train station. You know, droves of guys. Not knowing where to go and which train to get into, and all our luggage. Probably a good three hour trip to Christie. And then at Christie Lake Station, waiting on the dock to get into the freighter canoes—campers, milk, food supplies,"* recalled one young camper.[36]

The station stood directly across the lake from the camp, a distance of about 2.2 kilometers and the wooden slide leading down to the water provided a perfect diversion for the youngsters as they waited for the canoes from camp to come and pick them up.

A group of young lads from the camp heading out in their canoes.
(Courtesy: Carole Gagne Ince and Christie Lake Kids)

Chapter 6 ♦ Christie Lake Camp

"I was so small I couldn't carry my bag empty let alone full of clothes" [recalled one camper]. *"The stairs leading down to the dock at Christie Lake Station looked huge to me. That's where the bigger boys would take the canoes across to Camp. The little guys would be carried around to the Camp via horse drawn buggy. But, of course, some of the big boys, being tough, walked the seven and a half miles around the lake."*[37]

The individual responsible for transporting the smaller boys to the camp in his buggy was George Farrell, the farmer who lived next to the camp. Farrell was well-known around the camp for he also picked up the camp garbage, provided the kitchen with milk, did minor repairs and kept an eye on the camp during the off-season, even going so far as to clean out the camp latrines.

With no electricity or running water, the camp was lighted with coal oil lamps and cooking was done on a wood stove. Water was carried from the lake by pail, and campers soon discovered that by placing white rocks beside the trails it was easier for them to find their way to and from the water after dark.

Beyond the camp the surrounding countryside around the lake was used for hikes, nature walks and berry-picking, and once a week there was an overnight camp up the Tay River. Every second Saturday night, the boys were allowed to invite a few of the girls from around the lake over for dinner. Kathleen Hicks, daughter of Mervyn and Matilda Hicks, who often went with her cousin Nora and sister Mary, recalled sitting at the long table with the boys, whose favourite trick was to splash them with spilled milk.

"You learned to roll up the oilcloth covering the table quickly," recalled Kathleen, "or the milk ended up in your lap."

After dinner a space would be cleared; someone would get out a guitar and there'd be a dance. According to Kathleen that's when the chant would start: "So and so has a girlfriend! So and so has a girlfriend!"

"They were tough little nuts," said Kathleen, "straight off the streets of Ottawa. They loved nothing better than to sneak up and stick a snake under your nose. But as long as you simply said, 'Oh what a nice snake,' they'd back off."

By ten o'clock the girls were in their boat and headed home where Kathleen often found her mother waiting on the cottage porch for them.

Despite the odd bump, bruise or reprimand, life at the camp was an enjoyable experience for the city youngsters and continued to be so until August 22, 1926, when tragedy struck. That day "Chief" Carmichael and one of the tent leaders left to go across the lake to pick up the morning mail. They were on their way back when the weather took a turn for the worse, and a strong wind swamped their canoe, throwing Carmichael and the young lad into the water. The two clung to the canoe for fifteen minutes until Carmichael finally told the youngster to swim to the nearest island. Then overcome by the weight of his clothing or getting tangled in the weeds, Carmichael went under the water for the last time.

Upon making his way to Pickerel Island, the young camper looked back, only to discover there was no sign of his leader. The lad waited what must have been an excruciatingly long five hours until three o'clock that afternoon when summer resident William Neal, who was fishing nearby, saw him and came to his rescue. When Neal picked him up and learned of the tragedy, he quickly rushed the boy to the mainland and sought help. Although an immediate search was commenced, Carmichael's body was not found. News spread quickly through the camp.

"The reaction in the camp was like a contagion," said one camper. "Some young guys who were normally real little devils weren't that day. The whole camp was subdued and depressed until we were sent home the next day."[38]

Despite continued efforts, the body of the camp director was not found until seventeen days later when George Farrell, who had been patrolling the lake daily, eventually found it. Farrell removed the remains to the Christie Lake station where County Coroner Dr. Dwyre determined an inquest would not be needed.

The recovery of the body came exactly one week after a $10,000 trust fund had been set-up for Carmichael's wife and children. Established by a number of prominent Ottawa citizens, the fund was generously supported by members of the Christie Lake community and quickly reached its target. A large funeral was held in Ottawa and was attended by co-workers, friends, city officials and a number of boys who wanted to pay a final tribute to their Chief.

Chapter 6 ◆ Christie Lake Camp

Carmichael was succeeded as probation officer with the Ottawa Juvenile Court by Alexander Renton, a former detective with the R.C.M.P., who was also placed in charge of the camp at Christie Lake. That summer Renton helped plan a camp memorial service to be held on the anniversary of Carmichael's death. Led by the Perth Citizens Band, the campers and various visitors from around the lake left the camp in boats and proceeded to Pickerel Island, where the ceremony was held under the direction of Judge McKinley. Renton placed a wreath on the water at the spot where Carmichael had drowned. The large gathering stood in silence while the band played "Onward Christian Soldiers." The service closed with everyone standing at attention for the singing of "God Save the King."

In 1942 the camp suffered what many considered to be its most serious loss with the unexpected death of Judge McKinley. From the outset McKinley had been the driving force behind the camp. It was his dream and his dedication that had directed the camp through its formative years. Now it was in desperate need of someone who

Jack McKnight who became camp director after the death of Judge McKinley.

shared the judge's vision and determination. That person turned out to be probation officer Jack McKnight, who was named the new camp director.

McKnight was an inspiring leader, blessed with a deep caring and understanding for the kids, along with a fun-loving personality. In 1943 McKnight, who loved to give speeches, most of which began "Ya know boys camp doesn't just happen," hired Ottawa's Bill Martin to come on board as camp leader. Martin worked tirelessly for the next thirty years organizing camp circuses, minstrel shows and church services.

On the Sunday afternoon of July 25, 1943, a memorial cairn was dedicated at the lake to Judge McKinley. Several members of the Christie Lake community, as well as visitors from Perth and Ottawa, gathered at the lake to pay tribute to the camp's founder. In addressing the group, the Rev. Ian Burnett of St. Andrews Presbyterian Church in Ottawa commented, "Let us do honour to a good and great man. No monument is necessary to retain his memory. His real memorial is the camp and the lives of the young men who have passed through this camp" (*Perth Courier* 07/29/1943).

The cairn, located outside the camp dining hall, was constructed of stones gathered from around the Christie Lake countryside and

The view of Christie Lake from the Scout camp, Camp Opemikon, ca. 1945.

Chapter 6 ♦ Christie Lake Camp

placed at the base of a flag pole draped in the Union Jack. Serving as a guard of honour at the dedication that day were four scouts from nearby Camp Opemikon.

The Scouts had arrived at Christie Lake in 1938. That year, after having scoured hundreds of miles of back roads, Jack Armstrong, Executive Secretary of the Ottawa District Scout Council, had picked a site at Christie Lake for the district Scout camp. Subsequent negotiations led to the purchase of a hundred acres from Mrs. Annabelle Sweetman and fifty acres from George Noonan, with the camp to be owned and operated by the Voyageur Region of Scouts Canada. The name "Opemikon," meaning "by the way or near to road or trail" was adopted because of the camp's proximity to the Hanna Side Road.

When the first group of Scouts arrived at Camp Opemikon that summer their meals were cooked on open wood stoves and served in a marquee tent. A dining hall, however, was soon built by campers and staff using logs from the abandoned McManus farmhouse. Following that, sites were cleared for a chapel, health centre, patrol sites, cub cabins and various storage buildings. Swimming and boating areas were also laid out as were tent platforms and kybo shelters. Eventually, trails to O'Brien Lake and Farren Lake were also established. So it was that by the end of the 1940s Christie Lake was home to two of the best-known and best-run camps in the province.

By the end of the Second World War, the original Christie Lake Camp, now twenty-some years old, was in need of a physical overhaul. As a result, in 1945 a new boat house and workshop were built, along with a cold storage room under the kitchen. With limited space the camp had stored many of its belongings in the barn of Ray Erwin a neighbouring farmer. Unfortunately, in May 1946, Erwin's barn was destroyed by fire and the camp lost all its kitchen utensils, oars, paddles, sports equipment and worst of all the canvas sides for their huts.

A few years later, in 1948, with funds provided by the Lions Club, a new building was constructed at the camp that provided accommodation for four patients and living quarters for the camp medical officer. Officially named the Lions Club Medical Centre, the building was dedicated on July 28, 1948. Shortly thereafter the Lions' Den became the official residence of the camp director.

Among those thanked at the opening of the camp's medical centre was Christie Lake summer resident George James who sat on the camps' board of directors. Over the years, James, who along with his brother Lawrence owned the James Bros. Hardware in Perth (following the retirement of Daley Reid in 1921), had provided financial support, as well as many of the materials needed at the camp for repairs and renovations.

Mr. James, who was married to Charlotte Lister, had been coming to Christie Lake for many years having first purchased land in 1914 from R.J. Drummond. Located near Gravelly Bay, the James cottage stood just west of Judge McNeely's cottage. It was here that George's son, Alan, would spend his summers and just to the west of where Alan's son, George, would live year-round.

Like the senior Mr. James, there were other lake residents who took it upon themselves to help the camp whenever they could. Folks like the Erwins, the Noonans and the Jordans received deliveries, provided storage space, took telephone messages and kept an eye on the place.

A group of campers at the Christie Lake Camp gather at the water's edge. (Courtesy: Carole Gagne Ince and Christie Lake Kids)

Chapter 6 ◆ Christie Lake Camp

Following in the footsteps of George Farrell before them, Ed and Marcella Noonan were only too happy to have the leftovers from the camp kitchen to feed their pigs in exchange for keeping an eye on the property in winter. As well, Ed Noonan helped out with the maintenance work, while Marcella did the camp wash and spent hours mending the mattresses torn by the metal bed springs. It was also the Noonans' telephone that provided the camp with its link to the outside world.

In the early 1960s Ed Charby took over from Ed Noonan as camp handyman. A nearby neighbor, Charby was a colourful character whose favourite saying was "T'aint no use worryin' 'bout it!"

As the work increased, however, the decision was made to hire a live-in caretaker. Because it was a move that necessitated the construction of a suitable residence, plans were drawn up for a house that

Iris Fleetwood-Morrow with her daughter, Jane, at the Arliedale store where the campers often went for ice cream ca. 1958. (Courtesy: Penny Nault)

141

would include a room for board members to meet, as well as a garage and storage area. The house was to be located at the end of the road just inside the camp gate, but when the plans were finalized they inadvertently placed the building partly on property owned by the camp's neighbours Edna and Harry Chaplin. The Chaplins graciously offered to sell the small piece of land to the camp for a dollar and in 1976 the Chaplin's son Doug was hired for the caretaker position. For the next two decades Doug and his family lived in the house and kept an eye on the camp.

Activities such as swimming, canoeing, boating, camp craft and nature lore, as well as Jack Carmichael's boxing matches, Bill Martin's circuses, Jack McKnight's wrestling shows and Dan Offord's comical Olympics, formed the core of the Christie Lake experience for the young people. At the end of the camping session, ribbons were presented for life saving, wood craft, first aid, aquatics, athletics, rowing, swimming, canoeing and team games. One of the most hotly contested awards was for the cleanest cabin. The weekly reward for the tidiest cabin was an overnight hike, while the winners of surprise inspections in between were taken on a trip across the lake for ice cream at Arliedale Inn.

Over the years a number of Perth boys, including Merv Roberts and Peter Noonan, enjoyed the benefits of a stay at the camp. In 1946 Roberts was chosen as the best camper among the ten Perth boys who spent the week at camp. For his efforts Merv was presented with a prize donated by James Bros. Hardware. No one's experience at camp was more marked, however, than that of Gordon Stiller who lived on the family farm at Christie Lake.

GORDON STILLER, CHRISTIE LAKE CAMPER 1932

I went to Christie's Lake Boys' Camp when I was seven. My father had died when I was three, and we weren't too well off. We lived on the farm where I still live now, not too far from Camp. Things were scarce, but we managed because we had a good mother. I had just had my tonsils removed in the spring of 1932 and wasn't recovering too well. The doctor recommended that I go to camp, and I was lucky enough to be one of ten local boys sponsored by the Perth 100 Club. They paid our way and supplied our shorts, running shoes, socks and T-shirts.

Chapter 6 ◆ Christie Lake Camp

> *At camp there were a few boys from Ottawa you'd say hello to only if you thought they were in a good humour, otherwise you'd stay out of their way—just a few. Two of those tough guys we called "The Tow baldies" because they had their hair cut short.*
>
> *We had to do work in the kitchen in little groups. We only did this once or twice during the two weeks, but it was fun. George, the cook, was very good to me. He would cook great big pots of food and we'd help serve it. He was no amateur; anyone who could produce good food in those quantities had to know his business.*
>
> *They tried to keep the best possible order at camp, although on some days, it was a losing battle. There were a few boys who just didn't want to do what they were told. Camp had to be run strictly, but the leaders, the doctor and all the staff were very decent to me. It was a great experience for a guy like me; did me a lot of good. We lived out in the country; we didn't get away much. Anybody who could get to camp was pretty lucky.*[39]

Residents around the lake were always more than welcome at camp activities. While some were regular attendees at the Sunday church services held there, others came to hear the various musical performances conducted at the camp including several by the Royal Canadian Air Force Band. Marcella Noonan remembered being able to hear the music loud and clear from her house.

"We used to sit outside and listen," she recalled.

In 1938 George James arranged for the Perth Citizens Band to perform at the camp. The boys and their guests were treated to a medley of popular tunes presented under the direction of Richard Mills. Invited to join in on the choruses, the boys and their guests were said to do so "lustily and vigorously." "The Maple Leaf Forever," "A Long, Long Trail," "Anchors Aweigh," and a score of other well-known tunes comprised the repertoire "that made the rafters ring in the dining hall."

One evening George James, accompanied by members of the Perth Canadian Club, motored out to the camp for an evening of entertainment.

Arden Blackburn's Mail Route

Upon arrival at the camp the Club men received a hearty and spontaneous welcome. Bright-eyed young fellows crowded about the car and wanted to shake hands with all the visitors. It created an embarrassing situation for a moment as no one knew whom to shake hands with first. It was only at the whistle of the camp superintendent that sufficient control was secured to enable the friendly salutations to pass off with more dignity if with subdued enthusiasm (Perth Courier 07/24/1941).

The highlight of the evening was George James' annual copper shower.

By a magical formula which is one of the closely guarded secrets of Mr. James, coppers rained from the heavens and fell upon the ground causing a grand scramble and the exultant note of the victor as he exclaimed in triumph, "Gee, I've got it." This continued to a period of exhaustion both as to the magical copper supply and the physical endurance of the boys themselves. But when all had recovered their breath a great cheer of thanks resounded to high heaven for this act of kindness (Perth Courier 07/24/1941).

The cottage of longtime camp supporter George James located on Gravelly Bay. (Courtesy: George James)

Chapter 6 ◆ Christie Lake Camp

The evening concluded in the dining hall with Professor Gray at the piano leading the crowd through old-time favourites such as "Roll Out the Barrel."

On yet another occasion, the boys at camp were delighted when members of the One Hundred Club from Perth, accompanied by Brown's Orchestra, visited the camp and put on an evening's entertainment. The orchestra was said to have given a good account of itself with "old-time melodies, stream-line summer symphonies and rollicking roundelay." On that same occasion centenarian Chris Forbes, known to the boys as the "magician," lived up to his reputation with a bag full of tricks that mystified everyone.

There were times that even the camp cook, George Ouellette, took his place among the performers and sang several old time songs. A World War One veteran who joined the camp in 1932, it was rumoured that Ouellette had been a member of the Dumbells, the famous Canadian performers who got their start entertaining fellow soldiers during the war and continued as a touring group following their return home. Whatever his background, Ouellette remained a well-known figure at camp for over twenty years.

One year, Ouellette, whose theme song was "I Ate the Baloney," decided to stay at the camp all winter. He talked of banking earth up around his cabin for warmth and subsisting on porcupine if his food ran out. Some around the lake wondered if he was doing it because he had no place to stay in the city. Despite having reservations about the scheme, Judge Fraser relented when Ed and Marcella Noonan offered to keep an eye on Ouellette. While Ouellette stayed several winters, often accompanied by a few dogs and a goat, in the end, he would have to be "brought out because his legs had become weakened."[40]

Replacing George Ouellette as camp cook was no easy task. In 1948 the camp had brought in outside help for the preparation of the food when it hired Leo Noonan from Perth as a kitchen helper and made his wife responsible for the dining hall. It was a move that marked the end of the campers' doing chores in the dining hall. which resulted in a marked improvement in its appearance and cleanliness.

A group of campers gather in front of the dining hall at the Christie Lake Camp.

Now, however, they were in need of a cook, a fact that became painfully obvious one evening when camp director Ron Russell discovered there was nothing for dinner but coleslaw. It was the final straw for Russell, who sent Dan Offord into Dewitt's Corners to get the boys some hot dogs. Russell then phoned Jack McKnight to say that he was firing the kitchen staff. Russell eventually convinced a Mrs. McKinnon from Perth who had done a lot of cooking for the Catholic Church to cook for the camp. She enticed her friend Mrs. Tovey from Balderson to join her.

Once at the camp the ladies produced wonderful home-cooked meals, complete with pies for dessert. They organized the kitchen and had the boys help carry things and stir the big pots of food. The next year their husbands came to the camp to take on some of the heavy work such as the dishwashing. The women only stayed a few years, but everyone raved about the food that Mrs. McKinnon and Mrs. Tovey cooked.

When the ladies gave their notice, the issue of finding a cook for the camp once again proved to be problematic. At one point George James' son, Alan, recalled someone from the camp coming into James Bros. Hardware in Perth and asking if anyone knew of a local caterer.

Chapter 6 ♦ Christie Lake Camp

Alan James suggested Keith Blair, who at the time was cooking for both the Girl Scouts at Camp Davern and the Boy Scouts at Camp Opemikon. So it was that Blair started cooking at Christie Lake Boys' Camp in 1964 and for three years was the caterer for all three camps. One summer Keith claimed he served 106,000 meals.

"Cooking at Christie Lake Camp was not a lot of trouble; I was dealing with nice people…It wasn't financially rewarding, but it showed up on my resume and got me some brownie points," recalled Blair.[41]

Over the years life at camp was a rewarding and unforgettable experience for countless young lads, who took away from Christie Lake lessons that would stay with them for the rest of their lives. A highlight each year was the annual baseball game between the campers and the staff led by Judge McKinley who liked nothing better than to take to the pitching mound.

From the outset baseball was an integral part of life at camp, particularly under the direction of John Young, camp director from 1928–1939. Young was a gifted athlete, who had starred on several

John Young, a gifted athlete, who played on both the camp and community ball teams.

high school basketball teams while attending Glebe Collegiate in Ottawa. Although Young was a good enough basketball player to play for McGill University, it was the fact that he was a top-notch baseball player that delighted the judge. With Young as his catcher, McKinley pitched the staff team to many a win on the camp ball field.

♦ Chapter Seven ♦

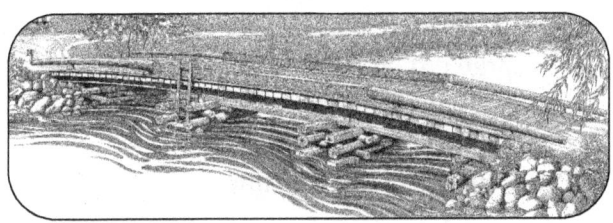

CHRISTIE LAKE BEARCATS

Baseball had long been a popular pastime at Christie Lake. It was a passion the Marks brothers had handed on to their children, particularly Jack, Joe and Ted, the three sons of Ernie and Kitty Marks, who were often seen playing on a diamond laid out on the hayfield adjacent to their Uncle Tom's Arliedale Inn.

One day in August 1929, while driving the foot of the lake, the three Marks lads noticed Alan James, Law Shepherd and the Conway boys playing catch. When they stopped to chat, the boys agreed that the two groups should get together for a baseball game. So it was that a match was arranged for August 14th of that year to be played on a field hastily marked out by Alan James at the Christie Lake School (S.S. No. 5 Bathurst).

When the day arrived and the hotly contested match was won by the head of the lake, the camaraderie was such that there was talk of even more games. Alan James suggested the two teams combine to form one Christie Lake team, which would then challenge other teams in the area. The proposal quickly met with enthusiastic approval and before long the newly-formed Christie Lake Bearcats were scheduled to play against a team from Perth.

Although the Bearcats ultimately came up short in the game against the boys from Perth, by a score of 23–9, the consensus among the Christie Lake team was that such a good time had been had by all that they should host a baseball tournament at the lake. So it was that a few weeks later a "mammoth picnic" was held under the auspices of the newly-formed Christie Lake Community Club. As expected, the highlight of the day was the Lanark County Softball Championship held in front of a large crowd on a field set out at the foot of the lake. The tournament was won by Ray Lee's All-Stars, a team from Perth, who were presented the championship trophy by P. J. Kehoe the president of the Community Club at the time.

The original team from the "foot of the lake" – Back L.– R. Ted O'Gorman, Law Shepherd, Jack Kinnear, Alan James. Front L.- R. Joe O'Gorman, Eddie Conway, Red Conway. (Courtesy: George James)

CHAPTER 7 ♦ CHRISTIE LAKE BEARCATS

Following the presentation of the trophy that day, hundreds of spectators gathered on the shore of the lake to watch a number of contestants take part in a one-mile marathon swim from the Kehoe dock to what was then known as Rocky Point and back. The girls' race was won by Mary Shaw and the boys' race by Billie Hogan. A horseshoe tournament was also held and won by Ed Noonan and Harvey Miller, who were declared Lanark County Horseshoe Pitching Champions. Trophies for all events were donated by George James, owner of James Brothers Hardware in Perth.

The day concluded with a potluck supper, after which The Aces furnished the music for a dance at the former Christie's Lake House, which was now owned by Dan Lee of Perth. Eventually an outdoor dance platform was built at the community grounds, complete with a railing and a stage, to accommodate the day's final activity.

A number of fans watching a game from the side of the hill adjacent to the community grounds at the "foot of the lake." (Courtesy: George James)

It was a fun-filled day very much in the grand Christie Lake tradition of Col. Balderson's regatta and the Marks brothers' rehearsals. All agreed that it should continue and so for the next seventeen years (1929–1946) the Christie Lake Picnic and Sports Day was one of the lake's most highly anticipated events.

Held each year on the community grounds at the foot of the lake, the day featured the softball tournament with hundreds of spectators watching the game from the natural seating provided by the slope of the hill next to the field. Among the most vociferous of supporters were Ernie and Kitty Marks, accompanied by Kitty's mother, whose shrill voice carried across the field and literally across the lake.

"C'mon, Teddie! C'mon, Teddie!" she cried loudly, much to the consternation of those around her.

The community grounds themselves were steeped in local history, sitting as they did next to where the bark factory had once stood and where Alexander and Isabella Palmer had once operated their popular Christie's Lake House. Just to the east of the grounds was the stone house originally built by George and Janet Gray. At the time of his death in 1893 Isabella's father, George, was hailed as the oldest settler in Bathurst Township. By that time, the elderly gentleman, who had first arrived as an eleven-year-old youngster on the Eliza, had spent close to eighty years at the lake.

Ernie Marks, his wife Kitty and Kitty's mother Mrs. Reynolds from Brockville, sit on a blanket to watch the boys play baseball. (Courtesy: George James)

CHAPTER 7 ♦ CHRISTIE LAKE BEARCATS

> **GEORGE GRAY 1804—1893**
>
> We record this week the death of the very oldest settler in the township of Bathurst—Mr. George Gray. His death took place on Monday, Sept. 18, at the age of 89 years. Deceased was born in the town of Banff, Scotland, in the year 1804, and came to Canada with his parents in 1816, with the very first lot of settlers. He lived at the farm at the lake ever since—seventy-seven years. He was uncle of Mr. J. G. Campbell and Mrs. Duncan McNee of this town. His only brother now living is Mr. Robert Gray of Pembroke. He leaves a widow and several children.
> Perth, September 22, 1893

Following the death of Isabella's mother in 1896, Alexander and Isabella Palmer had moved their family into the Gray homestead. When it became apparent that it was getting difficult to manage both the tourist home and the farm, Alexander and Isabella sold the Christie's Lake House to David Anderson and worked the farm where it was said "for the remainder of their lives, they were widely known, highly respected and esteemed" (*Perth Courier* 09/22/1893).

Over the years Alexander and Isabella Palmer were stalwart members of the Christie Lake community. When Alexander died on March 2, 1930, he was hailed as having been "a substantial citizen of Bathurst." It was said that Alexander Palmer's "genial nature and likeable disposition" had turned the Christie's Lake House into the most popular tourist destination in the area.

When Isabella Palmer passed away a year later, on February 2, 1931, she was recognized as one who had always been more than willing to reach out to those around her.

> *If there was sorrow in her community, she was among the first to be there with sympathetic counsel and practical helpfulness. It was in her Christian character that she was most highly respected and in her church, Calvin United, she was faithfulness itself. A kindly and peace-loving woman, the community in which she lived all her life is much the poorer because of her passing* (*Perth Courier*, 02/06/1931).

Following the death of Isabella Palmer another summer camp was established at the lake, this time on the site adjacent to where she and her husband had run their inn. In 1932 when the directors of the Shernfold School in Ottawa, a residential program for developmentally delayed girls, decided a summer camp was needed, the Anglican Diocese of Ottawa purchased the property at the foot of the lake where Colonel Balderson had built his Barracks. They subsequently renamed it Camp Haydon, in recognition of one of the school's founding members, Senator Andrew Haydon, who had passed away the previous November. Before long the location of the camp also became known as the "Snake's Rest" because of the large black water snakes that came to sun themselves on its porch and dock.

Designed to provide training and care for approximately fifteen "manually minded" girls, ranging in age from six to sixteen, the Shernfold School was maintained by fees paid by the parents of the girls. Because the tuition was rather steep, the school was populated primarily by the daughters of well-to-do parents. The school's program was overseen by a board of prominent Ottawa citizens, including Senator Haydon, who served as its first chairman, and future Ottawa mayor Charlotte Whitton, who at the time was the director of the Canadian Council on Child and Family Welfare.

During the summer, the camp itself was run by the Anglican Sisters of St. John the Divine, who often sent the girls to the Noonans' for the mail. Arden always knew when the girls were there and so did everyone else. They were said to be the friendliest and most outgoing members of the entire community. There was no one the girls wouldn't speak to and in a voice you couldn't miss.

Camp Haydon wasn't the first camp for girls on Christie Lake. In July 1921 the Y.W.C.A. of Perth had sponsored a program at the lake known as the Blue Triangle Camp. During the month of July that year a total of forty-four girls stayed at the camp, some for a weekend and some for a week. Each Saturday morning a bus left Perth with a load of girls headed for Christie Lake.

> *Boating and camping were the chief attractions of camp life and many of the girls learned to row and swim. Picnicking proved such a favourite pastime that practically every night saw the camp starting off armed with baskets and boxes, to have their tea at some new*

Chapter 7 ♦ Christie Lake Bearcats

and unexplored point on the lake. Evening singing of songs usually in the boat, became a regular part of the day's program and with frequent trips to the store and spring added to all the other camp activities, the days seemed all too short for the campers to do all the many things they wanted to do (Perth Courier 08/05/1921).

For one of those weeks the camp was operated as a Canadian Girls in Training Camp, a church-based program for girls and young women ages eleven to seventeen. That week eleven girls spent five days at the lake under the direction of Mrs. T. J. Farmer.

When Camp Haydon eventually closed its doors in 1948, the building was bought by George Kerr and Jim Cavanaugh for purpose of once again operating a tourist accommodation. It was known as Kelly's Holiday Inn and included a general store and snack bar that served hot dogs, hamburgers, cold drinks and ice cream. In 1952 it was announced that the store would be open from "8 a.m. until midnight."

Jack Palmer son of Alexander and Isabella Palmer and a well-known lake handyman. (Courtesy: Gray Palmer)

Arden Blackburn's Mail Route

During the years that Camp Haydon had been in operation, Alexander and Isabella Palmer's son, Jack, had come by each Sunday in his horse and buggy to take the girls to church. By this time Jack had become another of the lake's well-known figures, having inherited his father's genial nature and his mother's outgoing sense of compassion.

Born at the Christie's Lake House in 1886, like his parents before him, Jack Palmer spent his life at the lake. In 1915 he married Mabel Korry, and in 1931 the couple moved to the stone house of the Gray family to live and work just as Jack's parents had done before them. It was here that Jack and Mabel Palmer's three children—Elwood, Gray and John—were all to be born.

Jack Palmer and Norman Morris sawing down a tree at the Sproule cottage in 1935.

Chapter 7 ♦ Christie Lake Bearcats

While John died in infancy, Elwood and Gray Palmer grew up to help work on the family farm. The thirties were a busy time for the Palmers. Once food had been put on the table, the excess from the farm, including livestock, was sold to the neighbours or taken to town. Besides selling wool, syrup and firewood, the Palmers sold and delivered fruits and vegetables taken from their large summer garden. They also provided butter, cream and milk to the cottagers around the lake.

The proximity of the Palmers to the lake meant the winter task of cutting ice was another opportunity to earn a bit of money. Each year large blocks of ice were cut and stored in the Palmer icehouse before being delivered to the cottagers come summer. Ice cutting was not a simple task recalled Gray Palmer. A wet ice saw could easily freeze up if not maneuvered properly. After cutting the ice two men were needed to pull the blocks out of the lake and slide them up a ramp and onto a sleigh. The ice was then hauled to the Palmer home where it was stacked in the ice house and packed with sawdust for insulation. As a youngster, Gray learned quickly that as the stack got taller, the work got harder.

With the arrival of the train, Christie Lake had witnessed a dramatic increase in the number of visitors seeking accommodation at the lake. It was for this reason that Jack Palmer realized he could put his carpentry skills to good use. To be known as the "Handyman of Christie Lake," over the years Jack Palmer became busy opening and closing, as well as renovating and building, cottages around the lake, including one on an island for the Ramsay family.

"My father hauled local materials over there and built that whole thing for a couple thousand dollars!" recalled Gray Palmer.[42]

As Jack Palmer got busier and busier, he handed over more and more of the farm work to Norman Morris, a fellow who had arrived at the farm one summer looking for work. Norman had stayed to help with the harvest and never left. At the time, according to Gray, it was quite common for young men to be taken on for room and board, as well as a few dollars and the occasional bit of tobacco. Some, such as Norman, simply stayed on.

As a youngster Gray often watched as his father and Norman hitched up the team and left to spend a couple of days in the bush

Arden Blackburn's Mail Route

*Above: Amelia Rancier on the right and Mabel Palmer on the left.
Below: the same twosome in a canoe on the lake. (Courtesy: Terry Brooks)*

Chapter 7 ♦ Christie Lake Bearcats

cutting wood. In those days a bush cord of wood that took two men with cross cut saws the better part of two days to cut, split with wedges and deliver with horse and wagon (or sleigh) to Perth fetched a whopping $5.00. When the men came back from their time in the bush, Gray accompanied them into Perth where the men got paid for their wood and Gray got a glass of milk and a day-old donut for lunch.

Like Alexander and Isabella Palmer before them, Jack and Mabel Palmer were well known around the lake for the warm welcome they extended to those with whom they came in contact. Kathleen Hicks recalled how on numerous occasions Mrs. Palmer invited her and her sister into the Palmer barnyard to pet the animals. On one occasion when the girls took a shine to a little lamb, Mabel Palmer said they could take it home with them for a couple of days. With great delight the girls put the lamb in their boat and took it back to their island.

When the girls eventually returned the lamb to the Palmers, Mrs. Palmer suggested they might like to take one of the kittens for a while. It was another offer the girls readily accepted. When the girls got the cat home, however, they discovered that it did nothing but meow all night, a fact that didn't sit well with their parents.

Kathleen's sister Mary said: "I think it's constipated. I'm going to give it some medicine."

Mary then proceeded to give the poor kitten a healthy dose of laxative, which stopped the cat from meowing but set it to howling. So it was that the girls quickly returned the kitten to Mrs. Palmer, who thanked them very much for having taken such wonderful care of it.

During that time, Jack and Mabel Palmer not only raised their own family at the lake, but brought up a number of foster children as well, all of whom would miss the couple dearly when they were gone.

> **JOHN CECIL GRAY "JACK" PALMER 1886—1966**
> His life was an inspiration to his family and friends, and always young at heart, he enjoyed to a great extent the company of young people. He was interested in children's aid welfare and was a foster father to a number of children for the past thirty years, all who out of respect and love attended his funeral.
> Those who lived nearest to the warmth of his personality, his family, immediate relatives have suffered a deep loss that arouses the sympathy of neighbours and friends, among whom, although far removed there will always remain happy and pleasant recollections of him who lived through many years in the respect and confidence of the community.

It was obvious that from an early age Gray Palmer had inherited his parent's love of Christie Lake. Born to Jack and Mabel Palmer on Nov. 6, 1921, at the age of twelve Gray won the Bathurst Public Speaking contest conducted at the annual meeting of the Lanark County Educational Association. His address was aptly entitled "My Township" and began,

> *Concession line and cross road, river and lake, railway and highway, valley and hill, meadow and upland, clearing the woods, my township is the dearest and best place in all the world to me.*

and concluded,

> *I think you will all agree with me that every child in Bathurst has reason to feel proud of the place of his birth and as far as myself, I feel that the greatest gift my mother gave to me was my nativity in the good old, fine old, happy old township of Bathurst.*

> *Let others boast of city birth,*
> *Of high and proud degree,*
> *Wealth, station, honor and all things*
> *That make prosperity.*
> *But I am satisfied with this*
> *Wherever I may be.*
> *That Bathurst is my native home.*
> *The dearest home to me.*

CHAPTER 7 ♦ CHRISTIE LAKE BEARCATS

As a young lad Gray performed various jobs around the lake, including helping to get the community grounds next to his home ready for the annual ball tournament. In the early days, recalled Gray, playing on the field was no easy chore for the players who had to run in bare feet over freshly harvested corn stalks. Once the tournament was over, Gray's job was to make sure all the bats and balls were put back in the bag, before he headed to Alan James' cottage to start the player piano used to entertain the players as they gathered to relax and recall the day's best plays over a few cold drinks.

While Alan James set the standard by playing in all seventeen tournaments, in 1936 young Fred McLenaghan, the team's bat boy, set the standard for being the youngest player to play on the Christie Lake team when he did so at the age of fourteen. McLenaghan was an all-round athlete who would eventually play hockey for the Yale Bulldogs in the Ivy League. Following his graduation from Yale with a degree in engineering and management, McLenaghan became president of Burndy Canada, the world's largest manufacturers of electrical connectors.

Another view of a ball game taking place at the community grounds.
(Courtesy: George James)

Arden Blackburn's Mail Route

Helping with the ball tournament was only one of the many tasks Gray Palmer did to help earn a little cash. He also shot groundhogs and sold them for ten cents apiece to a local farmer who then fed them to the foxes he was raising for fur coats. With the fox farm being four or five miles away, Gray had to haul his cargo there by bike.

Another of Gray's jobs was to scrape and roll the tennis court at the McKinnon cottage with a heavy steel roller. By the time he was in high school Gray was occasionally being asked by Walter McKinnon to look after the children while the adults were away. It was Gray's responsibility, among other things, to ensure that while their parents were out, the children didn't fall down the steep hill to the lake or get hurt in any way.

As a teenager Gray knew exactly what he wanted to do with the money he earned. He wanted to buy a car. One of the first cars he bought was an old Chev for which he paid $20 and proceeded to paint a bright green, leading many around the lake to call it "The Curse of Ireland." When Gray arrived at the McKinnon cottage with the car, Walter MacKinnon displayed a keen interest in it. His interest,

Some of the Christie Lake gang in Ted Marks motor car. L. – R. George Carruth, Ted Marks, N. Berg, Ernie Marks, Carol Berg, and Grant Garrette. (Courtesy: George James)

CHAPTER 7 ♦ CHRISTIE LAKE BEARCATS

A young Gray Palmer sitting on the fender of the Chevrolet cabriolet that he bought for $280.00. (Courtesy: Gray Palmer)

however, had nothing to do with the colour. Curious as to whether Gray's car could safely get him and the McKinnon children to town should an emergency arise when the adults were away, Walter McKinnon queried Gray about the condition of the car's tires. When Gray admitted they weren't very good but that he didn't have the money to do anything about it, McKinnon told Gray to go to Jack McGlade's garage in Perth and get a new set of Dunlops. He told Gray not to worry about the price; there would be no bill. Gray did as instructed and discovered, much to his joy, that it was just as Walter McKinnon had said. There was no bill.

The arrival of the motor car at Christie Lake brought with it a new set of adventures and misadventures. While Irene Strong

(Kirkham) could smile about the time she and Gray and Art Kirkham drove up the frozen lake doing "donuts," Gray, himself, always chuckled over the time Jimmy Hogan and Mortimer Reid decided to go to town to get some beer. Knowing that Mortimer's dad, who was sleeping at the time, wouldn't approve of the purpose for their excursion, the boys decided not to turn the engine on until they had pushed the car up the hill to the road. Unfortunately, the car got away from them and ended up on the dock just inches from the water, a fact that brought a great deal of amusement to everyone, except Daley Reid and the two boys.

Members of the baseball team gather at Arliedale Inn. L. – R. Jack Marks, Law Shepherd, Jim Burke, George Carruth, Grant Garrette and Ted Marks. (Courtesy: Donna Walsh)

When he was finished high school Gray Palmer roomed in Perth and worked at James Brothers Hardware, six days a week, eight hours a day, for nine dollars. Each week, after paying five dollars plus a box of vegetables from his mother's garden to the two "old maids" he boarded with in Perth and purchasing the "weekend gas special"—

Chapter 7 ♦ Christie Lake Bearcats

five gallons for one dollar—for the drive home on Sunday, Gray was left with three dollars to do him the week.

Realizing that it wasn't going to be enough money upon which to live, in 1939, a month and a half short of his eighteenth birthday, Gray Palmer applied to join the air force. Following his acceptance, he was sent for advanced training to the trade school in Guelph, after which they asked him where he'd like to be stationed. Recognizing an opportunity to explore Canada's west coast, Gray announced that he'd like to go west, following which they immediately sent him east, specifically to Mont Joli in Quebec, as part of Canada's Eastern Air Command.

Gray remained there until 1945 when, as fate would have it, he met Charlie Bland, at the time the head of Canada's civil service and a summer resident of Ottawa Point. Bland recognized Gray and asked him how he liked his posting. When Gray informed Bland that he would rather be farther away or closer to home, it wasn't long before Gray received a transfer to the Uplands base near Ottawa.

Following the war, Gray returned to Perth, where he went see Lawrence James at the hardware store to inquire about the possibility of getting his old job back.

"Yes we want you back!" exclaimed Lawrence James. "We have you all nicely trained. You're an asset."

When Gray asked what the pay would be, Lawrence answered, "The best we could do would be $25 a week."

Believing he was better qualified now as a result of his air force training, Gray decided to talk to Les Smallwood at the Pepsi dealership in Smiths Falls. Following their conversation, Gray ended up at Pepsi with a job that paid him $70 a week and was the first of many jobs that Gray would hold in the area, including serving as the parts man for James Barr's Ford dealership in Perth, working for the McDougalls at Canadian Tire, and establishing Perth Motors with a couple of buddies on Highway 7.

In the end, however, Gray Palmer returned to the place he loved the best—Christie Lake. The gentleman who had once won the public speaking contest talking about where he lived, came back to take up residence in the former summer home of Daley Reid, next to where his grandparents had once operated their hotel. In the days ahead, Gray, like his dad before him, was to become a well-known handyman around the lake.

"The pay was good and I always had nice people to work for," mused Gray at the age of ninety.

◆ Chapter Eight ◆

CHRISTIE LAKE COMMUNITY CLUB

Expires December 31, 1940

POST OFFICE DEPARTMENT, CANADA

Division OTTAWA

CONTRACT

FOR

CONVEYING HIS MAJESTY'S MAILS

Over
Perth R.R. No. 4

AND

Contractor John A. Blackburn
Date of Contract January 1, 1933,
Duration of Contract December 31, 1
Frequency six times per week
Distance 27-7/8 Miles
Rate, $ 1201.51 per annum
Period of renewal four years
from January 1st, 193 7.

Arden Blackburn's Mail Route

300,000—24-6-30

IN ANY FURTHER CORRESPONDENCE ON
THIS SUBJECT PLEASE QUOTE
No. M-Perth
No. 4.

Office of District Superintendent of Postal Service

Ottawa, Mar. 9, 1934

Mr. John Arden Blackburn,
   Mail Courier,
      Perth, Ont.

Dear Sir,-

          I have the form filled in by you whereby you agree to accept the contract for the service, Perth R.R.No. 4, under the existing terms and conditions and desire to inform you that you will commence your duties as mail contractor for this route on March 15th, 1934.

          The Transfer of Contract forms to be executed in connection with this service are now in the hands of the Postmaster, Perth, and I should be obliged if you would have them completed and returned with the least possible delay.

          I am also enclosing some Declaration Forms which are to be subscribed to by you and the couriers employed by you before commencing the performance of the service.

          Please be governed accordingly and acknowledge receipt of this letter.

                  Yours truly,

                  District Superintendent

GMP/MR

Chapter 8 ♦ Christie Lake Community Club

In March 1934 the Christie Lake community received some welcome news when it learned that Arden Blackburn had been awarded the balance of John Thomas' mail contract. The job, which Arden had been doing on a temporary basis, had come open when Thomas accepted a permanent position at the post office in Perth. Folks around the lake had gotten rather used to having Arden around and were quite overjoyed to hear that Rural Route No. 4 was now officially under his command.

Among those happy with the news of Arden's appointment was Webb Krauser, the gentleman responsible for the sporting events at that summer's annual community fun day. Krauser had been one of the CPR officials, along with William Neal and Henry Suckling, to establish a summer home on Christie Lake following the construction of the railroad. As purchasing agent for the CPR, Krauser had flown over Christie Lake on numerous occasions, while making his way from Montreal to Toronto, before eventually deciding to establish a summer home there.

Having made the decision to settle at the lake, the Krausers purchased the property known as Arliedale Point on the eastern tip of Station Bay. It was here that Arlie Marks and her husband, Jim Perrin, had once had a cottage and would eventually be the site of the Sherman residence.

Once at the lake the Krausers built a large cottage that included a guest house and a boathouse. Outside they planted an extensive garden on the property which was their pride and joy. Much to their dismay one summer it was invaded by a herd of cattle, whose entry into the garden was deemed to be the fault of someone who had mistakenly or deliberately left open the gate to the property thus allowing the "pillaging" steers to enter and consume the entire corn crop in one devastating blow.

The issue of open gates was not a new one at the lake. There had been the time that Charlie Peters accused Joe Patterson of leaving the gate open at his place, thus allowing Charlie's cattle to escape. When Joe denied it, Charlie hid behind a bush at the top of the hill to set the record straight. When, as suspected, he saw Joe leave the gate open, Charlie confronted him. The war of words was reported to have turned ugly when Joe tried to stab Charlie in the neck with a pitchfork.

Arden Blackburn's Mail Route

Charlie, however, was said to have avoided any physical damage when he knocked Joe out.

Although the invasion into the Krauser garden was less dramatic than the purported foray into Charlie Peters' field, it did manage to elicit a veritable tirade of indignation from the local paper.

> *Now we have had people leave our gates open in the past, but it was always due to the fact that they were driving in a car or were careless about shutting the latch. But why anyone should deliberately let down five bars into a garden leading nowhere, and into which had gone an enormous amount of work and loving care, is something we'll never be able to figure out. The senselessness of the whole thing is appalling. It seems to us that there must be something more beneficial that people could do with their time than tricks like this* (Perth Courier 08/19/1948).

The home of the Krausers, who had two adopted children, Betty and Webb Guy Jr., quickly became a rendezvous for the local teenagers, who gathered there to swim off the dock. One of the attractions in swimming at the Krauser's was Betty herself, who wore a black bathing suit held together by a safety pin. At times accompanied by Ray Johnson, the well known organist and choir director of the Sweet Cap "Light Up and Listen" program, Betty was an excellent swimmer, and while she liked nothing better than to push others under the water, she also had a serious side and was often a successful competitor at the swim races held as part of the community fun days.

WEBB KRAUSER 1880—1949

We do not know a great deal about his past history—only that he was born in Pennsylvania in 1880 and was vice-president of the Canadian Cardwell Company in Montreal.

But we do know that he was one of the finest men we have ever been privileged to call a friend. We know that he was a keen and expert gardener and grew the finest corn we ever tasted.

He was a generous host and his cottage here was imbued with his sincere hospitality. His fondness for skiing, snow-shoeing and hikes through the woods were shared by many of us.

His generosity and thousands of acts of kindness will never

Chapter 8 ♦ Christie Lake Community Club

> be forgotten. He gave so much of his time and himself in bringing happiness to others. His joy and appreciation of the beauty and serenity of his beloved Christie Lake will always be remembered.
> Perth, 1949

The swimming races were but one of the many competitions held at the annual Christie Lake Picnic and Sports Day. Organized by a committee made up of some of the lake's best-known residents, the day continued to consist of a variety of games and races, including canoe and sail boat races and numerous novelty races such as a three-legged race, a wheelbarrow race, even a needle and thread race. Each year, as it always had, the event concluded with a supper and a dance on the outdoor platform the club had built for just that purpose.

COMMUNITY CLUB OFFICERS—1934

President—G. G. Garrette
Publicity—Joe O'Gorman
Baseball—Eddie Conway
Decorations—Wib Noonan
Sports—Webb Krauser
Refreshments—Mary Noonan and Jessie Hill
Dance—Alan James
Prizes—Daly Reid
Horseshoes—Jack Palmer
Treasurer—Alan James
Secretary—Ernie Marks Jr.

The sporting events being put together by Web Krauser for the 1934 fun day were, according to committee president George G. Garrette, among the best ever.

> "The races on land and water promise to be unusually keen," noted Garrette, "and several novelty events will be introduced which should thrill the large crowd. The committee is making a real attempt to secure handsome prizes and cups and a large list of entries is assured. Jack Palmer, in charge of the horseshoes, reports that that there will be more 'throwers' this year than ever before and that the

veterans had better look to their laurels" (*Perth Courier*, 07/20/1934).

Come the big day that year one of the lively topics of conversation at the supper, served by Mary Noonan and Jessie Hill, was how lake resident Reg Sproule had captured the prize for the fastest fish filleting by cleaning a fair-sized pickerel in less than ninety seconds. Reg, who operated a small snack bar during the fun day, seldom failed to entertain.

Following the 1934 fun day, the annual banquet of the Christie Lake baseball team was held at the Revere House in Perth under the chairmanship of out-going captain Eddie Conway. For the upcoming season it was announced that Alan James was to take over as captain of the team.

Alan James, who helped to establish the first Christie Lake ball team, played in every tournament from 1929 to 1946. Here he enjoys his 12' Peterborough sailboat. (Courtesy: George James)

Chapter 8 ♦ Christie Lake Community Club

Arden and Sophia Blackburn on the mail route shortly after they were married in 1932. (Courtesy: Ken Blackburn)

"Alan James steps into the captaincy which he so rightly deserves. 'Al' has a long and faithful record with club and his many friends at the lake and in Perth wish him every success" (*Perth Courier* 09/07/1934).

At the same meeting George Carruth was named coach and Wib Noonan was re-elected manager. The popular "Red," as Wib was known, was said to be "a canny leader" and in his first year at the job had surprised everyone with his grasp of the game.

The members of the ball team weren't the only ones looking to the future. When Arden officially signed the papers to take over the R.R. 4 mail route, the first person he told was a young lady from Snow Road Station by the name of Sophia McPhee. With the contract for the route now tucked carefully in his back pocket, Arden now felt comfortable talking to Sophia about a life together. So it was that on

Arden Blackburn's Mail Route

March 16, 1935, the couple was married at the Westminster Presbyterian Manse in Smiths Falls.

With no time for a honeymoon, Arden headed right back to the mail route with Sophia now by his side.

"I sat on the side where the boxes were and put the mail out," said Sophia.

He was "very regular with his mail," observed Sophia, who noted that Arden arrived at the post office by eight each morning to pick up the mail. After that he picked up the other things he needed in town before heading out on his route at ten.

"He always had to have a nice driving horse," Sophia shared. "When we got married in 1935, he bought a team of horses on a banknote."[43]

> *Dear Arden:*
>
> *This little gathering has been arranged by your friends of the Rural Mail delivery Service for the purpose of letting you know how greatly pleased we all were when we heard of the big event that took place a few weeks ago. Now that you are a married man and about to settle down in life we certainly do want to congratulate you.*
>
> *Married life is a new starting point in a man's affairs and usually at that time his friends gather around to wish him well. That is why we are here tonight, to wish all happiness possible to you and the good lady who is your wife.*
>
> *You have a lot of friends all around the country, sincere and true friends, and the men of the mail deliveries hope to be numbered among the very best. We all doing the same class f work, we knock around day by day along the concession lines and highways, meeting all classes of people, and we know the high place you hold in the opinion of the folks in this section of the country. That is a good thing to be able to say about any man.*
>
> *And so although it is now a few weeks since you got into double harness we believe you have been hitched right, and we expect to see the new team going on and on through years of happiness, holding the respect and esteem of their neighbours by good intentions, good words and good deeds.*

Chapter 8 ♦ Christie Lake Community Club

> *Just as a token of the friendship that exists between us all and of the fine wishes in our minds for peace and prosperity in your lives, we ask you to accept this little gift, a purse of money with our truest and best congratulations.*
>
> *May all good things be yours*
> *Home, wife and children dear*
> *And friendship that endures*
> *Through each succeeding year.*
> (Courtesy Ken Blackburn)

In the coming years Arden and Sophia Blackburn had two sons—Lindsay Thomas, born March 3, 1936, and Kenneth Arden, born February 23, 1937. Once they were old enough to do so, the boys often accompanied their dad on his route, and after the family had been raised Sophia would rejoin her husband. This time, however, because of new regulations, she had to be sworn in at the post office and fingerprinted.

The year that Arden and Sophia were married saw additional excitement at the Christie Lake Picnic and Sports Day when a seaplane from Ottawa flew to Christie Lake and took passengers for a trip at two dollars per person. While the plane created quite a buzz, the ball tournament remained the highlight of the day.

"Summer residents at the lake take their softball seriously, which was amply proven by the vocal support accorded their favourites and the rounds of vociferous applause which greeted every worthy play" (*Perth Courier* 08/16/1935).

When Eddie Conway leapt high in the air to grab a hot line drive and end the game, the team's supporters flocked on the field to congratulate the winners.

Thrilled as they were with the game itself, the residents of the lake weren't beyond mixing a little politics with sport. As a result after former lake resident John Conway thanked all present on behalf of the Community Club for their attendance at the game that day, he then proceeded to preside over a program of brief addresses given by a medley of political figures. Included were speeches by Mr. T. A. Thompson, M.P. on behalf of the Bennett government, Mr. Bert H. Soper of Smiths Falls, Liberal candidate in the past federal election,

ARDEN BLACKBURN'S MAIL ROUTE

Sophia and Arden Blackburn with sons, Lindsay and Ken, outside their home on Sherbrooke St. in Perth. (Courtesy: Ken Blackburn)

A seaplane landing on Christie Lake.

Chapter 8 ◆ Christie Lake Community Club

who spoke on behalf of the Hon. W.L. Mackenzie King, and Paul Dufresne of Perth, who spoke on behalf of the Stevens Party.

Ernie Marks, the recently elected mayor of Oshawa, was said to have deplored the conditions of the roads leading to Christie Lake and urged "the co-operation of the Bathurst Township, Perth Town Council and Board of Trade in securing better roads to the lake, from which Perth derives considerable business in the summer months" (*Perth Courier* 08/16/1935).

In conclusion, Conway urged whichever candidate was elected for Lanark County in the forthcoming Dominion elections to see to it that better roads were provided leading to Christie Lake.

The need for improved roads had been necessitated by the increasing number of motor cars now making their way to the lake. With the road from town at first being nothing more than a wagon trail littered with horseshoe nails, the trip was often a hazardous affair. On more than one occasion as her family travelled to the lake, Kathleen Hicks recalled how her father was often forced to get out of the car and fix a flat tire. Sometimes twice before they got to the cottage!

"No big deal. He just got out. Patched it up and we carried on," ventured Kathleen.

At times during the summer when the rest of the family was at the cottage, Kathleen's father remained in town to work. Should he be late arriving come Friday evening, Kathleen's mother would send her and her sister by rowboat over to the Noonan's, where for ten cents they could call Perth. Because the call went through the operator in Glen Tay, however, it was often never completed.

"Mr. Hicks has just gone through Glen Tay. He shall be at the lake shortly," announced the operator, thus rendering a call to Perth unnecessary.

Despite the challenges of travelling the road from Perth, the automobile was now a permanent fixture at the lake. So much so that in 1935 George Noonan installed a gas pump in front of his farmhouse to provide folks with the needed fuel. Like the bicycle and the train before it, the automobile brought a substantial increase in the number of visitors coming to the lake.

As the crowds continued to swell at the lake's annual fun day, a new feature was added in 1937 when George (G. G.) Garrette announced the results of the races, as well as the play-by-play of the ball games, over Blair Thompson's mobile amplifier. At the time, it was noted that the announcing was expertly done and proved to be a popular feature of the day.

The fact that George (G.G.) Garrette could handle a microphone came as no surprise to those at the lake who knew his background. Garrette had first visited Perth in 1920 as advance agent for the Canadian comedy troupe the Dumbells and had been drawn to the lake at the invitation of the Marks' family. In 1925 Garrette purchased land from R. W. Marks, and shortly thereafter it was reported that work had commenced on a cottage.

George G. ("G.G.") Garrette, a promoter for the well-known Canadian performing troupe The Dumbells. (Courtesy: Ralph Fish)

"Morley White, the contractor, has erected a big tent and the grounds look like a big circus going up" (*Perth Courier* 07/24/1925).

By 1928 the Garrette cottage, complete with three fireplaces, was a favourite gathering spot for many from around the lake and would eventually become the summer home of the Fish family.

While G. G. Garrette remained an integral member of the Christie Lake Community Club, his son, Grant, became a stalwart on the

Chapter 8 ◆ Christie Lake Community Club

Christie Lake ball club. Born in Victoria, B.C., in 1913, Grant Garrette grew up spending his summers at Christie Lake. With a love of nature fostered from his time at the lake, Garrette went on to study forestry at the University of Toronto and although he eventually went to work for the Famous Players and 20th Century theatres, for years he pursued his passions of canoeing, sailing and hiking.

Grant's sister, Jeanette, was also a familiar figure at the lake, but for a very different reason. It was well-known around the lake that, as a member of the famous Rockettes, Jeanette had the unfortunate burden of having to stay out of the sunlight so that her skin remained white, a prerequisite for appearing in the Radio City Music Hall spotlight.

At the lake Jeanette was often seen with a monkey on her shoulder. Although some residents were amused by the sight, others knew it wasn't the first time there had been a monkey at the lake. Years

G.G. Garrette standing on the dock at his cottage on Christie Lake.
(Courtesy: Ralph Fish)

before Joe Marks had had one. Problem with Joe's was that it wasn't a particularly friendly or well-behaved creature. On one occasion when Maizie Marks was hosting a dinner party, it was said that Joe's monkey took a swing on the chandelier above the table and managed to scoop a handful of mashed potatoes on the way by.

The Garrette cottage built by Morley White ca. 1926. (Courtesy: Ralph Fish)

The Garrettes were but two of the many show business families to follow the footsteps of the Marks family to Christie Lake. The Chamberlains and the Carruths had done it, so did Theodore Strauss, a well-known Hollywood producer, narrator and writer, and his wife Ludi. Strauss was well known in Hollywood for having written documentaries on John Dillinger, Marilyn Monroe and Theodore Roosevelt and received an Emmy for "America Salutes Richard Rodgers: the Sound of His Music." He also went on to write and narrate many of the Jacques Cousteau underwater documentaries.

For Strauss his time at the lake was a welcome relief from the glare of the Hollywood spotlight. In 1964 when he was asked to work on the documentary "Four Days in November" regarding the assassination of John F. Kennedy, Strauss commented: "I can't recall any assignment, anywhere that has been as exacting as this one. In the first place, to record these four unimaginable days accurately is a frightening

Chapter 8 ◆ Christie Lake Community Club

prospect alone. The world sat over our shoulders, and to select just the right words to tell the story is a rather nervous task at best."

Joe Marks and G.G. Garrette sailing on Christie Lake ca. 1933.

Although they continued to live in Santa Monica, Ted and Ludi Strauss came to the lake each summer and stayed as long as they could. When Ted died in 1989, Ludi continued to come with the couple's boys. Unfortunately on one occasion while Ludi and her family were away, a young lady broke into their cottage looking for liquor. She failed to find any but managed to set the upstairs curtains on fire, and the building burned down.

A Theatre Colony

Christie Lake, in Eastern Ontario, has become a theatre colony where celebrities of the stage spend the summer months, this spot being the home of the Marks brothers who were once prominent in touring road shows. Among those at the resort are Florence Rogge of Radio City Music Hall, New York and her sister, Hattie; Leon Leonidoff, producer and ballet master of the same theatre; Les Appleby of "Abbie's Irish Rose" fame; G. G. Garrette and Ernie Marks, the latter from Oshawa (*Box Office—The Pulse of the Motion Picture Industry*, August 26, 1944).

Another prominent show business couple to come to the lake was the Rogge sisters. In 1937, when Hattie Rogge married Willis Conklin, the couple bought the cottage that Morley White had built in 1922 for the Behan family. At the time Hattie was the wardrobe director for Radio City Music Hall, where, it was said, she thought "no more of purchasing 600 yards of tarlatan than a housewife does of buying a spool of thread."⁴⁴

Hattie and Florence Rogge enjoy some table tennis at the Conklin cottage. (Courtesy: Penny Nault)

Often accompanying the Conklins to Christie Lake was Hattie's sister Florence, who was a choreographer and ballet director for the Rockettes. Prior to the opening of Radio City Music Hall in 1932 Florence Rogge had been the premiere ballerina for S. L. Rothafel at his Roxy Theatre. She then moved with Rothafel to the newly-opened

CHAPTER 8 ♦ CHRISTIE LAKE COMMUNITY CLUB

Radio City Music Hall, where Rothafel's Roxyettes became known as the Rockettes.

It was at the Radio City Music Hall that Hattie Rogge had met Willis Conklin, then a purchasing agent for the famous New York showplace. Following their marriage Hattie and Conklin became regular summer residents at the lake. A graduate of the Cornell University School of Architecture, Conklin eventually put an addition on the cottage which was bought by the Perraults in 1973. For many years Willis Conklin served as the scorekeeper at the Christie Lake ball games and helped found the Christie Lake Golf Association.

At the 1939 luncheon of the Christie Lake Golf Association, held in the clubhouse at the Links O' Tay course in Perth, Mrs. Les Appleby was re-elected secretary of the group, while Mrs. Webb

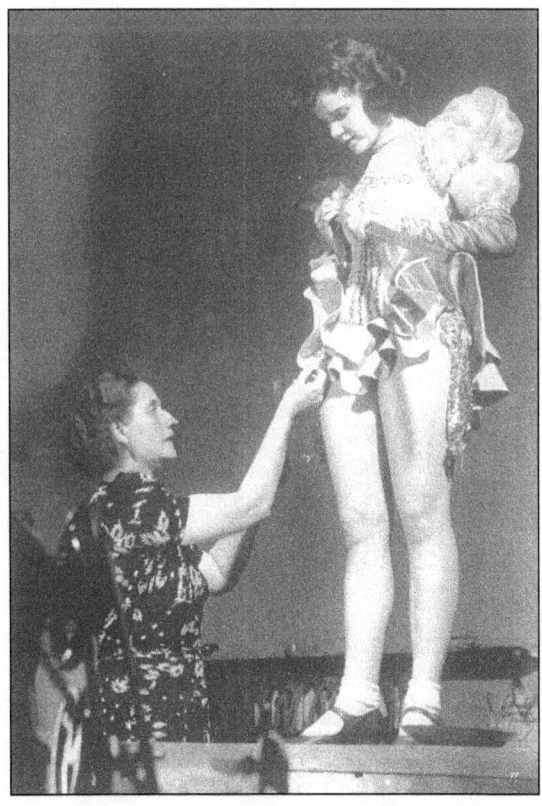

Hattie Rogge putting the finishing touches on the dress of a dancer at the Radio City Music Hall in New York. (Courtesy: Penny Nault)

Krauser was re-elected chairman of the arrangements committee. The handicap committee for the following year's tournament was composed of W. G. Krauser, Willis Conklin and G. G. Garrette. Before adjourning for another year, the association enthusiastically passed a vote of thanks to George S. and Lawrence H. James of James Brothers Hardware for their ongoing contribution to the day's enjoyment.

That same summer saw much rejoicing at the lake when the Christie Lake Bearcats earned their first trip to the semi-finals of the Eastern Ontario Softball Playdowns. The celebration, however, was short lived as talk at the lake quickly turned from the accomplishment of the baseball team to the ominous threat of war.

Arden with his pride and joy – Ken on the left and Lindsay on his right ca. 1937. (Courtesy: Ken Blackburn)

Chapter 8 ♦ Christie Lake Community Club

The Boys of Summer
By Jack Marks

The old ball season's over
You can hear the boys all say
And each and every player
Will soon be on his way
Back to school or college
Until another day
And when that day arrives, boys
We'll all be ready
To take the field and beat the teams
The way we used to do.
With Grant, Law and Donnie
Joe, Ted and Jack
We have an infield, boys
The old team all wants back
And good ole Wib and Alan
Eddie, Joe and Art
We have an outfield, boys
You can bet your life is smart
So let us give a cheer, boys
A real good hearty cheer
That all these boys
In the best of health
Will all be back next year.

♦ Chapter Nine ♦

NOONANS' GENERAL STORE

As a young girl Ruth Johnston (Brown) frequently rowed over to Noonans' store to pick up the mail and various other things for her mother. When she did, she often heard the adults discussing the latest news. It was in the summer of '39 that Ruth first noticed a tone in their voices that left her feeling a little uneasy.

"I remember especially the heightened atmosphere of impending world disaster which I heard in their talk in August 1939," recalled Ruth.[45]

That Labour Day weekend when a float plane came to the lake to pick up Ottawa Point resident Charlie Bland, the curiosity of those around him, including Ruth and her family, was immediately piqued. A native of Pembroke, Ontario, Bland had married Ethel Farrow' whose family first settled Ottawa Point, a property the Blands now shared with the Goodalls. At the time of his hasty departure Bland was chairman of the Civil Services Board of Canada, a position for which he'd eventually receive a honorary degree from Queen's University.

The reason for Bland's hurried exit from the lake that Sunday morning soon became clear for the Johnstons when their neighbour at the lake, Cyril Stiles, came to the top of the hill to inform them that war had been declared between Germany and Great Britain. The impact of Stiles' message sunk in around the lake a week later when a hastily assembled Canadian Parliament made it official with the declaration that Canada was also at war.

Charlie Bland, head of Canada's Civil Service Commission, came to Ottawa Point when he married Ethel Farrow in 1912.

The effect of this announcement first became evident in small ways at the lake. Before long, the Christie Lake ball team was forced to default the first game of the Eastern Ontario Playdowns when it was unable to field a team due to the departure of two of its members. One of the players absent was centre fielder Ted Marks, who was on his way overseas.

With every passing week, talk of the war dominated conversations around the lake. Each day a crowd gathered in the sunroom at the Stiles cottage to listen to the voice of prime minister Mackenzie King on the lake's only battery-operated radio, a piece of equipment Cyril Stiles had acquired as purchasing agent for the CBC.

The Stiles cottage, itself, was a landmark at the lake, having been built by Thomas Stiles in 1911 on land purchased the previous year from John and Martina Jordan for $150 ($1.50 per foot of waterfront).

Chapter 9 ◆ Noonan's General Store

Two different views of the Stiles cottage built in 1911 on property bought from John Jordan Sr. (Courtesy: Joanne Stiles)

An ordained Anglican priest, Stiles had married Charlotte Hicks, sister of Mervyn Hicks, and the aunt of Kathleen Hicks.

When at the cottage on weekends Reverend Stiles went down to the dock to conduct a Sunday service. On such occasions, residents from around the lake including Ottawa Point, anchored a short piece off the shore to take part in the service. Once the makeshift congregation was assembled and situated, suitable hymns were sung and Reverend Stiles delivered an appropriate homily.

The Reverend's wife, Charlotte, affectionately called "Tottie" or "Tot," was also known to offer up the occasional prayer of her own, a fact necessitated by her deathly fear of snakes. From the beginning of her time at the lake, the problem for Aunt "Tottie" was that the washroom was located a considerable distance from the cottage. To get there she had to travel a narrow path that took her between too large juniper bushes—the perfect habitat for her slithering nemesis. As a result, as soon as she left the kitchen door on her way to the bathroom, she began to sing "Country Gardens" in a voice loud enough to scare away any snakes currently on the path and give any

Jimmy Stiles sitting on the fence at the cottage renamed Red Gates after his father, Cyril, had painted the gates red. (Courtesy: Joanne Stiles)

Chapter 9 ♦ Noonan's General Store

that were about to cross an indication that she was coming. Whether her singing had any effect on the snakes was not known, but it made an impression on her neighbours who, as soon as they heard her voice remarked, "There goes Tottie Stiles to the outhouse."

In time Charlotte and Thomas Stiles had two children, Cyril and Margery, both of whom came to value their time at Christie Lake. While the Stiles cottage had been initially been known as The Retreat, Cyril Stiles precipitated a name change when he painted the gate red, thus providing the cottage with the new name of Red Gates.

Despite the name change, over the years the cottage on Christie Lake remained a retreat for Cyril Stiles, who looked forward to his time away from the meeting rooms of the CBC, where he had started as a purchasing agent but had eventually become the director of personnel. While at the cottage Stiles loved nothing better than to lie in the hammock or sink some tin cans in the ground for a quick round

Cyril Stiles ca. 1921 who became the personnel manager at the CBC. (Courtesy: Joanne Stiles)

of golf. One of his more unpleasant tasks while at the lake was to do the laundry, a responsibility that led him to plant a row of cedars along the road, so that those passing by wouldn't see him hanging up the wet clothes.

While Cyril Stiles found his time at the lake to be an enjoyable experience, his wife Louise found it to be less so. The couple's daughter, Joanne, recalled the time that one of the pigs at the Jordan farm had given birth. When news of the event got around, the Stiles' children along with those from Ottawa Point, including Margie Goodall, Allan Bland and Archie Graham, climbed on the fence to get a better look at the newborn pigs.

When Joanne's mother came along, she decided to do the same. Unfortunately just as Mrs. Stiles climbed on the fence the children all jumped off, causing the cedar rail to swing upwards, throwing the poor woman straight into the pigsty. While the children all froze in a state of panic, Joanne's mom picked herself up and calmly walked away. When she got to the top of the hill, however, she let loose and began to shriek at the top of her lungs, throwing quite a fright into poor Aunt "Totti," who watched in horror as her daughter-in-law, covered from head to foot in mud, ran to the dock and straight into the water.

While Joanne's brother Jim pursued a career with the RCMP, before becoming a municipal councilor for the Town of Perth, Joanne eventually found herself in Ottawa working for the Department of Foreign Affairs. That, however, wasn't her first job. Her first job straight out of secretarial school was with the National Hockey League (NHL) at its head office in the Sun Life building in Montreal. At the time, Joanne claimed to be the only girl in Canada to know the statistics of every player in the league.

During her four years at the NHL head office, one of Joanne's duties was to help look after the elderly father of league president Clarence Campbell. As it turned out, the senior Mr. Campbell was a huge Canadiens' fan and had a rail seat next to the visitors' bench at the Forum. Unfortunately, he was blind in one eye and because there was protective glass only at the ends of the arena, there was a concern that he might sustain a serious injury from a flying puck or errant stick. As a result, Joanne was often asked to accompany him to the games in an effort to keep him from getting hurt. Over time Clarence Campbell came to appreciate the fine job Joanne did and even accepted an invitation to visit her at the lake.

National Hockey League President Clarence Campbell and his wife relax on the dock at the Stiles cottage with the Jordan cottages in the background. (Courtesy: Joanne Stiles)

Whether Ruth or any of her family recognized the NHL president sitting on the dock next door is not known, but the Johnstons were certainly familiar with the lake and the comings and goings of its inhabitants. Ruth's family had been coming to Christie Lake since the 1890s when her great-grandfather David Hogg Jr. and his wife, Mary Louise, first arrived by horse and buggy. The Hoggs, who bought the Breezy Crest cottage of Nicholas Andison, eventually had six children—John and Mary Elizabeth, who died as infants, Edith ("Edie"), who married Dr. Richard Fowler, Mary Isabella ("Mamie"), who married Frank Hicks, William ("Will"), who remained unmarried, and Louise, who married Dr. Charles Bailey.

David Hogg Jr. and his wife, Mary Louise, with their grandson Arthur Fowler, in a boat at Christie Lake. (Courtesy: Hilary and John Fowler)

When Mary Louise Hogg died in 1918 without a will, the property went to her husband, David. When he died in 1928, however, four years passed before the property was deeded to their daughter Edith Fowler and her daughter, Isobel Johnston.

Earl and Isobel Johnston had four children—Ruth, her sister Helen (Sentence), and brothers David and Donald. Since her father was a high school teacher in Owen Sound, as a small child Ruth remembered the painfully long time the two-day trip to the cottage took, as it wound its way through a succession of small towns before eventually arriving at Christie Lake.

Once at the cottage Ruth quickly found herself quickly immersed in a whole different world of sights, sounds and smells, including the enticing aroma of the raspberry pies her mother baked in the wood stove with the berries Ruth and her sister picked nearby.

Life at the cottage for the Johnston sisters meant numerous trips to the Jordan farmhouse, where Mrs. Jordan used a ladle to fill the girls' pail with fresh milk scooped out of the large can that sat on the stoop. When all the work was done and the weather was nice, the girls

Chapter 9 ♦ Noonan's General Store

inevitably tried to convince their mother to take them on a picnic. If successful, they'd row up the lake for tea biscuits and deviled eggs.

While at the lake, Ruth loved nothing better than to row. It was little wonder, therefore, that one summer her attention was immediately drawn to the Sunnyside racer lying beside the road going into Perth with a For Sale sign on it. After convincing her dad to stop the car, Ruth was delighted to discover that the $15 she had recently won at school was enough to acquire the canoe, which she promptly did. Ruth's canoe then joined the family fleet, which included a skiff that seated four or five and a punt which their dad used for fishing.

Ruth Johnston's grandparents, Richard and Edie Fowler, who had two children – Isobel, who married Earl Johnston and Arthur, who married Margaret Hart. (Courtesy: Hilary and John Fowler)

ARDEN BLACKBURN'S MAIL ROUTE

Ruth's brother David and her first cousin John Fowler in the sandbox at Breezy Crest. (Courtesy: Hilary and John Fowler)

Over the years, Ruth and her sister, Helen, often rowed as their father trolled his favourite fishing spots, an endeavour that frequently resulted in a delicious feed of pickerel or bass. The girls also used the punt to row their grandmother across the lake to visit her cousins—Charlotte James, Edith Walker and Marion Sproule—with whom she often played bridge. Ruth and her sister would occasionally swim across the lake to visit Mary Lou Sproule.

Ruth remembered well the days she canoed down to the Noonan farmhouse to pick up the mail. Ruth watched intently as Arden brought the heavy canvas bag into the Noonan kitchen. Because Mrs. Noonan's hands trembled a bit, it was sometimes slow work for her to undo the padlock fastened on the bag.

"In the days before most of us had a phone and email hadn't been dreamed of, getting a letter from friends was important and we found it hard to control our impatience while the bag was opened and the mail sorted," recalled Ruth.

Over the years the neighbours of Ruth and her family had changed considerably. In 1921 Anslow Rudd had sold the adjacent Fern Cliffe cottage to Mary Alice Danner, the wife of William E. Danner. In 1923 the Danners bought the property next to theirs, which

Chapter 9 ◆ Noonan's General Store

A proud Arden Blackburn eventually gave up his horse and buggy for a motor car. (Courtesy: Ken Blackburn)

later belonged to the Thornbury family. It was also around this time that the Harris family arrived with their three children—Ellen, Murray and Loretta—and built a large white cottage between the Stiles and the Johnstons.

It wasn't long before the Johnstons and others at the lake learned that Mr. Harris owned a chain of popular eating establishments known as Murray's Restaurants. What had started as a small sandwich shop on Queen Street East in Toronto in 1924 by 1938 had grown to include seventeen Murray's outlets in Ontario and Quebec, all famous for their fast, courteous service and home-styled meals. The chain was so popular that noted Canadian pianist Willie Eckstein, well-known for having penned "Music Makes the World Go Round," even wrote a song about it.

> **"Won't You Meet Me at Murray's"**
>
> I'm going to sing you a song
> Just as I'm strolling along
> I'm in a hurry to go
> I'm headed for Murray's you know
> Won't you meet me at Murray's
> When the weather is fine
> Won't you meet me at Murray's
> The best place to dine
> When you're tired and hungry
> And your spirits are low
> Then you'll always find Murray's
> The best place to go
> The boy friend will like it
> The girl friend as well
> The good things they serve you
> You never can tell
> If you want to be happy
> And you want to feel good
> Say you'll meet me at Murray's
> Where the middle name's food.
>
> Words and Music by Willie Eckstein 1929

During the Second World War the newest Murray's Restaurant was opened in the recently built Lord Elgin Hotel in Ottawa where it was designed to provide regular room service for the hotel guests and also had entrances from the street to serve a walk-in clientele. It was the second Murray's Restaurant in Ottawa and its relatively simple menu was well-suited to the Lord Elgin which had been built to serve short-stay guests, particularly those who were in Ottawa on government and military business during the war.

As the war went on, anticipation for Arden's arrival at the lake grew even greater as residents waited anxiously for news of their loved ones overseas. By this time Arden had traded in his trusty horse and buggy for a Model A Ford purchased from James Brothers Hardware in Perth. While his motor car required slightly less maintenance than his

Chapter 9 ♦ Noonan's General Store

horses, it still needed to be tended to and on the coldest winter mornings Arden had to get up early to boil the water needed to pour over the manifold to ensure the car would start.

Arden loading up before beginning his route along with fellow postal workers L.– R. Arden Blackburn, Vince Bowes, Pat Henrietta, and Norman Darou. (Courtesy: Ken Blackburn)

To miss a day because of the cold simply wasn't an option for Arden, who knew folks had come to depend on him for much more than just the mail. So it was that, even in the worse winter weather, those who lived on Rural Route No. 4 listened expectantly for the familiar sound of the winter chains flapping on Arden's tires.

"We had a mailman called Arden who would deliver the mail in a Model A Ford," [recalled lake resident Elton Crandall Jr.]. "No back seat, but he would take your order one day...anything you wanted in Perth from milk to eggs, butter, anything, paint. You needed something and you wanted to save yourself a trip into town Arden would buy it and bring it out and you'd meet him and you'd pick up what you'd ordered and pay him. And that was for all the cottages not just one person. He had the back end of his car loaded.

Arden Blackburn's Mail Route

He'd pick up milk at Chaplin's dairy at Glen Tay. Good milk. Great chocolate milk."

By the end of the Depression, Arden Blackburn had become a vital link between those who lived at the lake and the things they needed in town. Each day in various mailboxes along his route, Arden would find a list of things that particular family wanted in town. The next day he'd return with his old Model A, minus the back seat, full to overflowing. Over time, it was all Arden could do to find a bit a room for his shotgun should he come across a partridge or a couple of pints of India Pale Ale should he get thirsty.

A crowd gathers around Arden as he arrives at the Noonan farmhouse in 1946.

As the years went by the arrival of Arden's motor car at the Noonan farmhouse remained one of the most highly anticipated events of the day. Here the crowd waited patiently as Arden had a coffee and Sarah Noonan took the mail from the canvas sack and placed it in the pigeon holes that lined her kitchen wall. No one, recalled Terry Brooks, was allowed to come into the kitchen until all of the mail was in its proper place.

CHAPTER 9 ◆ NOONAN'S GENERAL STORE

The property upon which the Noonan farm sat had been purchased by James Noonan from Isaac Corry in 1860. At the time, the farmhouse had only been half built. In May 1891 it was reported that James Noonan had moved to Perth and "disposed of his farm to his son George."

From the time that George Noonan and his wife, Sarah, took over the farm they planted a large garden, the produce from which they sold to their neighbours and other residents around the lake. Before long the Noonan's vegetable stand grew to include coal oil, kerosene and a variety of other supplies. In 1912, with the growing retail operation needing a space of its own, the Noonans took the summer kitchen off the farmhouse and rolled it down the hill and set it up at the edge of their property. There the Noonan store became a frequent gathering spot for folks at the foot of the lake, young and old alike.

The store and farmhouse of George and Sarah Noonan. (Courtesy: Terry Brooks)

According to Kathleen Hicks, her mother often issued her and her sisters a stern warning whenever they were sent to the Noonan store for ice.

"Whatever you do, don't get the ice until you're ready to come home," she'd caution the girls.

While the girls rowed over to Noonans' with the best of intentions, they'd always get sidetracked by someone they knew. So while Wib Noonan filled their canvas sack with the biggest piece of ice he could find, by the time the girls were done chatting with their friends, it was down to a fraction of its former size, much to the dismay of their mother.

It was shortly after the Noonans opened their store that construction began on the rail line along the lake, a fact that helped turn the Noonan store into a booming business. Not only did the blasting crews buy the bulk of their supplies at the store, but some of the workers boarded at the Noonan farmhouse as well. On Friday evenings George Noonan could be seen taking them by boat to the foot of the lake where they'd climb into a wagon destined to take them to Perth. Once in town, the workers would frequent the Perth Hotel or Revere House only to return late in the evening or early in the morning looking for a good night's sleep.

George Noonan outside the Noonan farm house in the early forties.
(Courtesy: Terry Brooks)

Chapter 9 ◆ Noonan's General Store

While most of the railway workers were allowed to run a tab with the Noonan's, few left without straightening up their account. One exception was a Swedish bridge worker who left a large ring as collateral for his room and board. In the end, he returned to Sweden without it, leaving the Noonan's with a rather stunning piece of jewelry as a reminder of his stay.

Mabel Palmer (left) and Amelia Rancier (right) all dressed up and ready to go. (Courtesy: Terry Brooks)

During the construction of the train station, George Noonan used his barge to haul building materials from the foot of the lake to the construction site. Such outings were not without their challenge as the waves would on occasion prompt a shift in the weight of the load only to see it end up at the bottom of the lake. Before long rumours around Christie lake surfaced that everything from barrels of nails to cases of whiskey had gone down. Eventually the barge itself went down, although no one has been able to find its remains.

Arden Blackburn's Mail Route

Once the train station at the lake was open George Noonan often greeted arriving visitors and helped them haul their trunks and bags and other belongings from there to their destination. Because the Noonans were familiar figures at the lake, few were surprised in 1914 when the government had designated their farmhouse as the site of the Christie Lake post office.

Although George Noonan was named postmaster at the time, it was actually Sarah who, over the years, looked after the mail. Because women were not allowed to hold the position of postmaster, it was George Noonan who ironically would receive a thirty-year service medal from the Postmaster of Canada.

No one enjoyed the camaraderie of the daily crowd that gathered to wait for the mail more than Amelia Rancier, who lived with the Noonans. Amelia had come to the farm in 1895 to help with the chores and those who arrived to pick up the mail were often met by the sight of her ironing the clothes or removing one of her freshly baked pies from the oven.

Amelia cleaned the house, milked the cows, did the washing, helped with the gardening and did whatever needed to be done around the farm. While she never had much in life, Amelia maintained she had all she needed. She never had a bank account, but kept twenty dollars rolled up in her shoe should she ever need it.

Before long Amelia became an integral part of the Noonan family along with George and Sarah's seven children—Verna, Ebert, Orville, Harold, Mary, Wilbur and Isobel. So closely united was she with the family that Amelia maintained the saddest day of her life was September 26, 1899, when Verna Noonan, the eldest child of George and Sarah, only seven years old at the time, passed away from inflammation. Amelia herself remained at the farm until the age of ninety. During that time she turned Roman Catholic, so she could be buried beside George and Sarah.

From the beginning, Amelia made no bones about the fact that she had no desire to leave the Noonan home. At one point, when members of the Methodist Church in Perth arrived at the farm with the sheriff, they took her into town to work at the Matheson House as a maid. Amelia complained that she wasn't one bit happy with the arrangement and before long bolted back to the Noonan's. When the

Chapter 9 ◆ Noonan's General Store

sheriff returned to the farm looking for Amelia, George Noonan suggested he get off his property, without Amelia, or he'd be forced to take matters into his own hands.

Those who knew George knew it was no idle threat. Residents around the lake were fond of telling the story about the time the local game warden, Forrest Richardson, had turned up at the Noonan farm looking for some lads who had been in the bush hunting out of season. According to Richardson, when he tried to put the run on them, they took a couple of shots at him. Thinking they may have been George's grandsons, Richardson arrived at the Noonan farmhouse with his tale of woe.

"Did they hit you?" asked George Noonan.

Sarah and George Noonan on the occasion of their 50th wedding anniversary in June 1941. (Courtesy: Terry Brooks)

"No. They missed," replied Richardson.

"Then they ain't no grandsons of mine," replied George Noonan.

As time went on George Noonan became a well-known cattle drover in the area, travelling often between Toronto and Montreal, and was eventually offered the position of manager at the stockyards in Winnipeg. It was a job offer he seriously considered, but, in the end, turned down for he couldn't convince his family to leave the lake. George informed the family that if they stayed at the lake, they would need someone to look after the farm since his cattle business left him little time to do so. It was then that the Noonans' youngest son, thirteen-year-old Wilbur, known around the lake as Wib, quit school to run the farm.

Over the years, Wib Noonan became a Christie Lake legend. The pale face, the freckles, the trademark crop of Noonan red hair (when the family went to Mass on Sunday, the church was said to be a sea of red), Kathleen Hicks remembered Wib well.

"Oh he was an awful one," smiled Kathleen. "I think Wilbur liked to shock us girls."

Kathleen recalled how when she and her sister Mary went to pick up the mail at Noonans', Mary, who was the shyer of the two Hicks girls, often sat on the bench that was there. Wib would say, "Be careful. There's a crack in that thing. It'll pinch your bum ya' know," following which poor Mary turned twenty shades of red.

When the Hicks girls climbed the fence to watch Wib and his sister Isobel milk the cows, Wib often squirted them in the face with warm milk.

"Can you imagine anything worse," exclaimed Kathleen who told how the milk was put in a trough near the water pump where the flies and other critters, including the barnyard cat, dropped by for a drink.

"I drank it too. Never sick a day," mused Kathleen at the age of ninety-five.

Dubbed the "Deputy of Christie Lake," Wib Noonan enjoyed the occasional drink, especially on the weekend. Come Friday night Wib headed to Perth with his faithful horse "Pete." Following a lengthy sojourn at the Perth Hotel, he climbed back into his buggy and promptly fell asleep. Because it was a routine followed with a good degree of regularity, "Pete" then followed the familiar path home

Chapter 9 ◆ Noonan's General Store

where he'd wait patiently outside the Noonan farmhouse for Wib to wake up.

It was a custom so familiar to folks around the lake that if they happened to be in town on the weekend and needed a ride home, they'd look for Wib's buggy outside the hotel. They would then experience what was, for the most part, a rather quiet ride home, punctuated only by the occasional burst from Wib who'd occasionally wake up hollering "Time for a beer!"

Despite his weekly forays into town, Wib Noonan hated to be away from home for any length of time. On the occasions when he and Amelia went over to their neighbours, the Jordans, for supper, Wib would hardly have finished his meal when he would say to Amelia, "Gotta go…gotta go…might be someone coming."

The only time he'd stay for a spell was when he'd had a drink or two recalled Alan Jordan. On those occasions he'd arrive at the Jordan's and sit himself down in the kitchen. He'd not bring any liquor in with him, but after a spell if no one offered him a drink, Wib would clear his throat and say to Alan, "I have a bottle out in the car if you care to get it." Once the bottle had been fetched, the evening would continue until such time as Alan decided to go to bed. At that point he would say to Wib, "Turn out the lights when you leave, would you?"

Despite the implication of the comment, sometime later Alan would hear Wib still mumbling to himself in the kitchen. Come the light of morning, however, Wib was nowhere to be seen.

What happened after Wib left the Jordan home became clear to Alan one time when he went to the Noonan's to borrow a shovel. Deciding it would be quicker to shovel the snow off the roof of his family's rental cottages with Wib's wide-mouth shovel, Alan went over to the Noonan farmhouse, where he found Amelia sitting in the kitchen. When he asked where Wib was, Amelia replied, "Wilbur isn't up yet."

Alan said he'd come back later. When he did, he was surprised to find Wib still in bed. At that point Alan told Amelia he was going to take the shovel and would return it the following day. When he went back the next day with the shovel, Amelia told him, "Wilbur missed a whole day yesterday."

Wib didn't miss many days though and if he was, as Kathleen Hicks maintained, bent on embarrassing the girls, he was just as intent on impressing the ladies. Often after a few drinks, Wib fancied himself a bit of a ladies' man, and so it was that one time upon entering the Jordan kitchen, Wib proceeded to kiss all the ladies present. Once finished Wib turned to Alan's Uncle George and asked where his wife, Lottie, was.

"I haven't kissed her yet," announced Wib.

"She's sick," stated George.

"Well that's too bad," said Wib.

"Yeah. She hasn't recovered from the last time you kissed her," said a deadpan Uncle George.

In keeping with his reputation Wib seldom missed an opportunity to assist the ladies. On one occasion when Doug Chaplin and a buddy were camping at the lake, they asked their wives to boil some water for tea. When the ladies protested, saying they were not going to drink anything made with dirty lake water, the boys suggested the girls go up and get some water at the Noonan farmhouse.

When they got there the ladies explained their dilemma to Wib, who said he would be only too glad to help. Going over to the kitchen

An elderly Wilbur ("Wib") Noonan still enjoying the occasional puff on a cigarette. (Courtesy: Terry Brooks)

Chapter 9 ◆ Noonan's General Store

sink, Wib turned on the tap and filled the pot with water, which he then graciously handed to the women, knowing full well it came straight from the lake. None the wiser the ladies heartily thanked Wib, who told them to think nothing of it.

When he wanted a night out after a hard day on the farm, Wib often headed to the dances in the Westport, where more often than not he'd end up on the wrong end of a scrap with one of the locals. Later in life when confined to a hospital bed in Perth, Wib discovered he was lying next to a fellow who had thrown him off the bridge in Westport thirty-five years earlier. By this time, all had been forgiven, if not forgotten, and Wib joked about how in the winter the Westport lads threw water on the hill at Foley Mountain where it would freeze, forcing unsuspecting motorists to pay them $2.00 to pull their cars the rest of the way up the hill with their horses.

As he promised his father he would, Wib Noonan looked after the family farm. He made maple syrup, sold cattle and trapped muskrat, mink and otter. Twice a week he delivered ice to cottagers, most of whom offered him a drink. He even tracked the height of the lake for the ministry, although he often did it from his kitchen. "Yup, looks the same as last week," Wib would announce while peering out his kitchen window.

Living with three elderly adults was not particularly easy for Wib, and in August 1950 when the barn on the Noonan farm was hit by lightning and burnt to the ground, an emotional Wib informed his father that he no longer intended to farm the property, saying instead he was going to build some cottages to the west of the house, which he would then rent and maintain.

Whether the decision mattered much by this time to the elderly George Noonan was difficult to say. A few years later, on June 13, 1953, Wib lost his dad, and the Christie Lake community lost one of its most-respected members when George Noonan passed away. A devout Roman Catholic his funeral was chanted by Father Meagher at St. Vincent de Paul Church in Dewitt's Corners where George and Sarah had been the second couple to be married there. Survived by his four sons and two daughters, as well as twenty-three grandchildren and four great grandchildren, George Noonan had left his mark on the lake he loved.

Arden Blackburn's Mail Route

The Noonan's gather at the time of George Noonan's funeral in 1953. L. – R. Isobel Noonan (Brooks), Irma Crawford King, Mary Noonan (LaFond), Red Noonan, Amelia Rancier (in front), Everet Noonan, Wilbur (Wib) Noonan, Orville Noonan. (Courtesy: Terry Brooks)

Like the home of Thomas and Margaret Marks, the home of George and Sarah Noonan had been a focal point for the Christie Lake community. It was here that folks came to get their mail; it was here they gathered each New Year's Eve to mark the passing of another year.

The annual New Year's Eve party at the Noonan home always drew a large crowd from around the lake. One year David Hill remembered his parents skiing to get to it. Featuring live music from the likes of Billy Dewitt and his piano, at midnight, after the pleasantries and best wishes had been exchanged, the kitchen door was thrown open to a great spread of food.

Given the number of gatherings and celebrations that took place at the Noonan's over the years, few were surprised when it was discovered following his death that Wib Noonan, the much-loved "Deputy of Christie Lake," had left $1,000 hidden under a stair tread at the farmhouse with instructions to have a party upon his passing.

Chapter 9 ◆ Noonan's General Store

A Tribute to George Noonan 1866—1953

Last Saturday, Christie Lake and the surrounding country lost one of their prominent and most beloved citizens in the passing of George Noonan. While feeling the burden of his eighty-six years during the past few months, he had been in relatively good health until the last days, but unto the end he was able to enjoy the company of his family and the good friends who dropped in to spend a few minutes with him, in accordance with long standing custom. He made the great transition quietly, with a little sigh and a quiet smile of greeting for his Sarah, whom he missed so greatly during his last three years, and who had been his wifely companion and steadfast friend through all of the many years of their life together. Now at last, he rests beside her in the little Roman Catholic cemetery at Perth, where are so many of his relatives and friends of bygone years.

It is given to few to have and enjoy so full a life as that with which Divine Providence saw fit to bless George and Sarah Noonan. They had an exceptional capacity to savour the happiness of each day as it came along, to regard the past with no regrets and to view the future with quiet confidence. They were people of integrity, loyalty to their family, their friends, the country in which they had their home and lived their lives and to their church. The fine imprint of their spirit and character has been left upon their children and the many grandchildren who mourn their passing and thus their fine qualities are indelibly impressed upon the future. In the persons of all of these young people, with the Noonan brand of red hair, so many of them, they leave to the country that they loved so well, a legacy of far-reaching and estimable value.

George was generously endowed with the peculiar Irish sense of humour, had a keen appreciation of a good tale, perhaps with a little spice in it and his chuckle is something to remember with a grin that is akin to his own. In his later years, it was his pleasant custom to sit at ease in the big farm kitchen of the home at the foot of the lake, where he was born and spent most of his days and to swap more or less tall tales with his companions. It is hard o say whether they or he derived the more fun from these visits, but they were enjoyed by all. As time went on the tribe of grandchildren increased and one of the best times of the year for him was when some of them would visit the old home, along perhaps with a sprinkling of nephews, nieces and some of their children and the walls of the place would ring again with the happy shouts of the youngsters. They made him think fondly of the days when Sarah and he were themselves the proud young parents of their group of red headed children and how they all looked to the future with confidence that later events proved to be fully justified.

He loved every day of his life, but at the end was quite prepared, as he would say, to "call it a day" and go on his way to even better things. So, while there is a tear in the eye and a pang in the heart of all of the many who loved him, and sorrow in the thought the human eye can no longer dwell upon his friendly countenance, there is none who would deny him his Great Experience, or the joy of joining his Sarah, with the both of them going hand in hand through the life beyond (*Perth Courier* 07/09/1953).

◆ Chapter Ten ◆

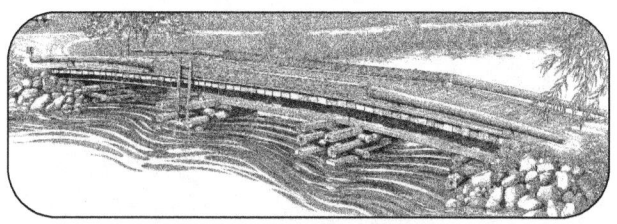

JORDAN'S BRIDGE

During his lifetime Wib Noonan had loved nothing better than to fish from Jordan's Bridge. He was, in fact, the only one to claim a designated spot on the old wooden structure. Whether anyone else acknowledged the reality of that fact mattered little to Wib, and over the years more than one unwitting fisherman caught an earful for being in the wrong place at the wrong time.

From the time he was a youngster, Wib seldom let a day go by that he didn't grab his gear and head across the road, there to take up his chosen spot on the bridge. Here he'd remain until the late evening when the neighbours and nearby campers heard his dad call out from the farmhouse, "Wilbur, you'd better come up now."

The fact that Wib laid claim to a special spot on Jordan's Bridge was made all the more brazen by the fact that his Irish Catholic background stood him in stark contrast to that of the Protestant upbringing of the Jordans, whose ancestors had been working the original Christy farm since 1863.

When Robert (b.1795) and Elizabeth Jordan (b.1803), both of whom were born in England, but later moved to Scotland, emigrated to Canada in 1837, they first settled in Drummond Township. When their son, George, born in 1830 in the village of Yetholm, Scotland, married Sarah McLellan of Bathurst Township on January 23, 1863, however, the couple took over the original Christy farm.

John and Martina Jordan bought much of the original Christy property from James Doyle. (Courtesy: Alan Jordan)

It was here that George and Sarah Jordan's son, John, was to be born in 1865 and where he'd spend the rest of his days. In 1895 John Jordan married Martina Miller and in 1897 the couple purchased the property outright from James Doyle for $700. Over time, John and Martina Jordan sold waterfront lots to a number of families including those on Ottawa Point, the Stiles and the Harrises.

When John Jordan, who resided all his life on the farm at the foot of Christy Lake, passed away in September 1950 it was on the eve of his 85th birthday and an occasion of much sadness within the Christie Lake community.

Chapter 10 ♦ Jordan's Bridge

An early view of the bridge leading into the Jordan farm. (Courtesy: Terry Brooks)

An automobile crosses Jordan's Bridge, a sight that sent shivers down the back of poor Sarah Noonan. (Courtesy of Libby Bandeen)

The Jordan home was ever a hospitable one, where the head of the household always found time to engage in friendly conversation and to perform some kindly act or unselfish deed. Thus John Jordan enriched his life and won for himself enduring friendships—the only real values in human life. Mr. Jordan always attended to his religious duties, acting as elder in Calvin Church for many years (Perth Courier 09/28/1950).

The burial service for John Jordan was held at the Jordan home with neighbours, Jack Palmer and Wib Noonan, acting as pallbearers. With John Jordan gone, his son John Jr. took over the family farm.

Over the years, the old wooden bridge at the entrance to the Jordan farm had became a popular summer hang-out. When the motor car first arrived at the lake, it was said that Sarah Noonan trembled in fear across the road on her front porch deathly afraid that some youngster would be thrown into the water by the bouncing of the boards as a car crossed the bridge.

"Seeing those poor kids knocked up and down as a car went across just about gave the poor woman a heart attack," recalled Kathleen Hicks.

The entrance to the Jordan farm was also one of the area's most popular fishing spots and word of a large catch at Jordan's Bridge quickly travelled around the lake. In the early forties, when Edward Danner, owner of the Wampole Pharmaceutical Co. in Perth, landed a lovely string of bass from the bridge, news of the catch spread like wildfire. It wasn't long before numerous other anglers stationed themselves at the bridge trying to emulate Edward's good fortune. It was said at the time, however, that "word had been passed around among the bass and only small fry attempted to swallow the bait, although one man was heard to say that he had hooked a five pounder, but that it got away" (*Perth Courier 08/06/1942*).

Over the years, tales from Jordan's Bridge added considerably to the lore of Christie Lake. In 1922 when Daley Reid accidentally fell off, they said, that while all that could be seen was his hat, there was "no official record of how much the river raised because of his presence in the stream."

Another oft-told tale was the one of the well-dressed Englishman, who showed up on the bridge with a fishing pole and some cheddar

Chapter 10 ◆ Jordan's Bridge

(Courtesy: Joanne Stiles)

cheese, which he declared to be his bait. The statement elicited more than a few raised eyebrows among those on the bridge, until the gentleman caught a four pound bass on his second cast.

There was also the time a fellow rented a wooden rowboat form the Jordans to go fishing on one of the islands. When it started to get dark the gentleman decided he would camp on the island for the night. So he threw his hat in the boat and pulled it up on shore. Unfortunately, he didn't quite get it quite far enough out of the water and so unbeknownst to him, it quickly drifted back out into the lake where it was hit by another boat making its way home. Seeing the hat floating on the water, the alarmed fishermen in the other boat set up an awful commotion thinking they had sent whoever was wearing the hat to the bottom of the lake. Much to their relief they realized their error when they heard the yelling that arose from the island.

It was during the Depression, when money was tight, that the Jordan family turned to the tourist trade to help generate revenue.

"I started with one cottage and 400 feet of white sand beach," the younger John Jordan once drawled pensively (*Perth Courier* 05/30/63).

As fate would have it, the Jordan's timing in inviting summer vacationers to their homestead couldn't have been better. Canada's economic recovery following the Second World War was swift and strong. As western oil and natural gas reserves yielded new sources of power for Canadian industries, the country's factories boomed once again. Before long Canadian workers were blessed with more disposable income than ever before.

By 1951 the Canadian government had announced a mandatory two-week vacation with pay for most workers which meant that many workers now had more free time than ever before. For families looking to escape the pressures of city living and to spend their leisure time in the great outdoors, the natural beauty and abundant fishing at Christie Lake was an obvious draw, and Jordan's Cottages and Campground, with its secluded border and sandy beach, was to be a favoured destination.

It was here that John Jordan Jr. and his wife Mary Elizabeth Scharf (married in 1933) raised their five children—Bob, Betty, Alan, Lloyd and Harold—all of whom worked on the farm and eventually helped oversee the family's growing recreational facilities.

Chapter 10 ♦ Jordan's Bridge

While the Jordans were met with an immediate steady stream of visitors, most of whom arrived in motor cars and many of whom came from the northern United States, their entry into the tourist trade wasn't without the occasional hiccup. In the beginning, they were dealing with people they didn't know, a fact that resulted in a few not being invited back.

On one such occasion a family gave their nine-year-old son a hatchet with which the youngster proceeded to destroy a number of cedar trees on the property. On another occasion two unwitting adults strung a wire across the road and doubled over laughing when it knocked young Jimmy Stiles off his bicycle. When informed of the incident, the Jordans were less than impressed. Undeterred by the occasional mishap, over time more and more of the Jordan's attention was devoted to their cottages and campground which could eventually accommodate 115 guests in 21 individual rental units.

John Jordan Jr. and his wife, Mary, on the occasion of their 26th anniversary in 1959 at the Harris cottage. (Courtesy: Alan Jordan)

Arden Blackburn's Mail Route

Because fishing was such a large part of what attracted folks to Christie Lake, particularly from the United States, the level of the fish population was a constant concern to the Jordans and other tourist operators, whose source of revenue depended upon the annual return of the anglers. As early as 1934 the Perth Fish and Game and Protective Association was involved in fish restocking on the lake. For years, Jack Newson, owner of Arliedale Inn, along with Morley White, had stocked the lake with smallmouth bass secured from government hatcheries. In 1954, however, the government halted its restocking program, a move that upset and angered John Jordan and the other resort owners.

By 1960 increased pressure on the lake's fish resources had resulted in the creation of the Christie Lake Hunters and Anglers Association ("Association") whose executive included Alan James, Wib Noonan and John Jordan. The Association carried out numerous activities to enhance the lake's fish resources, including coarse fish netting and the installation of marker buoys. As the level of the fish population became an increasing concern, the Association worked hard to help build a sense of responsibility among lake users and residents for protecting the lake and its resources for the long-term.

"'I'd like to see the lakes well-stocked to offset the heavy fishing pressure on this area. Why, you see thirty boats on the water today when you would see one or maybe two boats twenty years ago,'" noted John Jordan in the early sixties (*Perth Courier* 05/30/1963).

It took almost ten years of agitation by Jordan and others before the Ontario government finally reversed its policy in 1963 and once again started stocking the lake. In June of that year fishing enthusiasts from miles around braved the frigid weather to gather at the Jordan farm and witness the release of 500,000 pickerel fry under the direction of game warden Forrest Richardson of the Department of Lands and Forests. As hail and rain pummeled spectators and officials alike, boats pulled their way across the sandy shoals to watch and cheer as thousands of pickerel were dumped into the icy waters.

The Jordan farm had been chosen as the site for the fish release because of the family's involvement in the Christie Lake Hunters and Anglers Association, where John Jordan was its past president and his son, Alan, its secretary-treasurer. Each year the Association kept

CHAPTER 10 ♦ JORDAN'S BRIDGE

*Two more views of the Jordan homestead and campground.
(Courtesy: Penny Nault)*

the community informed by means of a report delivered at its annual dinner catered by Keith Blair who had cooked for the various camps on the lake.

By the mid-sixties the question of what type of fish should be put in the lake had become a burning issue. While many of the locals preferred pan fish that could be readily eaten, the resort owners preferred the sport fish that proved to be a greater draw for the tourists.

As for the expertise of those within the Department of Lands and Forests, at the time Alan Jordan commented, "Why, they say some of the biologists can't tell the difference between pickerel and rock bass" (*Perth Courier* 05/30/1963).

It was, in and of itself, an important distinction since the issue of whether Christie Lake should be a lake of pickerel or pan fish was beginning to drive a wedge between the various resort owners. The issue came to a head at the Association's annual meeting in 1964 when raised by Vic Lemieux proprietor of Norvic Lodge. At the time the question was said to have brought "a barrage of spontaneous wit, wisdom and ridicule from the 130 persons enjoying a sit-down supper meeting, in the 'Blue Room' at the Perth Hotel" (*Perth Courier* 04/16/1964).

A crowd enjoying some summer fun at the lake in front of the Jordan cottages.

Chapter 10 ◆ Jordan's Bridge

Another view of the Jordan cottages.

While Lemieux continued to assert that so-called "trash fish," such as perch and catfish, should be purged from the lake, Alan Jordan countered, "Some people like to catch trash fish if they can't catch the other. Right now they can't catch game fish and they can't catch fresh fish either" (*Perth Courier* 04/16/1964).

Despite the ongoing wrangling of the resort owners, fishermen continued to flock to Christie Lake. Even the community's mailman, who had a standing offer of a free rental boat from the Jordans, found time to do a little fishing. Although Arden Blackburn seldom, if ever, took a holiday, his son Ken recalled the times his parents packed up him and his brother along with a few belongings and headed to Ruby Island for an overnight campout. The island had been bought (or won in a poker game depending on whom you talk to) by Billie Burke, a buddy of Arden's from the Post Office.

When Arden and his buddy, Billie, did go fishing at Christie, nothing helped pass the time better than the occasional shot of whiskey. Fearing his friend, a rather short fellow, might fall overboard, Arden insisted on tying Billie to the seat of the boat, a fact that amused Arden's son Ken, who was brought along to row. According to Ken, when Billie wanted him to row a little faster he'd throw a quarter on

ARDEN BLACKBURN'S MAIL ROUTE

Arden Blackburn with fellow postal workers Billie Burke (left) and Percy Spalding (right). (Courtesy: Ken Blackburn)

the floor of the boat. Ken then picked up the quarter and picked up the speed.

Once after a hard day of fishing and the occasional drink, Billie discovered he had lost his wallet. When a long and frenzied search failed to locate it, it was given up as lost. A few weeks later, when a trio of the local ladies went fishing, they hauled in a nice catch including a good-sized Northern Pike.

> *A fish dinner followed at the home of Joe Patterson and all the fish were eaten except the worthy pike. It reposed outside the door in a basket to show off later to the envying population. However, Joe's cat got a whiff of the luscious delicacy and made short work of eating it completely. Yes, all except an indigestible wallet which was found among the finny remains and which bore the inscription: W. B. Perth Post Office (Perth Courier 06/10/1948).*

The wallet was then returned to its proper, if somewhat embarrassed, owner.

Chapter 10 ◆ Jordan's Bridge

With his complimentary rental boat, Arden Blackburn wasn't the only one to be on the receiving end of the generosity of the Jordan family whose reputation for helping others was well-known around the lake. A life-long resident of the lake, John Jordan was not only a prominent member of the Christie Lake resort owners, but a familiar figure in community organizations such as the Calvin United Church, the Bathurst Township Council (1955–1961), the True Britons Lodge, the Land of lakes Shrine Club and the Canadian Woodmen of the World.

The sudden loss of the sixty-year-old Jordan, who died of a heart attack on August 15, 1965, while water skiing at the lake, came as an unexpected shock to many.

Kenny Kirkham and his wife, Vera, in 1947. (Courtesy: Doris Kirkham)

"Christie Lake will not be the same without his cheerful greeting and wonderful community spirit," remarked one lake resident (*Perth Courier*, 09/09/1965).

Among the pallbearers at John Jordan's funeral were Wib Noonan and Kenny Kirkham. Kirkham was a close family friend and another familiar figure at the lake, having taken his place in a long line of Christie Lake handymen who, like Morley White and Jack Palmer, were often seen helping out around the lake. Over the years Kenny Kirkham seldom missed an opportunity to lend a hand come threshing time. When he wasn't helping folks on their farm or working on his own, Kenny could be found fiddling with things. Blessed with an inventive mind, it was said that Kenny Kirkham could "jig" up a solution to most problems in life.

> **SIMPLIFIED ICE CUTTING AT CHRISTIE LAKE**
>
> Kenneth Kirkham of Bathurst this winter constructed modern ice cutting and loading equipment capable of handling thousands of cakes of ice per day. Six sleighs drawn by teams can be loaded with large blocks of ice within a very short time, revolutionizing the ice cutting business at Christie Lake. Mr. Kirkham deserves commendation for his ingenuity and industry. Mr. Jack Palmer assisted Mr. Kirkham in building the new loading device, which this winter proved to be a great labour saver (*Perth Courier* 03/10/1939).

In the winter Kenny used a V-nose plow fashioned out of wood and attached to the front of his 1946 army truck to plow snow. On more than one occasion, after a major snow storm, a lake resident invited Kenny to drop over for a few beers and reminded him "to leave the blade down on your way in."

In the summer Kenny planed wood using a second-hand lathe and automobile spring he got from Sam Kelford. With his homemade machine powered by an old Case tractor, Kenny provided much of the lumber needed for building projects around the lake.

Kenny's popularity around the lake was bolstered by the fact that he grew the largest crop of hops in the area and used them to produce some of sweetest-tasting home brew south of Highway 7. Despite his

Chapter 10 ◆ Jordan's Bridge

ability to solve problems and fix things, later in life Kenny lamented the fact that he hadn't had more education. On those occasions, Alan Jordan reminded Kenny that others came to learn from him, not the other way around.

Kenny's 90th birthday party was a typical Christie Lake affair with a caterer, a band and a large crowd of people. At the end of the night, Kenny told everyone to make sure they came back in five years for his 95th. Many did and so did Kenny. Following another grand get together, Irene Strong, penned an article entitled "He Danced His Way to 95." It was a fitting farewell to Kenny, coming as it did just weeks before he passed away.

"We lost a good one when we lost Kenny," reflected Alan Jordan. "People around here just don't need each other as much as we used to."

The Blackburn family in the early forties.

Arden Blackburn's Mail Route

In acknowledging Kenny's passing, Alan Jordan touched upon what had long been a defining characteristic of the Christie Lake community—a willingness to help one another. It was a trait found in their day-to-day lives, as well as the fanciful tale of the bet between Joe Thompson and Bill Fournier.

According to the story, Thompson bet Fournier that he could drive his car to town without ever having to start it. What happened, according to Alan Jordan, was that Joe pulled out the distributor cap so the car wouldn't start and proceeded to ask people if they'd give him a push. Eventually, so the story goes, folks ended up pushing him all the way to Perth. Whether real or imagined, it was a story that captured the strength of the Christie Lake community.

Nowhere was the community's willingness to help one another better exemplified than in their mailman. Through the years residents at the lake had come to depend more and more upon Arden Blackburn.

> *"Our daily bread—particularly in winter—literally depends on our mailman, Arden Blackburn," recalled Bill Sproule. "It is he, who does all our shopping, brings our milk, picks out the best vegetables and meat and matches a ball of yarn. Even after we have failed miserably, he finds us a pound of butter" (Perth Courier, 06/15/1948).*

With his car piled high with groceries, dry cleaning and prescriptions from the apothecary, not to mention the highly anticipated Sears and Eaton's catalogues, Arden was a familiar sight on the North Shore Road. According to his wife, Sophia, on one occasion Arden was even asked "to exchange corsets at Shaw's clothing store for one particular lady," a fact that even years later brought a smile to Sophia's face.[46] It was an undeniable fact that those who waited for Arden did so for a myriad of reason.

> *"Arden has been a household word for us," remarked one summer resident. "We're always on the lookout for him and checking to see if he has come by yet. Always when we met him, he always seemed to have a few moments to spend with you, always he was smiling and helpful and positive."*[47]

For every item Arden hauled from town he often took one back, be it pots and pans to the local tinsmith or an item to be repaired at

Chapter 10 ◆ Jordan's Bridge

James Brothers Hardware. In the early days he even transported the odd resident to and from town, particularly in the winter when the wooden cover he had built over his cutter provided many a passenger with welcome refuge from the cold and snow. Arden even managed to get a small stove in the right front corner of the cutter and hot bricks on the floor to warm one's feet.

Among those fortunate enough to enjoy a cozy ride to town on a cold winter's day, courtesy of Arden and his cutter, was Bill Sproule, whose sweet tooth occasionally sent him scurrying to Perth to see the dentist. Born in 1928, Bill had moved with his family to the lake in the early thirties. Bill's first memory of being there was as a relieved three-year-old who had just peed off the family dock.

From that time on Bill's childhood at Christie Lake was filled with hours of games and swimming interrupted only by the occasional scare of a water snake or the energy boost of a brown sugar sandwich. As he got older Bill often made his way to the Noonan store to buy the chocolate-covered marshmallows known as "brooms." Unfortunately Bill's sweet tooth occasionally caught up with him. When that happened his dad asked Arden to take him to town. After the visit to the dentist, Bill stayed the night in town with his grandfather only to return to the lake the next day with the mail.

It was said that Bill's parents, Reg and Marion Sproule, had come to Christie Lake to seek a fresh start. Once among the well-to-do, it was said they had the misfortune to have lost everything in the market crash of 1929. It was for this reason that the couple and their two children, Bill and Mary Lou, had come to live at "Oak Lodge," the summer home built in the early 1900s by Marion's grandfather, Alexander Kippen.

Whatever the reason for his arrival there, Reg Sproule quickly established himself as one of Christie Lake's most colourful characters. A natural-born athlete, Reg Sproule loved the outdoor life afforded him at the lake and was a well-recognized and much-loved figure amongst the community, despite having some rather peculiar habits.

As a young volunteer in the Canadian Army Artillery, Reg Sproule had been severely wounded by German guns and was to be afflicted with nightmares for decades to come. Bill recalled his dad being given regular hospital treatments with a powerful magnet to

Two different views of Gravelly Bay in 1956. Top: Truman boathouse on the lower right and Dr. Kidd's boathouse in the bay. Bottom: L.-R. Truman cottage, Iley cottage, Craig cottage and Alex Montgomery's cottage. (Courtesy: Bob Chaplin)

Chapter 10 ♦ Jordan's Bridge

try to draw the shrapnel away from his heart. So it was that over the years the community around the lake came to forgive Reg Sproule for the odd misdemeanor.

Few complained at the Maberly Fair when, as others enjoyed a drink in the community hall, Reg slipped away to remove a turkey or two from those sitting in the back of a car and destined to be donated as prizes. That's just the way it was. No one was surprised or upset. The same was true of Sarah Noonan on the occasional Sunday morning when she came home from church only to discover that the roast she had put in the oven that morning was gone.

It was Dr. Kidd who eventually came to the conclusion that forgiveness only went so far. Over the years the doctor had come into possession of considerable property at the lake in exchange for medical treatment provided members of the Patterson family. Dr. Kidd, whose property stretched from Gravelly Bay to May A. Bell

Reg Sproule with his son, Bill, boiling sap at the lake. (Courtesy: George James)

Point, built his cottage just west of Gravelly Bay, and it was no secret that Reg occasionally entered it in search of a bit of booze. Finally getting fed up with the frequency of such occurrences, Dr. Kidd decided to mix up a harmless, but powerful, potion of medicine and mineral spirits, which he then poured into an empty liquor bottle. Before long, as Dr. Kidd anticipated, Reg was complaining of stomach pains, an ailment that cured him of entering the doctor's cottage without an invitation.

In the summer Reg Sproule often set up his booth at the community fun day to sell drinks and other confectionaries, while in the winter, he was seen out cutting ice.

"Our ice house never got nearly empty," recalled his son Bill.

The ice would be cut near winter's end just before the spring break-up when the lake produced a range of sounds which, according to Bill, were so loud they'd wake up many people most of whom were part of a bet as to when the break-up would occur.

The winter was not an easy time for the Sproules, whose home contained little to no insulation. With Reg attempting to keep out the cold by hanging pictures over the knotholes on the wall, the family eagerly awaited the coming of spring. While the end of winter signaled some relief from the cold for the Sproules, it also signaled an increase in work for everyone.

There were trees to be tapped and pails to be hung, recalled Bill. Then there was the endless walking from tree to tree collecting the sap which had to be boiled. Knowing that forty gallons of sap were needed to produce one gallon of syrup, cords of firewood kept a constant fire going day and night, burning under a large evaporating pan. While the end result was highly prized by city folks, they knew little, claimed Bill, about the work involved in producing that liquor bottle full of liquid gold.

As well as making maple syrup, Reg Sproule trapped wild mink, which he cleaned and tanned; he also netted white fish that provided some of the best fillets ever. In the rock bluff behind their house Reg blasted an eight foot deep root cellar. Protected as it was by a thick insulated door, it allowed the Sproules to preserve their vegetables and various other food items for months to come.

CHAPTER 10 ◆ JORDAN'S BRIDGE

Another view of Reg Sproule boiling sap at the lake.

On one occasion the cellar became home to an unlikely visitor in the form of a horse named Gerry. Gerry had unfortunately broken its leg. With the animal doomed to be put down, Reg took Gerry in and kept him in the cold storage room where he rigged a belly harness which he placed under the horse and tied to the roof. The homemade sling was left under the horse until it had recovered enough to stand on its own.

Reg's patience for Gerry was not an attribute that he extended to all animals. When the family Doberman, Rusty, had trouble following orders it so irritated Reg that he would occasionally grab Rusty by the two hind legs and was said to swing him up against a tree. It wasn't long before Rusty came to mind and wound up sitting on the

Sproule's sofa howling away as the family sang the old army ballad "For they wear no pants in the southern part of France."

Reg Sproule was an ardent fisherman, who claimed to set the record when he pulled a twelve pound pickerel out of Christie Lake with a rod and line. The fish was thirty-one and a half inches in length and was to hold a place of prominence in the window of James Brothers Hardware. At the time, Reg made it a point of letting it be known that he didn't approve of some of the current methods of fishing at the lake.

> *He was a firm believer in the old-fashioned method of fishing, in which the fish is given a sporting chance and is caught or lost by the fishermen's strength and skill. Trolling from a motor boat, which was formally unlawful, he considers very harmful to fishing interests, many fish being killed by this method (Perth Courier 10/22/1937).*

As time went by, more than a few Reg Sproule tales managed to find a permanent place in the folklore of Christie Lake. There was the one about the time he decided to go Christmas shopping in Perth. When he couldn't get his car started, Reg borrowed a cutter from the Palmers. On his way back home Reg discovered Bill Mitchell had put his car in the ditch. Doing the neighbourly thing, Reg tried to help him out by tying a rope around the cutter and then around the car. He then commanded the horses to take off, which they did, promptly pulling the box right off the Palmer's cutter.

Then there was the time a summer visitor was said to have launched into a violent sneezing attack while out fishing and lost his dentures. The story went that Reg, who was an excellent swimmer, offered to retrieve the sunken teeth. Using a pail and a heavy stone, Reg was said to have jumped out of the boat and had the teeth on the second try.

As much as anyone, Reg Sproule personified the ability of those around the lake to pardon their own. In the end, despite his peccadilloes, Reg Sproule was a much-loved member of the community. It was only fitting, therefore, that it was Reg who painted the big white letters on a rock at the foot of the lake the sign that said "Welcome to Christie Lake."

♦ Chapter Eleven ♦

CHRISTIE LAKE SCHOOL

One of the many roles filled by Reg Sproule at the lake was that of emcee at the annual concert held at the Christie Lake School (S.S. No. 5 Bathurst). Considered to be a major social event in the area, the concert brought together parents, relatives, friends and neighbours to watch the talent and antics of the young people as they performed on stage. Each year the parents of the students taking part in the concert were asked to provide a white sheet prior to the show so that a curtain could be made and stretched across the front of the stage. Most of the sheets were new, recalled Bill Sproule, for no one wanted to be accused of sending in one with "tattletale grey."

The Christie Lake School had been an integral part of the community since the late 1800s when teachers, such as Miss Tillie Doyle and Miss Kate Forrest, came to live and teach at the lake. The importance of the teacher's role in the community was a familiar one to Irene Strong, whose family owned the farm adjacent to the Christie Lake Camp. From an early age, Irene was keenly aware of the value her father placed on a good education. In fact, as a child, Irene attended a school built on land donated by her dad and known as the Strong School.

While many of her friends left school to get a job or to work on the family farm, Irene's dad insisted she attend high school. So it was that once she finished her elementary school program, Irene headed off to

Perth for three days to write the entrance exams for the Perth Collegiate Institute. When the names of those who had been successful were eventually posted in the *Perth Courier,* Irene's name was there among them. So come the fall Irene was off to Perth.

Like most of the high school students who came from the country, Irene roomed in town, looking after herself and getting her own meals.

"You grew up quickly in those days," recalled Irene.

Because of the poor conditions of the roads, most students didn't get back home until Easter unless they were able to avail themselves of the services of the train or Arden Blackburn's buggy. For some it was a long period and Irene recalled the time she got lonely and decided she'd walk home one Friday night after school. She got as far as DeWitts Corners before her tired legs and empty stomach prompted her to turn off at her grandparents.

Irene Strong ca. 1936 when she began to teach at the S.S No. 5 Bathurst School at Christie Lake. (Courtesy: Irene Kirkham)

Chapter 11 ♦ Christie Lake School

After high school Irene was granted permission to attend teachers' college a year before she was eligible and, as a result, was just eighteen when she started teaching at the S.S. No. 5 Bathurst School in September 1936. Irene's youthful appearance one day led the school inspector to question her about a rather tall, mature young man sitting at the back of the class. Despite being old enough to drive a car, the lad was a student at the school and not, as the inspector had first suspected, Irene's boyfriend.

Irene spent the next four years at the Christie Lake School teaching thirty to thirty-five students each year from primer to first year high school. While delivering a course of study prepared by the provincial government, Irene was paid $500 a year. Out of this, she took care of her room and board, bought the necessities of life and covered the summer courses offered at the Kemptville Agricultural College needed for her to get her permanent teaching certificate.

In the fall and spring Irene rode her bicycle from home to school, but in the winter she boarded at the home of Kenny Kirkham, who'd often hitch up a team of horses and use his sleigh to bring Irene and the neighbouring kids to school. Each year Irene chose one of the boys who lived nearby to come in early to sweep the school floor clean and to get the fire going.

The S.S. No. 5 Bathurst schoolhouse at Christie Lake. (Courtesy: Gray Palmer)

Arden Blackburn's Mail Route

Despite the fact that it was filled with wood, according to Bill Sproule, the big stove in the middle of the schoolhouse threw off limited heat.

"On the coldest days the girls were allowed to sit closest to the stove, while the displaced boys shivered and ground their teeth in righteous indignation," recalled Bill.

In fact, there were often times when Irene and the youngsters arrived at school to find the ink wells frozen, only to have to place them on the wood stove to thaw out.

In the early days, the washrooms were a pair of outhouses that stood in a corner of the schoolyard, one on each side of the wood shed at the back. Eventually, however, new washrooms were built inside the school at the end of the boys' and girls' cloakrooms. When an evening was set aside to celebrate the opening of the new facilities, Bill Sproule claimed some dignitaries from the school board were on hand to christen them in a most appropriate manner.

Inside the schoolhouse, the various grades faced the raised stage at the front—the youngest on the right and the oldest on the left. There was usually one grade per row, with the teacher's table on the stage. According to Bill, the seating arrangement allowed the kids to get a repeat of the previous year's lessons by turning to the right or a preview of the next year's lessons by turning to the left.

On the front left wall was an old set of *Encyclopedia Britannica* which someone had donated to the school. When a student's work was done, including their homework, they were allowed to read one of the encyclopedias. By the seventh grade Bill Sproule claimed to have scanned the whole set twice.

Despite its obvious merits, being successful in school also had its downside, as Bill's sister, Mary Lou, discovered when she won the annual school spelling bee. Following Mary Lou's achievement, the mother of the other finalist, who had previously provided the Sproule family with butter, wrote the Sproules' a curt note that simply said, "Expect no butter from me!"

The two mile walk to and from school each day provided Bill and Mary Lou with a fair degree of exercise, as well as the occasional moment of excitement. There was, Bill recalled, one corner on the road to school which had a rotting old tree stump with a hole in the

Chapter 11 ♦ Christie Lake School

one side of it. Their dad would sometimes hide apples or cookies in it for them as an unexpected treat.

The corner, however, was also home to a massive bull, and Mary Lou was convinced that should the bull be provoked, the old wooden fence would do little to prevent him from leaving the field. While she bemoaned the fact that her parents had bought her a red raincoat, she later credited her track and field prowess at the collegiate in Perth to the training she received in trying to quickly put a substantial distance between her and the bull.

It was with great fondness that Bill Sproule recalled the days he and Mary Lou didn't have to go to school because there was "water on the bridge," a low-level timber affair under which water drained from the adjacent meadow into the lake. The Sproule children had strict instructions to never cross the bridge if there was water on it. So it was that on warm spring mornings when the melted snow had raised the water level ever so slightly above the height of the wood, the children raced back home declaring they couldn't go to school because there was "water on the bridge."

Bill and Mary Lou Sproule waiting by their mail box on the North Shore Road. (Courtesy: George James)

Arden Blackburn's Mail Route

It wasn't that Bill and Mary Lou didn't like school, they did. Come lunchtime when they had finished their sandwiches and cookies and had a drink of water from the well, they liked nothing better than to join the other kids in a game of hide and seek or baseball or to join Boyd McLaren and the others in tossing the ball over the schoolhouse roof in a game of "Auntie Over." In the winter they made snowmen and snow forts, before the spring came and they went to the river to check out the return of the fish and other wildlife.

During one particular noon hour as the children played, Irene Strong, who was the teacher at the time, heard a sudden uproar coming from the playground. Upon going to the yard she found Gordon Stiller, the more cantankerous of the Stiller twins (as opposed to his sister Margaret), cursing at the top of his lungs. It seemed Gordon

Irene Strong when she enlisted with the Royal Canadian Air Force in 1942. (Courtesy: Irene Kirkham)

Chapter 11 ♦ Christie Lake School

was having a particularly bad day. Irene had no choice but to tell the lad to stay after school, at which time she administered the strap—giving him a slap on each hand. The reprimand did little to diminish Gordon's fondness for his teacher, for once chastised Gordon offered to see Irene safely home, thus demonstrating that even the bad-tempered have a good side.

The respect that Gordon Stiller accorded his teacher was indicative of the general regard with which Irene Strong was held by the students and parents alike. Despite her ability to be compassionate when called upon, Irene could also rule with a firm hand, a fact pointed out by Reg Sproule when it came report card time. As her middle name was Marion, Irene signed the student report cards "I. M. Strong." Reg took it upon himself to remind his son Bill that "she dammed well needed to be" given the size of some of the boys who towered over her.

While handling a variety of ages and ability levels, Irene did her best to ensure that all the children took part in all school activities, including the annual concert. So it was that when Percy Truelove had trouble remembering his lines, Irene had Margaret Stiller and some of her better students coach him.

On the night of the concert Percy arrived at the school, all decked out in his finest and with his proud parents in tow. Despite his teacher's and Margaret's best efforts, however, when it came time for Percy's part, he could recall only one of his four lines, a fact that didn't deter the large crowd from giving him a thunderous round of applause, much to the delight of his beaming mom and dad.

The audience at the school that evening, as it was for every concert, was a mixed lot, a microcosm of the lake community itself. Some were there to see family members; some were there simply for the entertainment. They came from near and far, the well-to-do and the not-so-well-off, and each year among them was a couple that stood out from all the rest.

From the time they arrived at the lake in the mid-1920s, Les and Jean Appleby seldom missed a concert at the school. A tall, dark-eyed beauty, said to have "the fine ebony-ivory complexion of an Argentine senorita," Jean Appleby often arrived at the school dressed in fur and with her hair pulled back tightly in a bun. Her husband

Les, with his Douglas Fairbanks' looks, matching spats and homburg hat, cut no less a striking figure.

Born in England, Les Appleby, with his unmistakable accent and impeccable manners retained very much the air of a British aristocrat even while at the lake. Les had risen to prominence in the entertainment world as manager of the Dumbells, Canadian soldiers turned singers and performers, who had gone from doing shows on a makeshift stage in France during the First World War to becoming the most famous of the Canadian army "concert parties." Formed to raise the morale of the troops on the front lines, the group took its name from the Third Division's emblem, a red dumbbell that signified strength. Upon their return to Canada following the war, the Dumbells were reformed as a vaudeville troupe and performed as civilians completing twelve cross-Canada tours over the next thirteen years.

As Les's reputation as an advance man and entertainment manager grew, he eventually toured with Sadler's Wells and Ballet Theatre, as well as American actress Bette Davis, with whom he

The first Miss Toronto contest held in 1926 with the winner Jean Tolmie in the middle with the white bathing suit.
(Courtesy: City of Toronto Archives Fonds 1244 Item No. 1028K)

Chapter 11 ♦ Christie Lake School

lasted but a year, finding her far too difficult with which to deal. Over the years, Les was associated with the tours of various stars, including Sir John Martin Harvey and comedian George Formby. A writer for the *Saskatoon Star-Phoenix* once remarked, "In the twenty-nine years the writer has known him, Les has never press-agented or managed a turkey."[48]

It was as business manager of the Dumbell's Capt. Merton Plunkett and his touring revue that in 1926 Les had met the beautiful twenty-one-year-old Jean Tolmie. In August of that year Jean was named winner of the first ever Miss Toronto contest. During the competition particular attention was paid to Jean's hair, which, as usual, was parted in the middle and tightly held together at the nape of her neck.

"No, I would never think of having it bobbed," she said at the time. "I think bobbed hair looks terrible on a tall girl."

It seems the judges agreed.

"Miss Tolmie is not only beautiful, she is intelligent," said one of the judging committee. "Anyone is intelligent who has sense enough to wear her hair like that."[49]

By the end of the event Jean was the obvious choice of the five judges to represent Toronto at the 1926 Atlantic City Miss America beauty pageant.

Once in Atlantic City Jean again wowed the judges, a fact that put them in quite a quandary since she was a Canadian and therefore ineligible for the title of Miss America. In the end Jean's "remarkable beauty" was said to have forced the Atlantic City judges to create a special award for her, a fact that led to her being presented with the first Miss Congeniality award in recognition of her "beauty of face and grace of carriage."[50]

Following the competition Jean insisted that she had no desire to enter the world of show business. "My ambition is to get married and have children," she declared at the time.[51] Come fall, however, she found herself on a coast to coast tour with Capt. Plunkett's Revue. It was while travelling with the troupe that Jean encountered the charming and dapper Les Appleby. When the company disbanded in the spring, Jean returned to Toronto, but dearly missed her English squire, and so it was that come fall she left for Fort William where on September 19, 1927, she and Les were married.

After their marriage Les and Jean bought land from R. W. Marks at the head of the lake, following which Les began the process of almost single-handedly designing and building a showpiece summer home that eventually became the residence of Bruce and Mary McIntyre. With a boathouse, storage area, work room and spare bedroom on the ground floor, upstairs were two bedrooms, bathroom, kitchen, dining room and breakfast nook. A large wood-panelled sunken living room faced the lake.

After a winter full of travelling, Les and Jean were always happy to get back to the lake they loved so much. On one occasion it was reported that Les "was so overcome with joy, that he executed a nimble entrechat on the station platform, to the delight of the delegation who greeted the train" (*Perth Courier* 05/01/1947).

To showcase the view from their summer home, Les bought a huge plate glass window from a department store supplier in Toronto. The large window provided the Applebys with an abundance of light, as well as a breathtaking view of the lake. While it was a mystery to many how Les got the window from the train station to the cottage, Bill Sproule, who had once watched Les use a block and tackle system to set a massive fireplace mantle by himself, knew that Les was capable of most anything. It was Les' ingenuity that led the couple to having a dumbwaiter in the cottage to bring things up from the water to the kitchen, including firewood for the stove.

Meanwhile outside the cottage was a large terraced garden that gave Jean Appleby space to utilize her considerable gardening skills. Unfortunately in her later years Jean was struck by a disease that left her paralyzed and confined to a wheelchair, thus unable to tend the yard she had taken such pride in. When Jean passed away in 1978, Les never got over her loss. He spent the winters at the Park Lane Hotel in Ottawa, where he whiled away the hours watching a condo going up across the street. In the summer he returned to the lake where he would eventually pass away in his sleep at the cottage he and Jean had loved so much.

The attention garnered by the Appleby cottage was at times a source of worry for their next door neighbor, Josephine (Josie) Jacques, who was concerned that distracted boaters might damage her water system. As a result, those caught up staring at the Appleby cottage were often

Chapter 11 ♦ Christie Lake School

A gathering of friends at the lake, including Iris Fleetwood-Morrow (top left) and (bottom left – right) Les Appleby, Jean Appleby and John Fleetwood-Morrow. (Courtesy: Penny Nault)

brought up short by the elderly Mrs. Jacques, who cautioned them about the water pipe that extended out from her shoreline.

"Mind me pipe, mind me pipe," she scolded the passing boaters.

It was Josie Jacques who first introduced the Applebys to John Fleetwood-Morrow. Like Les Appleby, Fleetwood-Morrow had come to Canada from England in the 1930s. A professional fashion photographer with the T. Eaton Co., Fleetwood-Morrow was a member of Toronto's Arts and Letters Club where, when he recounted his experiences as the official photographer with the Canadian Forces during the Second World War, John was acknowledged as no mean raconteur.

"His hair-breath escapes were told with modesty and restraint," reported the club in its monthly newsletter.[52]

It was while in Belgium during the war that John Fleetwood-Morrow met Iris Cross and the two were married. Once back in Toronto the couple was invited by members of the Jacques family to visit the Jacques' cottage on Christie Lake. It wasn't long before the Fleetwood-Morrows bought a cottage of their own on a point just west of Station Bay, later to become the home of Dr. Oesterbaum and his wife.

The arrival at the lake of John and his wife, Iris, unfortunately spelled an end to their marriage. It was shortly thereafter that the couple divorced, and John married Janie Church, whose family also had a cottage on the lake. Following their marriage, John and Janie bought a cottage just up from the Krausers (later to be the Hoard cottage) and became good friends with the Conklins and Jimmie Kinloch, a senior news editor at the CBC. A native of Perth, where his parents ran the Birkacre Tea Room, Kinloch had once worked at the *Perth Courier* before quitting to join the CBC. In the summer of 1948, Kinloch, with the help of Les Appleby, built a cottage on Christie Lake known as the "Kin–Loch–Up."

As the Kinloch cottage was nearing completion, a group of lake residents came over to attend "the hanging of the door," a ceremony celebrated around the lake to officially open a newly-built or renovated building. When they arrived, however, there was no sign of their host and they were informed by Les Appleby that Jimmie had retired to nurse a sore thumb which was in pretty bad shape from filling numerous nail holes with putty.

Chapter 11 ♦ Christie Lake School

John and Iris Fleetwood-Morrow on the dock at the Appleby cottage ca. 1950. (Courtesy: Penny Nault)

The visitors hung around awhile and enjoyed a cup of tea courtesy of Jean Appleby's sister Kate Tolmie but eventually came home feeling pretty disappointed. The joke around the lake was that when Jimmie tried to go to sleep and forget his throbbing thumb, he actually found himself counting putty holes instead and got up more tired than when he lay down.

The "hanging of the door," like the concert at the school and the annual fun days, were events that in the early days brought the community around Christie Lake together and demonstrated its capacity to be inclusive. It was a trait that didn't necessarily mean everyone in the community was equal, but rather that everyone in the community had a place.

It was for this reason that Irene Strong believed every child deserved their moment in the spotlight and why the Applebys could cheer as loudly for Percy Truelove as for any professional performer of the day. It was why George and Sarah Noonan left a Christmas dinner each year at the door of John Burns, the lake recluse. It was why Don Bell's mom sent him with a pie for Aaron Bolger, a hermit with an affinity for

Dickie Patterson relaxing on the porch of the Sunrise/Sunset cottage with Dave Rogers. (Courtesy: Dave Rogers)

Chapter 11 ◆ Christie Lake School

machines, who dove into the pie with such vigour that an incredulous Bell was prompted to ask, "Don't you want to save some?"

Nowhere, however, was the capacity of the community to take care of its own more evident than in the case of Dickie Patterson, a developmentally delayed lad, who, as a classmate of Irene Strong's, languished in the early grades despite having been in school for a number of years. Often finding fault with what they saw as his misbehaviour or inattentiveness, teachers frequently became frustrated with Dickie.

On one such occasion, recalled Irene, Dickie was told by their teacher to stay in at lunchtime. Forgetting, or misunderstanding, the directive, when lunch was over Dickie headed outside. As fate would have it, as he left the school building Dickie stepped on a loose board, the squeaking of which alerted the teacher to his departure. The teacher gave chase, catching Dickie with one leg over the school fence. Grabbing him by the other leg, the teacher hollered for a student to "Go and get the strap!" With the strap in hand the teacher began to hit Dickie. It was a painful memory that stayed with Irene Strong and no doubt accounted, in part, for the compassion she had, as a teacher, for students like Percy Truelove and Dickie Patterson who struggled "to keep anything in their head for more than a day," as she put it.

Dickie Patterson had grown up at Christie Lake, the son of Sarah Geary and Bob Patterson. Despite his weaknesses Dickie grew up to be a trustworthy lad, who worked hard and was a valued member of the community. Folks around the area hired Dickie to run errands, to do odd jobs, and Dickie did whatever was asked of him. He raked leaves; he cut grass; he dug gardens. But what Dickie liked to do more than anything was to guard things, for Dickie took great pride in the believing he was an officer of the law.

So it was that when there was a dance at Wemyss, Dickie donned his conductor's cap and stationed himself inside the front door as a security guard. Invariably, at some point in the evening, someone asked Dickie to "give us a little step dance." At which point Dickie removed the cigarette package and countless other items from his shirt pocket and proceeded to do a step or two which prompted a loud round of applause from the crowd.

The summer that Irene Strong's older sister got married was a stressful time for the Strong family. Her sister was a stickler for

Arden Blackburn's Mail Route

Dave Rogers helping Dickie load his bicycle into the trunk of Dave's car. (Courtesy: Dave Rogers)

detail and could be quite demanding. A teacher at Broadview High School in Ottawa, she had informed the Strong family that the "Broadview" people would be coming to the wedding and everything was to be just right.

Come the day of the wedding things were running quite smoothly until Dickie Patterson rode in on his bicycle, wearing his best black jacket and white shirt, and began to usher people to their seats. Irene's dad didn't want to hurt Dickie's feelings but knew his daughter would be mortified if she became aware that Dickie was greeting the guests.

Aware of Dickie's affinity for guarding things, Mr. Strong said, "Now Dick, I appreciate what you're doing, but we need someone to keep an eye on the farm while everyone's at the wedding. Would you do that for us?"

"Yes, Mr. Strong. Yes, Mr. Strong," replied an eager Dickie.

On another occasion when Dickie was asked to guard the plane of CPR president William Neal, some passersby became suspicious about a "strange guy" hanging around the plane. When they asked Dickie what he was doing, Dickie replied, "I'm the pilot."

CHAPTER 11 ◆ CHRISTIE LAKE SCHOOL

Whether his interrogators believed his answer or whether they could even understand it was doubtful, since it was difficult for those who didn't know Dickie to comprehend what he was saying. Not only did he have few, if any, teeth, which hindered his pronunciation, but, he often interjected random phrases such as "eyesy-piesy" into the conversation, thus making him even more unintelligible.

During his lifetime Dickie was seldom seen without his trusty bicycle. No matter the time of year or the time of day, Dickie rode it everywhere, often pedaling only fast enough to keep him and the bike from falling over. When the winter snow got too deep and Dickie was forced to push his bike, it was a fact quite obvious to those at the lake who recognized the mark of the bike tires running alongside the tracks of Dickie's shuffling feet.

When Dickie's dad passed away, Dickie inherited the home near the railroad track by the mailboxes. From there he wore a path to the dump.

"Dick was a pack rat," recalled Elton Crandall Jr. "He'd go to the dump and bring back everything by wheelbarrow. He had a huge wheelbarrow. He'd bring back fridges that didn't work...He would get old mattresses and pile them up in his room and sleep on top of them covered in blankets."

Dickie Patterson and Morley White cutting wood on Morley's farm ca. 1940.

Eventually it became next to impossible for Dickie to open the door of the house, a fact that forced him to put his back to the door and shove and then shimmy inside to the top of his stuff. For the last fifteen years of Dickie's life, Jeff Nault was the social worker assigned by the County of Lanark to look after Dickie and his financial affairs.

"At times he saw me as his best friend and at times he saw me as his worst enemy," mused Jeff.

Knowing that Dickie's house was heated by baseboard heaters which were now completely covered, Jeff hired Perth electrician Bill Shafer to come out and install an industrial heater above Dickie's door. Despite the best of precautions, the inevitable eventually happened and Dickie's house burned to the ground.

Following the fire a 12 x 16 foot hunting camp was brought from Fallbrook and set near the entrance to the dump. Unfortunately, it eventually suffered the same fate as Dickie's previous home and was leveled by a fire. When that happened Gray Palmer gathered up a few others from the community, and they built Dickie another home complete with a nice new outhouse. Dickie, however, would have nothing to do with the outhouse.

Dickie Patterson standing in front of a load of wood at the Sunrise/Sunset cottage of the Rogers brothers. (Courtesy: Dave Rogers)

Chapter 11 ◆ Christie Lake School

"Dickie, this is for you," they said.

"I don't like it," Dickie said. "I'm not gonna use it."

True to his word, Dickie continued to go up the hill to use his old outhouse, which was really nothing more than an open-air rail suspended between two blocks of wood.

Dickie displayed the same degree of defiance when Gray built a box around Patterson Spring, a bubbling supply of ice-cold water, located not too far from where Dickie lived. For years Dickie (as well as CPR president William Neal and numerous others) had been using the spring as a source of drinking water. They shared the water, however, with various salamanders, frogs and other critters, a fact that prompted Gray to build a cover made of cedar with a hinged top. When Dickie discovered the box, however, he promptly ripped it off and threw it in the swamp.

Dickie displayed a similar disregard for proper hygiene. As a result, the only time he came clean at all was when he got caught in the rain or took a dunk in the lake. So it was that lake resident Ernie Rogers often tried to convince Dickie of the recreational benefits of going for a swim. If successful, Ernie then provided Dickie with a new set of clothes from the Salvation Army. The problem was Dickie insisted on putting the new clothes over his old ones.

Ernie Rogers was another familiar face at the lake. Following the war, he had sold the family farm near Brooke and bought the Sunrise and Sunset cottages originally built by R. W. Marks for his children. Born in 1898 Ernie Rogers had been one of two boys and five girls born at the family homestead near Brooke. He had worked on the farm until 1915 when a fellow by the name of Adair came looking for help to run the telephone lines from Brooke to Glen Tay. Ernie agreed to help him and the next year when Adair didn't show up, Ernie finished the job. He then went to work for a telephone construction company in Rochester, New York, before moving to Buffalo. In 1963 he retired to his property at the lake and helped watch over Dickie.

It was Ernie Rogers who christened the local dump the "Christie Lake Boutique" and gave Dickie the job of looking after it. Through the years many in the area claimed the dump was never as well maintained as it was when Dickie Patterson looked after it. Living in his ramshackle shed full of newspapers and bicycle parts, Dickie was in his element at the dump. His closet was the fence where folks hung articles of clothing in the hope that others could use them. It was here that Dickie recovered the fur coat that he wore both summer and winter.

"I'd go over to see him," recalled Elton Crandall Jr. "and I'd say, 'Hello Dick, how are you?'

"He'd say, 'Fine, Mr. Marks.'

"He'd call me Mr. Marks, because he knew I was Maizie Marks' son. I didn't tell him I wasn't Mr. Marks because he wouldn't remember that anyways. I just let him call me Mr. Marks."

Names weren't the only thing to confound Dickie. Although he attempted to use the sun to tell time, in the end, the time of day meant little to Dickie. He ate when he got hungry; he slept when he got tired. Getting a job done was more important to Dickie than the length of time it took to do it.

One evening Dickie had been splitting wood with Wib Noonan when Wib said he was going to call it a day and suggested Dickie do the same. Eventually Wib went to bed only to get up the next morning and discover that Dickie had worked all night and left the entire pile of wood cut and stacked.

Once when an inspector from the Ministry of Labour came to visit the Noonan farm, he asked Wib if he ever hired anyone. Wib responded that on occasion he did. As the inspector began to ask more questions, Wib spotted Dickie coming down the road on his bike. He beckoned Dickie over and told him that this particular gentleman wanted to ask him some questions.

The inspector asked Dickie if he ever worked for Wib.

"Sometimes," giggled Dickie, pleased as punch at being the centre of attention.

"And what does he pay you?" asked the inspector.

"Me no tell you," replied Dickie, giving Wib a sly grin.

When the official attempted to pry a more suitable answer from Dickie he continued to receive a string of non sequiturs that prompted him to eventually throw his hands up in despair. It was a gesture that clearly indicated to Wib that, in Dickie Patterson, he had found an appropriate answer to government interference in private enterprise.

If time meant little to Dickie, money meant even less. What little money Dickie had went for cigarettes or batteries for the radio he

Chapter 11 ◆ Christie Lake School

listened to all night. Once when Jack Briggs asked Dickie to shovel the road into his house, it took Dickie a couple of days to clear the drive of snow. When Jack went to pay him with a crisp twenty dollar bill, Dickie refused it. The perplexed Briggs remained at a loss as to why Dickie refused what was, for him, a considerable amount of cash. It wasn't until Jack broke the twenty into numerous smaller bills that he realized Dickie now thought he had more money and went away a happy man.

As the years went on, Jack Briggs' wife, Millie, and her sister, Janie Fleetwood-Morrow, helped look after Dickie, often bringing him food and other needed items. Their valiant attempts to steer him in a healthier direction, however, often proved to be fruitless. On one occasion Dickie managed to drag a freezer full of spoiled food home from the dump where it had been abandoned by someone who had suffered a prolonged power outage. No one wanted to think about what happened to it after that.

While some suggested that Dickie be placed in a home, most at the lake knew that such a move would spell the end for Dickie. So the community took care of him and kept him in relatively good health despite his less than ideal living conditions.

As it turned out, Dickie had built up such a strong immune system that he was seldom sick. On the rare occasion when he was forced to seek medical attention, Dickie went to see Dr. Kidd at his office in Perth. When he did, he never had to wait long. The nurse, recognizing that the less time Dickie spent with folks in a closed room the better, would immediately say, "Mr. Patterson, the doctor will see you now" and quickly usher him into another room.

On the odd occasion when he did have to go to the hospital, Dickie presented a considerable challenge to the medical personnel.

"When he did get sick and went to the hospital, they had an awful time trying to clean him up," recalled Elton Crandall Jr. "because it took two or three days to give him a bath and get him to where he was presentable."

The Herculean effort put forth by the hospital staff, however, never had a lasting effect.

"When he got home from when he was in the hospital, he'd get right back to his old tricks, same old Dick," said Crandall. "But he

Elton Crandall Jr. with his mother Maizie Marks and father Elton Crandall Sr.

was a legend at Christie Lake for many years. He was a legend, Dickie Patterson was."

The one person Dickie did visit on occasion was his old classmate Irene Strong. When Irene and her husband, Bob, moved to back to the Christie Lake Road after being away for a number of years, Dickie often stopped in on his way to or from town to have a cup of coffee.

"Now Miss Strong would, would you have a cup of coffee?" Dickie would ask.

"Yes I would," Irene would reply, knowing she'd have to call upon her strong constitution given Dickie's aversion to using a handkerchief.

Chapter 11 ♦ Christie Lake School

On one such occasion Dickie motioned to Irene to come closer. Irene was well aware that when Dickie thought he had something important to say he'd whisper it, so she leaned over and listened intently as Dickie asked her if she would take him to see Suzette Burgoyne, a nice young lady with a bright red convertible.

"I know Suzette and I like her," whispered Dickie in his "this-is-important" voice.

While Irene ensured that Dickie got a ride in the car, it was to be but a passing fancy, for Dickie would pedal his bicycle for the rest of his days. Following his death on March 6, 1997, Dickie was buried in the Anglican church cemetery in Brooke with a sketch of him on his bicycle inscribed on the headstone.

CHAPTER 14 • CHRISTIE LAKE SCHOOL

♦ Chapter Twelve ♦

CHRISTIE LAKE AFTER THE WAR

The Second World War took its toll on the Christie Lake community. On June 6, 1942, residents around the lake were saddened to learn that Ted Marks, well-known son of Ernie and Kitty Marks, had been declared missing in action and presumed dead. The popular centre fielder of the Christie Lake ball team never returned.

On the home front, the lake lost another prominent member in 1943 when David (Daley) Reid passed away at his home on Gore Street in Perth. Reid, the son of Thomas Reid and Elizabeth Hogg, had been predeceased by his son, Mortimer, who died in 1934. It had been back in 1893 that Reid and friend, George James, had established the James and Reid Hardware in Perth. During his twenty eight years with the firm Reid was in charge of office administration and prided himself on knowing every customer.

"He took a deep interest in people, and his understanding and friendliness won a wide circle of friends," it was noted at his passing (*Perth Courier* 07/29/1943).

A church warden and member of the choir at St. James Anglican Church for nearly five decades, over the years Daley Reid's voice had added a touch of beauty to many functions at the lake. He had also taken a keen interest in all community events including the annual fun day for which he often arranged the prizes.

Before the end of the war, the lake lost yet another summer resident when George Reed, a warrant officer in the Royal Canadian Electrical and Mechanical Engineers (RCEME), drowned in the lake on April 8, 1945. Reed and his two sons, nineteen-year-old Albert and six-year-old Neville, had been about two hundred feet from shore when a strong wind capsized their canoe throwing all three into the icy water. While the others clung to the canoe, young Albert swam to shore and returned in a rowboat into which he managed to pull his younger brother. His father, however, had already sunk out of sight.

Throughout the ordeal, Reed's wife, Evelyn, had been in the cottage with their two daughters, Helen and Katherine, unaware of the tragedy unfolding outside. On being alerted to what was happening, Evelyn and neighbour Morley White applied artificial respiration to young Neville, who was unconscious at the time. When Dr. Hagyard arrived, Neville was conscious, but running a temperature due to the shock and exposure. As a result, the young lad was brought to the Great War Memorial Hospital in Perth for treatment. Neville would survive the ordeal. His dad would not be so fortunate.

Born in England in 1899 George Reed had arrived in Canada with his parents in 1910. He grew up to be an electrician in Ottawa prior to entering the services of the Royal Canadian Ordnance Corps where he served as both a soldier and a civilian employer. As a member of the Canadian Army permanent force, Reed was a highly-regarded N.C.O. whose officers expressed great regret when informed of the fatality. Reed had been on a ninety-six-hour leave and had taken advantage of the time to take his family to their summer cottage on May Bell Point.

When the war in Europe was finally over, time came to remember those who had fulfilled their duty and, in particular, those who had given their lives in doing so. So it was that on a beautiful June afternoon in 1946 hundreds of residents gathered on the community grounds at Christie Lake to honour the returned veterans of Bathurst Township. The assembly was presided over by Reeve C. J. Mather, who welcomed the large audience, acknowledging in particular the ex-service men and women.

Mather then called upon Alex Armour, the longest serving councillor at the time, to unveil the Township Honour Roll upon which

Chapter 12 ♦ Christie Lake After the War

was inscribed one hundred and ten names. After the unveiling, the names of the veterans were called, and the reeve and council presented each with a certificate of honour and a fountain pen. A moment of silence was observed in memory of those from the township who had not returned including Ted Marks, Squadron Leader Lloyd H. Cameron, Corporal Harold B. Clyne, Pilot Officer William J. Kyle and Flying Officer George A. White.

Dr. W. G. Blair, M.P., a native son of the township and a veteran of World War One, recalled how a similar presentation had taken place in the township twenty-seven years earlier. Dr. Blair warned the veterans that their fight was not over yet. He advised them to take part in their country's affairs.

"You must help combat hatred and greed and intolerance which might lead to another war, which, with the atom bomb, could mean the end of Christianity if not of the world" warned Dr. Blair (*Perth Courier* 06/20/1946).

On June 4, 1947, the area lost another of its servicemen when twenty-one-year-old Fred McParlan of Perth drowned after falling from a boat on Christie Lake. McParlan, who had been with George Findlay of Perth at the time, had been in the stern of the boat operating the outboard engine when a sudden lurch caused him to be hit by the handle of the motor and thrown overboard. Although Findlay

A sugar shack at Christie Lake as sketched by Franc van Oort.
(Courtesy: Franc van Oort)

dove from the boat, he could not recover his friend. McParlan, who had become bridge master of the Tay Canal following the death of his father, had served in the Royal Canadian Air Force overseas during the war.

*George James watches on as Reg Sproule boils sap at the lake.
(Courtesy: George James)*

Chapter 12 ♦ Christie Lake After the War

> **SPRINGTIME AT THE LAKE**
>
> Things are bustin' out all over. The cats are having kittens, new chicks are arriving, and Morley White's cow, Ida, had twin calves last week—Jack and Jill. Morley has been ill with a cold for quite some time, and was taken to Perth Hospital on Tuesday morning, full of pneumonia bugs. He was shipped home on Saturday, full of pep and rarin' to go (*Perth Courier* 05/22/1947).

As it always had, each spring continued to usher in a new season at the lake. The warmer weather meant the sap began to run and folks around the lake again set themselves to "a-gatherin' and a-boilin," including Joe Patterson who was said to tap over 600 trees. Meanwhile, come Easter, the womenfolk at the lake staged their unofficial fashion show.

"Fifth Avenue had nothing on Christie Lake on Easter Sunday morning when all the ladies were out on parade in their Easter bonnets," noted one lake resident (*Perth Courier* 04/01/1948).

With the rise in temperature came the inevitable threat of fire. In the summer of 1947 a crew of lads, including Willis Conklin, Webb Krauser, Grant Garrette and Morley White, were forced to carry the buckets and man the stirrup pumps to put out a blaze on Chapman's Island. Unfortunately, two days later the fire was going again, a fact that didn't sit well with the lake's local reporter, who wanted folks around the lake to be a little more careful with their cigarettes and campfires. "It is some consolation to know that these fires are contained to islands; but all of us wish that the people who start them so lightheartedly would be as joyous about seeing that they were out" (*Perth Courier* 08/14/1947).

The following spring when a brush fire started just below Patterson's cattle crossing on the Bush Road, it was hard to find anyone to put it out. Except for Dick Newson and Jack Marks, it was said every man in the district had gone to Perth or was attending a sawing at Crawford's or was laying ties at Feldspar. So it was that Jean and Jack Marks, Dick Newson and Dot Marks rushed to the scene where after a hectic ninety minutes of pounding and whacking with shovels and cedar boughs brought the pesky fire under control.

Arden Blackburn's Mail Route

In the summer of 1948 the threat of fire at the lake was dramatically heightened by a serious lack of rain. That year when one blaze spurted up the back of a nearby cottage, Bob Marks, who was said to be "lollygagging" in his front yard at the time, was the first to spot it and sound the tocsin. Following which, motorboats full of "husky rangers" arrived on the scene and assisted the local residents in squelching it before it did any damage beyond burning a wide stretch of ground. The cause of the blaze, although undetermined, became somewhat apparent when it was discovered that a certain father, who was missing his cigarettes, had a son who had turned an interesting shade of green.

While the arrival of fall lessened the danger posed by fires, it brought a different hazard to the lake, this time in the form of overzealous hunters who seemed to be everywhere.

> *At first we thought that possibly this world was in for another war, but soon discovered it was Stuart Chapman of Ottawa, who is here to bag a deer, giving his slick new telescopic sight a workout. We decided to go for a walk to lap up the peace and quiet and pin-ng!! right past our good ear. Luckily we are a whiz at ducking* (Perth Courier 11/13/47).

Arden Blackburn with friends J. Millar and M. Crain. (Courtesy: Ken Blackburn)

Chapter 12 ♦ Christie Lake After the War

While talk around Noonans' was often full of wild claims about wolf tracks, howls and near misses, none was more spectacular than that of Charlie Peters.

Peters reported that while going for his cows one evening, his dogs suddenly shot ahead of him barking furiously and then disappeared from sight. Quite a flurry ensued and by the time Charlie arrived on the scene, it was said that "one of his cows was minus her tail" (*Perth Courier* 10/16/1947). Charlie was another in the long list of well-known lake handymen who did a lot of work around the lake, including the dock at the Appleby cottage. In 1940 Charlie had bought Sunrise and Sunset, the former cottage of R. W. Marks, which he then sold in 1946 to Ernie Rogers.

Unattended fires, errant bullets and cow tales weren't the only sources of excitement at the lake in the late forties. When a silver seaplane, belonging to the Canadian Pacific Airways, landed on the lake one Sunday afternoon in 1947, it created quite a scene as a crowd gathered on the station dock to get a closer look. Motorboats roared in from every corner to catch the excitement.

"Presently the plane took off, circled for thirty minutes and came in again. A prettier piece of landing and leaving we never did see" noted one witness (*Perth Courier* 06/26/1947).

That summer even Arden got in on the excitement when he received some rather unexpected attention from his superiors at the postal headquarters in Ottawa. Arden's good fortune came about when S.C. McEvenue, president of the Canada Life Assurance Co., was making his way by car from Toronto to Ottawa and discovered he had lost his wallet containing over $200 in cash and valuable papers.

Early the next morning McEvenue was informed by the OPP that the wallet had been found by a Mr. Blackburn who, having no thought of holding it for a reward, had immediately turned it in at the police station in the hope it could be returned to its rightful owner as soon as possible. McEvenue was so appreciative of Arden's action that he drew his honesty to the attention of the postmaster general, who sent Arden a note. (See next page.)

Arden Blackburn's Mail Route

Ottawa,
August 12th, 1947

Mr. Arden Blackburn,
Courier,
R.R. N0.4,
Perth, Ontario

Dear Sir:

Mr. S.C. McEvenue, President of the Canada Life Assurance Company, Toronto, has brought to my knowledge the fact that you found on your route his wallet containing $200.00 which you handed to the Provincial Police for return to its owner.

Although I am convinced that the majority of the postal employees are honest it is most gratifying to receive such a report and I wish to congratulate you on your very creditable act.

Yours sincerely,
Ernest Bertrand

Ernest Bertrand

Postmaster General

Chapter 12 ◆ Christie Lake After the War

It wasn't all good news at the lake. After the war, the community received the rather unwelcome news that the Bell Telephone Co. was not taking over any more rural telephone companies for at least two or three years because of a shortage of equipment and materials. This meant that if the Perth and Christie Lake Telephone company was to expand its coverage, it would have to do so on its own.

When the decision was made to proceed with expansion, it was announced that a charter was going to be drawn up to form a new company. A thousand shares of stock in the new company were to be issued with each shareholder of the former Perth and Christie Lake Telephone company to be issued five shares in the new company after they had signed over all rights of ownership to their present telephone.

Over fifty shareholders attended the inaugural meeting of the newly-formed Perth and Christie Lake Telephone Association on Feb. 7, 1948. Considerable discussion took place as to the pending allotment of shares. Eventually under the direction of T. A. Rogers, owner of the first telephone in the area, the list was completed and the shareholders elected a board of directors with J.W. Newson holding the position of president and John P. Cameron elected vice-president.

A view of the lake from the rail line.

Come spring, lake residents received news that a second train was to be added to complement the service of the original Christie Lake Flyer.

> *For lo these many years, one tired little train has been doing the entire job of hauling freight, express and passengers into and out of our station, wary unto death to the very core of its overworked engine. But one day last week, civilization hit Christie Lake with the coming of a sister—or is it brother?—train to take its share of out transportation. Now we are on the map—two trains a day, by golly!—and we can whoop into Perth whenever we wish* (Perth Courier 05/13/1948).

Along with the arrival of a second train, the summer of '48 also saw the arrival of smaller and faster boats to the area. Mitt Cameron was the first to own a Sea Flea on Christie Lake and loved to run it with the engine wide open. One day he decided to test the common understanding around the lake that you didn't go between Alan's and Greer's Islands.

"One day Mitt got into the sauce and, with his boat all tuned up, roared through there with it wide open, ripping the bottom off the poor old 'Sea Flea," chuckled Gray Palmer.

It was a no less a worse fate that befell Bob Peters who, running his Sea Flea full speed towards shore, was caught by a wave and thrown into the side of Vic Lemieux's boathouse. With his Sea Flea still lodged in the wall of the building, it was said Peters immediately disengaged the motor from the boat and threw it over his shoulder, hoping to be long gone with it before Lemieux discovered the damage.

The appearance of smaller, faster boats on Christie Lake brought with them the advent of outboard motor racing. It started in 1948 when Eldon Crandall Jr. of Auburn, New York, arrived at the lake with a twelve foot Thompson driven by a ten horse Mercury. One day as Elton sped across the lake, three boats from the foot of the lake shot forth to challenge him, but Elton was said to have skipped away from them—the undisputed victor. The challenge was on.

A week later, Ronnie Romeiser arrived at the lake with a twelve foot mahogany run-about he had built during the winter in Ottawa. Powered by a sixteen horse Johnson, the craft was said to be "held

Chapter 12 ♦ Christie Lake After the War

together by Scotch tape, bobby pins and faith" (*Perth Courier* 08/19/1948). Despite its haphazard appearance, when launched, Romeiser's boat not only didn't leak, it actually attained a speed of 3.5 m.p.h. provided, it was said, there wasn't a headwind.

Not satisfied with such a meagre speed, Romeiser removed the plate from the engine's muffler, a move that increased the boat's speed only marginally but increased the noise to a level that it gave many lake residents a lasting headache. No sooner were folks plotting to dump Ronnie's motor into the lake than "like the speed of a thousand bombers with faulty engines roared in Brian Noonan" (*Perth Courier* 08/19/1948).

Following Romeiser's lead, Noonan had removed his muffler plate as well. This was all too much for Jack Newson who proceeded on several occasions to phone the local OPP, who arrived at the lake to talk to both Ronnie and Brian. In an attempt to bring peace to the lake, Elton Crandall declared his boat was now "strictly a pleasure craft." His racing days were over

Crandall's surrender came just as Ronnie Romeiser arrived at the lake with a new racing boat said to have been built back home on his dining room table. Powered by a sixteen horse Johnson, Romeiser's new craft was capable of reaching speeds of fifty miles per hour. It was said that Romeiser travelled so fast across the lake that it took "two men to see him, but only one to hear him" (*Perth Courier* 08/03/1950).

While life at Christie Lake in the days after the Second World War had a certain devil-may-care attitude, it also shared the rest of the country's uneasiness with the "Cold War" being waged between the United States and the Soviet Union. With each super power seeking the ultimate weapon of mass destruction, the world had been plunged into an "arms race" that brought with it everything from bombing drills to fall-out shelters.

In North America the rush to develop nuclear weapons to defend democracy against Communism had transformed uranium from a simple disposable by-product to a highly desirable detonator. Now known as the "Cinderella" mineral, by 1949 a ton of good uranium ore was worth $1,500, forty-five times the value of gold!

Countries in the hunt for uranium did everything in their power to locate large deposits. The United States offered a bonus of $40,000 for the first twenty tons of reasonably rich uranium ore from any single strike. Across Canada prospectors, armed with the government-issued *Prospector's Guide for Uranium and Thorium Minerals in Canada*, combed the countryside with picks, shovels and Geiger counters. So intense was the search for the radioactive metal that when news surfaced of a strike at Christie Lake, it sent a veritable flood of curious visitors and inquisitive reporters scurrying to the doorstep of Joe and Bertha Patterson.

While the Patterson strike would become the area's best known mineral discovery, mining, itself, was not a new pursuit around the lake. It had been active there since the mid-1800s when Perthites William Morris and Dr. James Wilson operated the Christie Lake Iron Mine on the north shore of the lake. The area's first mining "magnate," Dr. Wilson, was a combination of medical humanitarian and industrial visionary.

Fresh from medical school in Edinburgh, Wilson had emigrated from Scotland to Ontario in 1818 at the age of twenty, first settling in the village of Lanark, before moving to Perth and setting up a rural medical practice in 1822. As time went on, Wilson began to take a strong interest in the various rock outcrops that he encountered as he made his rounds through the countryside in his horse and buggy.

FOR SALE: James Wilson's undivided half of lots eighteen, nineteen, and twenty in the third concession of the Township of South Sherbrooke.
The above lots contain a very rich iron mine.
Perth, 4th September 1863

In part because of the ongoing efforts of Dr. Wilson and his contact with Sir William Logan, the founder and first director of the Geological Survey of Canada, the presence of minerals in the area began to attract the attention of foreign investors.

> *The mineral wealth of this section of country is getting more and more developed every day. The inexhaustible supplies of the most valuable minerals in our very midst are beginning to attract the attention of British and American capitalists and their operations*

Chapter 12 ♦ Christie Lake After the War

are to be seen everywhere. An American company is now engaged in taking out a quantity (fifty tons) of magnetic iron ore from the deposits in South Sherbrooke, near Christy's Lake, and shipping it to Cleveland, there to be treated by practical mineralogists. If the report is favourable we may soon expect to hear more about it (Perth Courier 10/07/1864).

When a mineral strike did occur, it invariably sent the "penny" stocks of mining companies soaring, usually only to have them eventually tumble leaving many a latecomer with a hefty loss. It was a fate that often led to disappointment and frustration for those involved, including those at Christie Lake.

At various times we have heard of the formation of companies whose object was to work the deposits of iron, mica, phosphate and other valuable minerals that were known to exist in the vicinity of Perth. Some of these companies have made a pretence of opening up and

Charlie Peters and Will Truelove stand at a limestone kiln built on the fifth line and used to cook limestone and pound it into powder before mixing it with water and sand to make cement. (Courtesy: Les Peters)

working some of the mines, but the most of them have merely acquired mining leases from the owners of the lands, and then held these lands for speculative purposes, and at such high rates as to prevent those who really wished to go to work from doing so (Perth Courier 10/07/1864).

The exception to the "boom and bust" rule appeared to be the mining operations of Thomas Aspden, who had established the Christie Lake Bark Factory. Having ample capital and unlimited credit, Aspden was said to be quite successful "in working the mica and phosphate deposits of the Township of Burgess, and for the past two years, has moved large quantities of these minerals, giving employment to large numbers of men and horses" (*Perth Courier* 02/28/1868).

The untimely departure of Thomas Aspden and his family for London, Ontario, in 1872 meant that mining operations around the lake slowed down and wouldn't recover until the railway arrived and provided an economical means of shipping the minerals across the country. When that happened the busiest site in the area was the O'Holloran feldspar deposit on the farm of Michael O'Holloran, Lot 1, Concession 2, Bathurst, a short distance from Christie Lake. The feldspar mined on the site was shipped by box car to Montreal where it was used as a filler in paints and as a glazing in ceramics. The O'Holloran site, which contained a contractor's hoist and vertical boiler as well as a horse wheel and a derrick, was said to keep eighteen men employed under the direction of Albert McGonegal the foreman.

Despite the success of the O'Holloran operation, over the years mining in the Christie Lake area remained a relatively low-key affair and stayed that way until the uranium strike on the Patterson farm. With the price of uranium soaring daily, when news of the strike at Christie Lake hit the headlines in September 1956, it brought a deluge of strangers and reporters to the Patterson farm, a quarter of a mile west of the Christie Lake train station.

A tall, friendly man Joe Patterson had lived his entire life on the farm his family had established in 1871. Throughout the years he had worked hard and by the time of the strike Joe was ready for a rest. At the time of the mineral discovery only twenty-five acres of the three hundred and eighty acre farm was actually under cultivation. The

Chapter 12 ◆ Christie Lake After the War

Mining sand in Jordan's Bay. The sand was lifted by bucket and passed through a screen into a wagon and then shipped by train to a foundry in Montreal to be made into castings for plow points etc. (Courtesy: Doris Kirkham)

rest, stretching from Christie Lake westward to Little Silver Lake, was bush that was accessible only by narrow gravel roads running south from Brooke.

While it was said that Joe wasn't inclined to get too excited about the discovery of the brannerite ore (uranium oxide) around his home, he did admit that it could be "a godsend." Fifty-six years of age and partly disabled, Joe said he'd be more than willing to retire to a corner of the farm, if the price was "fair" for the rest of it.

The strike on the Patterson farm was made by Bob Sybal and John Gregor, who, when they had no luck fishing one day at the lake, decided to turn their attention to prospecting. They crisscrossed acre after acre of rough slope around Christie Lake until their Geiger counter went wild on the Patterson farm.

On their next visit to the farm, Sybal and Gregor were accompanied by a third gentleman, Mike Polak, along with maps of all the lots in the area. The men asked Joe to assist them in staking out the area. Although Patterson was somewhat amused by the antics of the men in the bush, particularly when they had come face to face with a black bear, Patterson found them to be "amicable and trustworthy and considered them as good friends."[53] While there were some at the lake who didn't take a shine to the strangers, in the end, Joe offered to help them and said he hoped the uranium strike would be beneficial not only for himself, but for his neighbours as well.

"Even if I don't get a nickel, it would be a great stir for Perth and Smiths Falls," remarked Joe at the time.[54]

Following the initial discovery on the Patterson property, several more square miles of land was marked around the lake as more and more prospectors moved into the area. Soon the area being staked included not only the Patterson property, but land owned by Charlie Peters, Dick Newson, Gerald White and Lloyd Fournier as well. It was said the claims even reached into the bottom of Christie Lake itself and also took in the railway station and other Canadian Pacific Railway property.

When a geologist's report on the ore discovered at the Patterson farm indicated that the mining of uranium in the staked area seemed "possible, profitable and practical," Gregor, Sypal and Polak immediately closed the Patterson property to the public, a move

Chapter 12 ♦ Christie Lake After the War

that not only served to increase the level of curiosity of those around the lake, but also the animosity.

CHRISTIE LAKE MINES LTD.

To diamond drill the uranium show south east of Perth, Ontario. The property consists 1600 acres and the show is identified as Brannerite which is essentially an oxide of Uranium and Titanium.

Recent offerings of 200,000 shares of stock at 25 cents per share were oversubscribed. We offer now, acting as agents for the Company, a limited number of shares at a price of 35 cents per share.

Christie Lake Mines is a speculative issue.
Complete information supplied on request.

C.R. Jenner and Co. Ltd.
357 Bay Street,
Toronto, Ont. Mar. 22, 1957

By May 1957 Christie Lake Mines Ltd., with Bob Sypal as its president, had begun drilling on the company's holdings at Christie Lake. No sooner had the work commenced, however, when a disturbance was reported in the area known as Sleepy Hollow, adjacent to the Christie Lake Camp, on the south shore of the lake. Residents there claimed to know nothing about any staking activities and were said to be running prospectors off their land with a shotgun. When the OPP tried to get the bottom of the rumours, however, they ran into a stone wall.

"If residents on the south shore of Christie Lake know anything more than they told provincial police who investigated a reported shooting there over the weekend, they are certainly not telling," reported the *Ottawa Citizen*.[55]

When OPP constable Stuart Pearce questioned farmers in the Sleepy Hollow area about the shooting reports, few admitted to knowing anything about them.

It was true that many residents were surprised and angry when told they didn't own the mineral rights to their own property. One farmer, who owned several hundred acres of land between the Scout

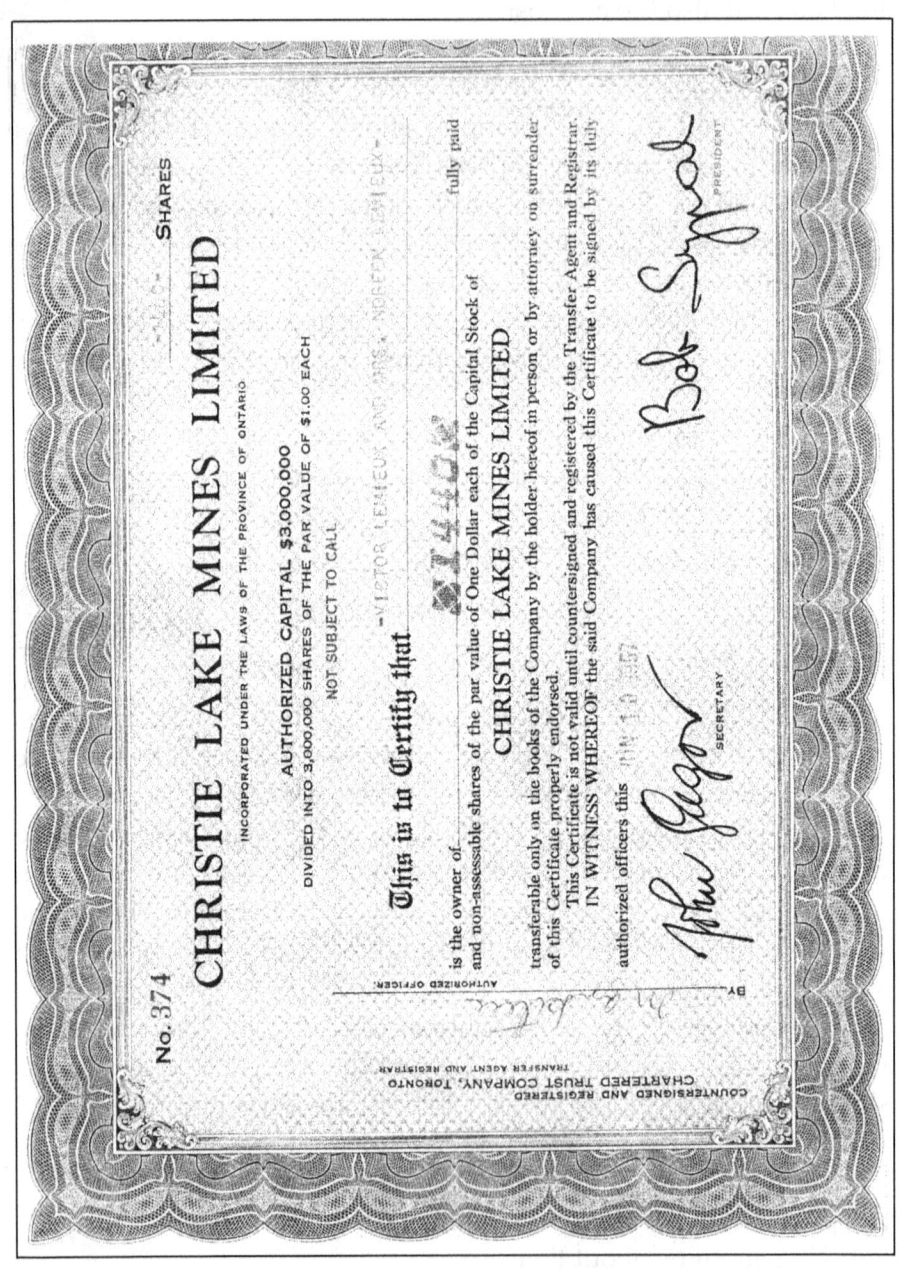

A stock certificate belonging to Vic and Noreen Lemieux. Like many the Lemieuxs were to be disappointed by its failure to amount to anything.

Chapter 12 ♦ Christie Lake After the War

Camp and the Christie Lake Camp, said he had known nothing about the claim staking until he noticed fresh blaze marks on one of the trees in his sugar bush and followed the cuts until he came to the swamp. He said he later identified the markings as the procedure used by prospectors in marking the boundaries of a mining claim.

The word around the lake concerning the gunshot blasts was that some men from the mines had gotten into a heated discussion with one of the farmers, who then ordered the miners off his land. As they left it was said they heard two shots, fired from a shotgun and coming from the direction of the irate farmer. The miners could not positively state whether the farmer had fired into the air over them or if the shots came from somewhere nearby. They said they had taken no chances and cleared out.

When the reports of the mysterious shotgun blasts reached the national news, some around the lake thought things were getting blown out of proportion.

"I think they are making a big story out of nothing," remarked Lloyd Fournier's wife, whose family owned considerable property in the area. "I did hear shotgun blasts during the break-up in the early spring, but did not know exactly where they came from. I think the people responsible were shooting ground-hogs" (*Perth Courier* 05/09/1957).

While the farmers in the area denied taking part in any "shotgun settlement," several did report seeing a strange black car in the area. Frank Tysick said he saw the car parked in his laneway early one Saturday morning and a man carrying an axe coming across his fields from the north of the road. He did not bother to question the man, who was in the company of a woman, and, according to Tysick, the couple got in the car and went up the road.

Meanwhile Wilbur Murphy, a farm neighbor to the west of Tysick, said the same car and its occupants had stopped at his well for a drink later that morning, but he didn't talk to the man either. Ronnie Fournier, who was working on his father's farm at the time, said he saw the mysterious black car speeding off towards Perth at what was said to be "an alarming rate."

A short while later a couple of prospectors were reported to have arrived in Perth at the dry goods store of Norman Levine. They had with them mineral samples they said they had found just outside

Perth. Their Geiger counter had been acting up, however, and upon hearing that Lavine was an amateur prospector who owned such a device, they had come to see if he would check the radioactivity of their samples for them. When Levine confirmed that their sample was definitely radioactive, he said the men told him they were off to Toronto to register their claims.

When it was later discovered that unidentified prospectors had blasted a shallow excavation and removed a "considerable quantity of samples" from one of the claims previously staked by the Christie Lake Mines, claim jumping was suspected and believed to be the work of the same pair who had sought the aid of Lavine's Geiger counter. Upon further investigation, it was determined that sixteen mining claims belonging to the Christie Lake Mines had been restaked by a gentleman by the name of Kenneth Whyte, accompanied by a friend from Perth.

When Whyte filed a complaint against the mining company, a hearing was conducted in Toronto by the Commissioner for Mines J. F. McFarland. When he was called upon Whyte testified that he "could find no indication of writing on any of the original claim posts."

Asked by the commissioner if he had seen any work going on at the time of the restaking, Whyte replied that he had not, this despite the fact that a drilling crew was at work on one of the highest points on the lake, clearly visible from at least a mile away. Whyte told the court he had observed each post in question very thoroughly prior to re-staking and that on none of the posts in question was there any indication of writing. He did admit that the official metal tags issued by the Department of Mines were in place.

When confronted with several photographs made the week before the hearing which clearly showed considerable evidence of inscriptions still on the posts, Whyte conceded that the pair must have missed these. He later admitted to the fact that there may have been writing on the posts, but not enough to be able to tell what it said. When shown one of the posts Whyte was able to identify both letters and figures. In this case, and in all cases, Whyte's new posts could be seen in the photographs propped up behind those of the mining company.

Two hours after the hearing had convened, Whyte's lawyer, J. Arnold Shapiro, requested a meeting between the commissioner and

Chapter 12 ◆ Christie Lake After the War

the counsel for the mining company. When the trio returned to the courtroom a half hour later, Shapiro threw in the towel, and Commissioner McFarland noted that the dispute lodged by Whyte had not been done so on solid grounds whatsoever.

"Therefore the case is dismissed," declared McFarland (*Perth Courier* 07/11/1957).

So ended one of Christie Lake's most-publicized misadventures, following which life at the lake returned to normal, or as normal as life in the fifties and sixties anywhere could be.

During the years following the Second World War Canada's population had grown more quickly than at any other time in its history. Returning soldiers and their brides had come home looking to raise a family. Over four million babies were born in Canada during the fifties, and for the first time "teenagers" became a driving force in Canadian culture, a fact evident even at Christie Lake.

No one had to tell Vic and Noreen Lemieux there were more young people on the lake than ever before. With a teenage daughter

Noreen and Vic Lemieux in front of their lodge on Christie Lake.
(Courtesy: Penny Nault)

of their own, they saw firsthand the number who hung around the marina, often looking for something to do. Vic thought a little water skiing in the summer and a little downhill skiing in the winter might be just the ticket, both for them and for his business.

Opened in the summer of 1952, Norvic Lodge and Marina sat on a piece of property formerly owned by Colonel James W. Spalding an inspector with the Royal Canadian Mounted Police, the same J.W. Spalding who had once shot Tom Marks in the foot. Spalding's grandfather had held a commission in the British army and was given the land at the lake as a recompense for his services. When Colonel Spalding retired from the RCMP in 1938 he returned to live at Christie until 1944.

Next door to Colonel Spalding was the Vergette family. Barbara Vergette (Hutton) had first come to Christie Lake as a twelve-year-old in 1933 in the rumble seat of Phil and Lois Wheeler's Model A Ford, a seat she shared with the Wheeler's son and family dog. Initially Barbara and her mom (Vera) stayed at the Wheelers' cottage until such time as Barbara's mother, separated from her husband since Barbara was six, could purchase some property and build a cottage of her own.

The cottage Barbara's mom built was to be one of the first, if not the first, pre-fab cottages on the lake. The kit bought at Davis Lumber in Ottawa was brought by train to the Christie Lake station and then hauled to the cottage site on George Noonan's barge. Barbara's mother hired an elderly French-Canadian carpenter to assemble the cottage and erected a tent for the men to sleep in and provided them with meals as they worked.

Eventually Barbara's mother built a road into her cottage using the services of men in the area looking for work during the war. At the time, Colonel Spalding was more than a little upset because he had built the bridge into the area and thought that Barbara's mother should help pay for it since she now drove over it as well.

Following the war, Barbara's mother brought electricity onto the site by cashing in her war bonds. Once that happened, Barbara recalled, they were able to install a refrigerator. Prior to that it had been necessary for her and her mother to go by boat to Morley White's to get ice, although when they did they took the opportunity

Chapter 12 ◆ Christie Lake After the War

Welcome TO A JOYOUS VACATION

You will have a REAL vacation here with us. You will come to us over picturesque highways . . . and park your car near your cottage accommodations, or in our shaded parking lot. You may, or may not, use it again until you leave us, for here at Norvic Lodge you will find many things to do . . . and you will have many pleasant hours.

Your accommodations will be in private cottages, each with complete modern bath service . . . the very best of beds . . . plenty of blankets for those cool evenings... all the towels you need -- and complete, daily maid service to keep everything in order.

You will be served those good, old-fashioned country meals . . . with many of the foods fresh from nearby farms . . . and everything prepared by folks who love to cook . . . and prepare foods in many different ways.

. . . and we are on duty at all times to look after each and every detail . . . to give you all those little personal services that go to make a vacation so delightful.

  Noreen and Vic Lemieux

to fish for pickerel, which often resulted in the provision of a tasty meal. Life at the lake was an enjoyable time for the Vergettes, even if it meant the occasional run-in with her neighbor Vic Lemieux.

While the Lemieuxs offered a special Sunday brunch in the dining room at the lodge with a dinner bell to summon the fishermen from the lake, they also ran a snack bar in the boathouse in the hopes of attracting the increasing number of young people who frequented the lake.

In 1960, in an effort to turn Norvic Lodge into a year-round operation, Lemieux opened a ski hill onsite which was to become home to the Tay Valley Ski Club. With busloads of young people arriving from Perth, the ski tow and snack shop were run by Neil Stewart who had bought Arliedale Inn from the Newsons in 1957.

> **TAY VALLEY SKI CLUB**
>
> The Tay Valley Ski Club, located at Norvic Lodge on Christie Lake, twelve miles west of Perth, is about to enter its second season.
>
> Results of the first year were so gratifying that the Club has carried out an extensive program of development during the off-season in the bulldozing, blasting clearing and grading of an entirely new hill which will be available for skiing as soon as there is snow.
>
> In order to service this new hill a rope tow is now being installed and will be in operation on the weekend throughout the season. The Club intends to expand its junior ski development program with free instruction and in addition it is intended to provide free transportation to and from the Club on weekends for those children who are in need of a lift (*Perth Courier* 11/09/1961).

In the summer months Lemieux introduced skin diving at the lodge and sponsored water skiing shows which took place on Wednesday and Sunday afternoons. As many as seventy spectators gathered on the shore to watch the young "Christie Lake Surfers" put on their water skiing exhibition which included events such as slalom, clown, turnaround, mixed doubles, pyramid, ballet, shoe skis and flag parade stunts.

Chapter 12 ♦ Christie Lake After the War

Pulled by a seventy-five horsepower Johnson, driven by "Pudge" Rogers, the six skiers—Peter Cotton, Brooke Briggs, Jill Wooding, Dave Blair, Diane Wilson and Judy Lemieux—performed to such musical hits as "Ghost Riders," "Canadian Sunset" and "Goodnight Irene," all of which was piped over a loudspeaker system. An announcer, often Alan Gilhuley, filled the gap between routines.

While Brooke Briggs performed as the resident clown among the group, others took turns entertaining the crowds by skiing on every manner of object including an outhouse door. At other times the male skiers formed a pyramid that held Diane Wilson aloft. Before long their performances began to attract considerable attention.

"In chatting with several sportsmen from Ottawa, they were high in their praise of the efforts being put forward by these youngsters. So their reputation is gaining far and wide," noted one newspaper columnist (*Perth Courier* 08/01/1963).

Throughout the sixties the quick-talking Lemieux worked tirelessly to attract new business to the lake. In the spring of 1964 he decided the "personal touch" was what was needed to pay dividends in tourist dollars, so, as President of the Rideau Lakes–Thousand Islands Tourist Council, he announced that he and Norman Freeman from Battersea were going on a thirty-day selling spree. Armed with 10,000 pieces of literature tucked in their luggage, the pair planned to attend sportsmen shows throughout the northern states including Philadelphia, Baltimore, and Rochester.

"We're not just sending literature on tourist attractions in this area," commented Lemieux at the time. "We are going to personally back up our claims. There are 32 tourist regions in Ontario. We aim to prove we are one of the more active areas. It's the personal touch that makes a difference. Just wait and see" (*Perth Courier,* 02/20/1964).

To further emphasize his point Lemieux announced that they would also be taking a prize-winning pickerel and a smallmouth bass that had been caught in Christie Lake. Both fish had been mounted and were to be used to whet the appetite of the American fishermen.

Despite his best efforts to attract tourists to the area, the financial strain of running the lodge took its toll on Vic and he became bitter and at times downright ornery. Some said he was made miserable by the fact that he had lost considerable money in the Christie Lake

THIS IS A PLACE FOR *Family* VACATIONS

While FISHING is always one of the chief sports on a vacation... and many of our guests do a lot of fishing... this is more than a fishing camp...

We have shuffleboard, darts, table tennis, volley ball, badminton, cards, a fine children's playground — and a lot of spontaneous entertainment generated by our guests.

There are outdoor picnics... shore dinners... movie and slide shows, put on by guests who have been here before. There are trips to the interesting town of Perth, with all its historic old buildings and its many interesting stores. There are scenic trips out into this beautiful lake country.

MANY WATER SPORTS

SWIMMING... from a fine anchored swim dock, with diving boards... or from our main dock; water skiing... surf boarding... outboard trips... or just rowing along the shore. There are many beautiful places along our shore line for picnicing or picnics.

There are swings and other equipment in our play yard for children.

Yes, we have replacement tackle, live bait, outboard fuel... gas service at our dock for all boats — and we have winter storage for boats and motors.

There is a fine tuck shop at the dock where you can get gifts... refreshments... just about all the things you might need in a hurry on a vacation.

You will fish for walleyes... smallmouth bass... northern pike... whitefish and largemouth bass — and you will get all you want to eat... some to take home, if you wish, and you may get a lunker, for many big fish are taken in these waters. You will have many hours of pleasant fishing.

FROM THE TIME YOU ARRIVE...

... you get our personal service. Most of our guests come back year after year, because they are well-looked-after here. They know that they will have comfort in our cottages (some of which are shown below). They know that they will have good fishing. They know that we cater only to those fine folks who fit into a happy vacation picture.

Norvic is a beautiful spot. It is away from the rush of traffic. It has a beauty of flowers... trees and lawns — and from every cottage there is the view of the sparkling waters of the lake.

Come to us and sample what we have to offer. Make a reservation ahead of your arrival — or drop in when you are in the neighborhood. Have a meal with us... stay overnight (we'll bet you'll stay longer)

... just come and see what a fine vacation place Norvic really is.

CHAPTER 12 ♦ CHRISTIE LAKE AFTER THE WAR

mining fiasco; others maintained that he was simply driving himself too hard. On one occasion he closed down the road to the marina making life difficult for his neighbours.

"He was working so hard, he wasn't enjoying himself much," recalled Barbara Vergette's mom. "He was disillusioned. He got a little testy."

Like others at the lake the Vergettes had come to rely on Arden Blackburn to keep their cupboards at the cottage stocked. Each day Barbara or her mother met Arden at the entrance of the road to the marina and paid him ten cents for each pick-up he had made on their behalf.

On many occasions Arden was accompanied by his sons, Lindsay and Ken, who enjoyed the journey if only for the chocolate milk at Chaplin's Dairy in Glen Tay and curd at the cheese factory in Dewitt's Corners. The bag of curd was so big, according to Ken, that "it was all a young lad could do to carry it."

Both Lindsay and Ken attended Perth and District Collegiate Institute before going to work at the shoe factory in Perth. In the winter of 1954, however, Ken Blackburn contracted encephalitis and spent sixty-one days in the hospital, at times unconscious with a fever

The front view of Norvic Lodge ca. 1964. (Courtesy: Penny Nault)

Arden Blackburn's Mail Route

Arden and Sophia Blackburn on the mail route with their son Lindsay in 1938. (Courtesy: Ken Blackburn)

of 107 degrees. He received several blood transfusions, most with blood donated by the employees at the shoe factory, before eventually being sent home much to the relief of Arden and Sophia.

Like most boys growing up in the fifties, Ken and Lindsay Blackburn relished the freedom brought by the automobile and seldom missed an opportunity to join their friends on the road. It was shortly after Ken was released from the hospital that he and his brother, Lindsay, were passengers in a half-ton truck driven by their buddy Allan Blair. The three boys were headed home from Smiths Falls when, as they crested a hill just east of Perth, they encountered a car backing out of a driveway onto the highway. Having little time to react Allan Blair swerved to avoid the car. In so doing the truck with the boys skidded on the muddy shoulder of the highway and struck a telephone pole. While Ken was thrown clear of the truck and escaped with only cuts and bruises, Lindsay Blackburn and Allan Blair were taken to the hospital with life-threatening injuries.

"Everything happened so fast," recounted Ken at the time. "I saw the car, and then I came to on the side of the road...I didn't remember

Chapter 12 ♦ Christie Lake After the War

a thing until I came to and found myself lying in the mud on the side of the road" (*Perth Courier* 04/08/1954).

Because the vehicle carrying the boys struck the telephone pole on the driver's side, the impact pinned both Lindsay and Allan against the seat. A tow truck and a chain had to be used to pry them loose before they were taken to hospital in Perth with severe head and body injuries.

Four days later, April 10, 1954, the Blackburns received the news that is the nightmare of every parent. Their nineteen-year-old son, Lindsay, had passed away. Arden and Sophia were devastated.

Among the remembrances they received was a letter from the Honourable George Doucett, Minister of Highways, and a floral arrangement from the residents who lived on Rural Route No. 4. Just as he had reached out to them over the years, now they would reciprocate.

In the days and weeks ahead, at every stop along the way, Arden received the compassion and comfort of those who lived on his route. It was a show of support that was richly deserved, for over the years the residents of Rural Route No. 4 had found in their mailman a kindness and generosity of spirit that they held dear as a reflection of what their community was all about.

"If a contest for the area's top hero is ever held," maintained Bill Sproule, "my nominee would be Arden Blackburn. This unsung Samaritan delivered our mail, summer and winter. But that was just the start."

Arden Blackburn's Mail Route

ONTARIO
OFFICE OF
MINISTER OF HIGHWAYS

TORONTO,
MAY 20,
1 9 5 4.

Dear Mr. and Mrs. Blackburn,

    I know how stunned and distressed you must be by your son's tragic death and my heart grieves for you in your great sorrow.

    It will be hard to reconcile yourselves to this stroke of Fate -- time alone can heal this wound. But this is the inevitable sorrow we all have to face sooner or later in life; it is how we face-up to these experiences which gives it a fuller meaning.

    He would not want you to sit and mourn - to grieve and grow hard and embittered. He has gone out of your life and you must keep faith. Death, I think, only strengthens the faith between those who have it.

    I just wish you to know how deeply sorry I am and to extend my heart-felt sympathy.

Yours very sincerely,

Chapter 12 ◆ Christie Lake After the War

Arden Blackburn standing in front of the old Dodge panel van used during his later years of delivering mail to Christie Lake. (Courtesy: Ken Blackburn)

Epilogue

On August 23, 1967, Assistant Postmaster Ken Cowie presented Arden Blackburn with an envelope containing a cheque and a letter.

> *Dear Arden,*
>
> *We wish you to accept the enclosed as a token of our gratitude for the many years of service you have given us.*
>
> *Your handling of the mail and all those extra bits of shopping and carrying you have done for us have been greatly appreciated and we want you to know it now.*
>
> *We hope you will continue to serve us for many years to come.*
>
> *Sincerely,*
> *Your friends on RR4 Perth, Ontario*

From its earliest days, the community at Christie Lake had demonstrated a great willingness to reach out to one another and a deep pride in the mailman whose dedication had come to embody that trait.

> *To the many and numerous friends of RR4 Perth, I wish to express sincere gratitude for the overwhelming gift given me as an expression of your faith and trust during almost forty years of service. It has been a pleasure serving as a mail carrier on RR4 and I have enjoyed many happy associations over the years. I wish to thank everyone for their part in this wonderful "token of gratitude."*
>
> *Arden Blackburn,*
> *Perth, Ontario, 1967*

Arden Blackburn's Mail Route

On February 1, 1969, Canada Post announced that Saturday mail delivery in Canada would be discontinued. It was a declaration with which Arden Blackburn could not abide. Folks had come to depend upon him six days a week, not five. So it was that, despite the cutback and without pay, Arden Blackburn continued to cover his route on Saturdays and did so, faithfully, until his death on February 5, 1976, one month short of his 65th birthday.

About the Author

John McKenty (b. 1948) is a retired high school principal living in Perth, Ontario, with his wife, Zeta. His previous books include *Square Deal Garage: Sixty Years of Service to the Motoring Public* (2000), *Follow the Crowd: The James Boys of Perth* (2008) and *Canada Cycle and Motor: The CCM Story* (2011).

ENDNOTES

1 Edward Shortt, ed., *Perth Remembered* (Perth: Perth Museum, 1967), 16.

2 Shortt, *Perth Remembered*, 18.

3 Shortt, *Perth Remembered*, 19.

4 Harry Walker and Olive Walker, *Carleton Saga* (Ottawa: Runge Press, 1968), 167.

5 All quotes from Bill Sproule are taken from notes made by him and sent to the author.

6 Doyle eventually sold the rest of the original Christy farm to John Ritchie and John Jordan Sr.

7 Kitty Marks with Frank Croft, "My Life With the Original Marks Brothers," *Maclean's Magazine,* June 21, 1958, 16.

8 Diane Pinder-Moss, "A Rural Mail Carrier for 48 Years, Arden Blackburn Bore the Stamp of Dedication," *Mississippi Weekender*, October 13, 2006, 12.

9 Michael Taylor, *The Canadian Kings of Repertoire: The Story of the Marks Brothers* (Toronto: Natural Heritage, 2001), 29.

10 Taylor, *Canadian Kings*, 29.

11 Taylor, *Canadian Kings*, 31.

12 Taylor, *Canadian Kings*, 12.

13 Taylor, *Canadian Kings*, 20.

14 Ralph Willsey.

15 Taylor, *Canadian Kings*, 52.

16 Taylor, *Canadian Kings*, 50.

17 Taylor, *Canadian Kings*, 79.

18 Taylor, *Canadian Kings*, 80.

19 All quotes from Bob Marks are taken from the interview conducted by Ralph Willsey and printed in the *Kingston Whig Standard*, April 9, 1979.

20 All quotes attributed to Elton Crandall Jr. are taken from a taped interview he did with Stan Seymour.

21 Kitty Marks, "My Life," 17.

22 Taylor, *Canadian Kings*, 54.

23 Austin Cross, "A Place Where Nature Has Been Reckless with Her Favours," quoted in Beverly Ensom, *Christie Lake Camp: The History* (Ottawa: M.O.M. Printing, 1997), 46.

24 All quotes attributed to Jessie Hill (McKinnon) are from notes provided by Peter Higgins and Gord Hill.

25 Taylor, *Canadian Kings*, 43.

26 Taylor, *Canadian Kings*, 127.

27 *Granby Leader—Mail*, 10/22/26.

28 *Ottawa Citizen*, 10/27/1923.

29 Ralph Willsey, quoted in "Chimney Is Monument to Marks Brothers' Vaudeville," *Kingston Whig Standard*, April 9, 1979.

30 Stan Seymour.

31 Isaac Corry, letter to his brother, quoted in "George Corry (1807-1875) and Margaret Climie (1814-1875)," *Corry Family History*, accessed February 01, 2012, http:corry-history.blogspot.com.

32 Jean S. McGill, *Pioneer History of Lanark County* (Toronto: Clay Publishing, 1968), 170.

33 All quotes from Jessie McKinnon (Hill) are taken from the papers provided by her to Peter Higgins.

34 Reflections regarding the Shepherd family come from notes put together by Marnie Milne (Shepherd).

35 Ensom, *Christie Lake Camp*, 20.

36 Ensom, *Christie Lake Camp*, 48.

Endnotes

37 Ensom, *Christie Lake Camp*, 48.

38 Ensom, *Christie Lake Camp*, 65.

39 Ensom, *Christie Lake Camp*, 30.

40 Ensom, *Christie Lake Camp*, 112.

41 Ensom, *Christie Lake Camp*, 115.

42 All quotes from Gray Palmer are from conversations with the author and George James or Stan Seymour.

43 Pinder-Moss, "Rural Mail Carrier," 12.

44 *The American Magazine* 85, no. 2 (February 1938): 83.

45 All quotes from Ruth Brown are taken from papers sent by her to the author.

46 Pinder-Moss, "Rural Mail Carrier," 12.

47 Pinder-Moss, "Rural Mail Carrier," 12.

48 *Saskatoon Star-Phoenix*, 10/05/1949.

49 *Border Cities Star*, 08/25/1926.

50 *Ottawa Citizen*, 09/20/27.

51 *Border Cities Star*, 08/25/1926.

52 *The Monthly Letter, Arts and Letters Club*, June 1946.

53 *Ottawa Citizen*, 09/17/1956.

54 *Ottawa Citizen*, 09/19/1956.

55 *Ottawa Citizen*, 05/07/1957.

Bibliography

Bebee, Ed. *Fish Tales: The Lure and the Lore of the Rideau.* Smiths Falls: Friends of the Rideau, 2007.

Cross, Austin, "A Place Where Nature Has Been Reckless With Her Favours," quoted in Beverly Ensom, *Christie Lake Camp: The History.* Ottawa: M.O.M. Printing, 1997.

Ensom, Beverly. *Christie Lake Camp: The History.* Ottawa: M.O.M. Printing, 1997.

Marks, Kitty (with Frank Croft). "My Life with the Original Marks Brothers." *Maclean's,* June 21, 1958.

McGill, Jean S. *A Pioneer History of Lanark County.* Toronto: Clay Publishing, 1968.

Pinder-Moss, Diane. "A Rural Mail Carrier for 48 Years, Arden Blackburn Bore the Stamp of Dedication." *Mississippi Weekender,* October 13, 2006.

Shortt, Edward, ed. *Perth Remembered.* Perth: Perth Museum, 1967.

Taylor, Michael. *Legacy of Logging.* Perth: *Perth Courier,* 2003.

Taylor, Michael. *The Canadian Kings of Repertoire: The Story of the Marks Brothers.* Toronto: Natural Heritage, 2001.

Turner, Larry. *Perth: Tradition and Style in Eastern Ontario.* Toronto: Natural Heritage, 1992.

Willsey, Ralph. "Chimney Is Monument to Marks Brothers' Vaudeville." *Kingston Whig Standard,* April 9, 1979.

Walker, Harry, and Olive Walker. *Carleton Saga.* Ottawa: Runge Press, 1968.

www.ingramcontent.com/pod-product-compliance
Lightning Source LLC
Chambersburg PA
CBHW071620170426
43195CB00038B/1500